This book traces the political evolution of the Iberian peninsula from a collection of late Roman imperial provinces to the Spanish and Portuguese monarchies of the fifteenth century. That evolution is explained initially as a product of the interaction of the geography of Iberia and the successive invasions of it by the Visigoths in the fifth and sixth centuries and the Muslim invasion of the eighth century. The character of the Muslim organization of peninsular society is discussed and its failure to achieve a stable political order is assessed.

The rival cultures of Iberia came increasingly under the influence of Europe north of the Pyrenees and, as the peninsula developed agriculturally and institutionally, acted as the vanguard of that western European culture. Nevertheless, the different opportunities offered by the peculiarities of terrain and the relative weakness of the Islamic power confronting them led to the emergence of the variety of Christian kingdoms whose partial consolidation had only just begun by the late Middle Ages.

Cambridge Medieval Textbooks

THE MEDIEVAL SPAINS

Cambridge Medieval Textbooks

This is a series of specially commissioned textbooks for teachers and students, designed to complement the monograph series Cambridge Studies in Medieval Life and Thought by providing introductions to a range of topics in medieval history. This series combines both chronological and thematic approaches, and will deal with British and European topics. All volumes in the series will be published in hard covers and in paperback.

For a list of titles in the series, see end of book.

THE
MEDIEVAL
SPAINS

BERNARD F. REILLY

Professor of History, Villanova University

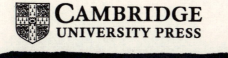 CAMBRIDGE
UNIVERSITY PRESS

Published by the Press Syndicate of the University of Cambridge
The Pitt Building, Trumpington Street, Cambridge CB2 1RP
40 West 20th Street, New York, NY 10011-4211 USA
10 Stamford Road, Oakleigh, Melbourne 3166, Australia

First published 1993
Reprinted 1994, 1996, 1999

Printed in Great Britain by
Athenæum Press Ltd, Gateshead, Tyne & Wear

A catalogue record for this book is available from the British Library

Library of Congress cataloguing in publication data

Reilly, Bernard F., 1925–
The medieval Spains / Bernard F. Reilly.
p.   cm – (Cambridge medieval textbooks)
ISBN 0 521 39436 8 (hardback) – ISBN 0 521 39741 3 (paperback)
1. Spain – History – 711–1516. I. Title. II. Series.
DP99.R375 1993
946'.02–dc20 92–23379 CIP

ISBN 0 521 39436 8 hardback
ISBN 0 521 39741 3 paperback

CONTENTS

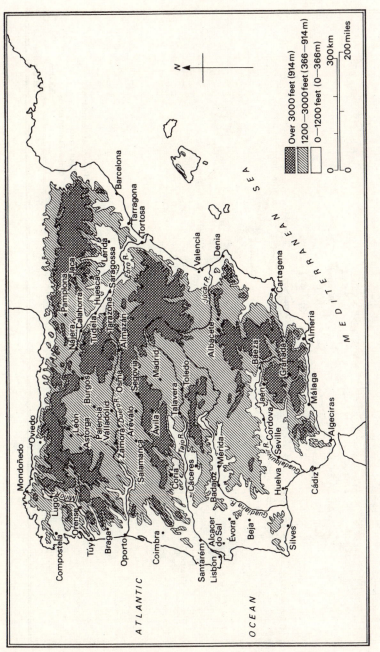

Map I Physical Iberia

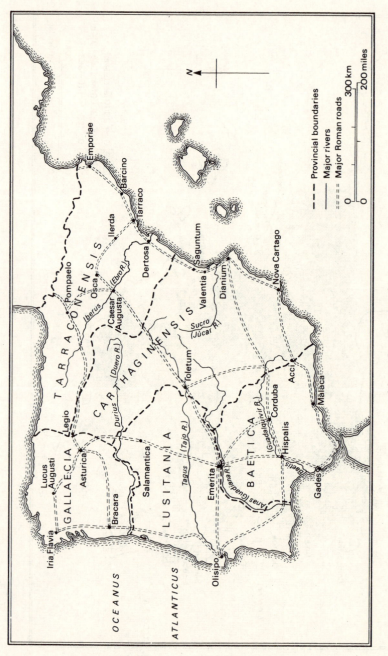

Map 2. Late Roman Iberia

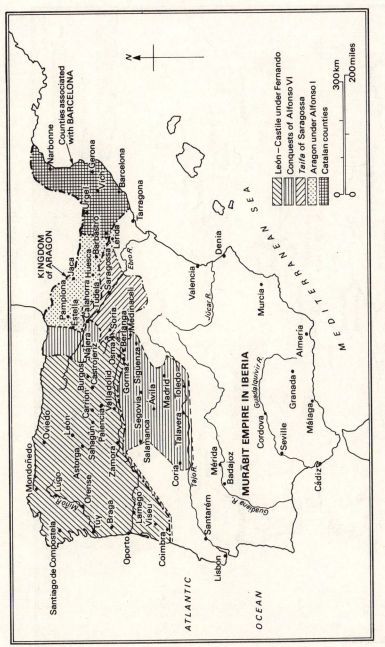

Map 3 Iberia at the end of the eleventh century

Legend:

León–Castile under Fernando
Conquests of Alfonso VI
Taifa of Saragossa
Aragon under Alfonso I
Catalan counties

MURĀBIT EMPIRE IN IBERIA

KINGDOM of ARAGON

Counties associated with BARCELONA

Narbonne
Gerona
Vich
Barcelona
Tarragona
Urgel
Barbastro
Lérida
Saragossa
Huesca
Jaca
Pamplona
Estella
Calahorra
Tudela
Nájera
Soria
Berlanga
Medinaceli
Osma
Gormaz
Sigüenza
Burgos
Castrojeriz
Carrión
Palencia
Valladolid
Sahagún
León
Astorga
Oviedo
Mondoñedo
Lugo
Orense
Tuy
Braga
Santiago de Compostela
Zamora
Salamanca
Segovia
Ávila
Madrid
Toledo
Talavera
Coria
Lamego
Viseu
Oporto
Coimbra
Santarém
Lisbon
Mérida
Badajoz
Cádiz
Málaga
Granada
Seville
Cordova
Almería
Murcia
Valencia
Denia

Miño R.
Tajo R.
Guadiana R.
Guadalquivir R.
Júcar R.
Ebro R.

ATLANTIC OCEAN
MEDITERRANEAN SEA

N

300 km
200 miles

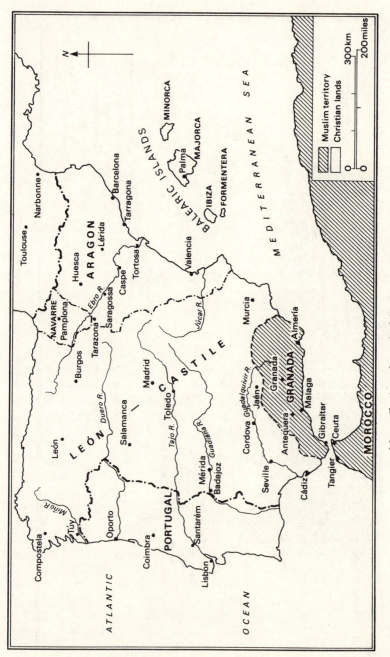

Map 4 Iberia at the end of the thirteenth century

I

AT THE EDGE OF EMPIRE

The political and cultural entity that constitutes modern Spain did not exist in antiquity and came into being during the medieval period only gradually. The Iberian peninsula was populated far back into the Paleolithic period but those shadowy, indigenous peoples of Iberia had been overlaid in part and in turn by Phoenecian, by Carthaginian, by Greek, and by Celt. But of these intruders none had brought unity until Rome gradually had extended her control over all of its peoples, beginning with the Second Punic War (218–201 BC). During the next six hundred years Roman rule there became an imperial order and the fundamental structure of the Roman Empire was always the province. Still at the beginning of the Middle Ages Iberia was simply a collection of Roman provinces politically, the westernmost peninsula of the Roman world geographically, and a participant in a common culture which we style classical.

The geography had imposed its conditions upon the Romans as it had and would upon everyone who attempted to govern Iberia. By European standards, the Iberian peninsula is large, more than 581,000 square kilometers. That is more than four times the size of England and a little bigger than France. Iberia is also very dry, on the average, with an annual precipitation of less than 1,000 millimeters. The westerlies off the Atlantic see that the northern and western coasts are mostly well watered, but the mountains of Cantabria in the north and of Galicia and Portugal in the west drain the Atlantic winds of most of their moisture before they reach the interior. There a central *meseta* averages 600 meters above sea level and constitutes almost half of the peninsula. The coastlands of the south and the east belong to the drier world of the Mediterranean. The agricultural civilization of Iberia, then, has always depended upon its river valleys to collect the precious water that is otherwise so scarce. Iberia has lived by its five great river basins.

The first and greatest of these is that of the Guadalquivir River whose 842 kilometers drain a watershed of 58,000 square kilometers. Since Phoenecian, Greek, Carthaginian, and Roman approached the peninsula from the east, which coast offers only one good entree to that land mass, it was usually simpler to sail through the "pillars of Hercules" and land at Cádiz. This originally Phoenecian port controlled the entrance to the Guadalquivir which was navigable all the way to modern Seville and, intermittently, to Cordova. But the river provided life-sustaining water from the eastern foothills of the Sierra de Cazorla with their towns of Ubeda and Baeza down through what would much later become the seat of the caliphate at Cordova. This basin and the narrow strip of coast along the Mediterranean to the south became the Late Roman Imperial province of Baetica. Its center was at Hispalis (Seville) and its northern limits were formed by the mountains of the Sierra Morena and the lower reaches of the Guadiana River.

Just north of these two lies the watershed of the Guadiana River, 839 kilometers long and draining a basin of 69,000 square kilometers. However, its flow is the weakest of all of the major rivers, much weaker than that of the Guadalquivir despite its considerable extent to the east. The river partially formed the border between the provinces of Baetica and Lusitania as it largely does that of modern Spain and Portugal. Its center was at Emerita (Mérida), the highest point to which it was navigable, and its northern border was constituted, in good measure, by the mountains of Toledo. Joined to the Guadiana basin in the Late Roman province of Lusitania was the Portuguese coastline as far north as Portucale (Oporto) and the lower portion of the watershed of the Tajo River.

This latter basin comprised some 81,000 square kilometers and the river itself stretches for more than 1,100 kilometers. It was useful for agriculture and stockraising but it drops down from the central plateau to the coastal plain of Portugal and to Santarém and Lisbon so steeply that it is hardly useful for transportation much beyond the former. To the north the Tajo basin was bounded by the great central chain of the Guadarrama Mountains and to the east by the Sierra de Albarricín. Like Baetica, Roman Lusitania too was easiest of approach from the Atlantic.

On the eastern side of the peninsula, of the two provinces oriented toward the Mediterranean, only Tarraconensis offered easy access to the interior. Tarraco (Tarragona), its capital, sat in the basin of the Ebro River.

This watershed of 85,000 square kilometers and its 928 kilometers long heart stretched, between the Pyrenees to the north and the Sierra de Albarracín to the south, from the mountains of Cantabria to the Mediterranean below Dertosa (Tortosa). It was a world in its own right as well as a province. The volume of water that the Ebro carries is the second greatest of the five rivers of Iberia and its flow is the most regularly distributed over the year.

Carthaginensis, on the other hand, took its name from its port at Carthago (Cartagena) which had little hinterland itself. The province included the major portion of the eastern Mediterranean coast and from there stretched northwest up onto the central *meseta* of Murcia, La Mancha, and Castilla La Nueva. At its northwestern end it even included most of the Duero River basin. That latter watershed of 98,000 square kilometers is essentially broken into two parts by the violence of its drop from the plateau down to the Atlantic at Oporto. Its 700 kilometer length in Spain and its 200 kilometer length in Portugal are, socially, two separate rivers. Both supply the essential water but only the latter is navigable for a short distance from the Atlantic. But if the province of Carthaginensis was a unit in some sort it had to be held together by administrative means. It had no such natural artery or center as had Baetica, Lusitania, and Tarraconensis.

The same may be said of the fifth province, Gallaecia, in the far north-west. Bounded by the Duero to the south, the Atlantic to the west, and the Bay of Biscay to the north, it stretched inland through the mountains to the edge of the *meseta* of Castilla la Vieja at Asturica Augusta (Astorga). It had a capital at Braccara Augusta (Braga) but geography oriented the province, essentially a group of mountain valleys and a narrow coastal plain, towards the Atlantic and the ports of Portucale (Oporto) and the more northerly Iria Flavia (Padrón). Were it not for the stubborn inventiveness of Rome, Gallaecia would have been merely what was left over from the remainder of the peninsula.

Indeed, Iberia's geography predisposed it to remain a series of separate human communities. The coasts, except as one of the great riverine systems reached them, everywhere were separated from its interior by substantial mountain ranges. The coasts themselves differed. Those of the Bay of Biscay, Galicia, and northern Portugal were well watered, even lush, while those of southern Portugal and the Mediterranean were dry, semi-desert. The first group lacked a navigable river for access to the interior. On the other hand, the rivers of the second group led only into their own watersheds. If mountains divided the coastlands from the interior, the Guadarrama divided the northern *meseta* in the Duero basin from its southern counterpart in the basin of the Tajo. The mountains of

Toledo divided the Guadiana basin from that of the Tajo. Finally, the Sierra Morena divide the Guadiana basin from that of the Guadalquivir. Even in our own times, the motor car, the railroad, and the airplane, only partially suffice to draw these well-defined regions together into one human community. The Romans had to attempt to unite it by means of roads alone.

Surely, the most significant material improvement made by Rome in Iberia was the construction of a comprehensive network of roads which covered and connected most of its physical surface. The prime purpose of this road system was military, i.e., to speed the movement of troops, their supplies and replacements, and the communications essential to their coordination. Although the Roman dominance in Iberia was not challenged during the first four centuries of the Christian Era, nevertheless that road system was constructed as a precaution and maintained as a convenience. In all the centuries after the disappearance of Rome from the peninsula, it was to remain the basic communication, commercial, and military grid of every Iberian society down to the coming of the railroad.

In part, it was a coastal network. From the port of Padrón in Galicia it ran sough through Braga, Coimbra, Santarém, and Lisbon in Portugal, and thence south and east to Seville. From that point it continued on to Algeciras, Malaga, and to Almeria, where it turned north through Cartagena, Denia, Valencia, Tortosa, Tarragona and Barcelona, and from there around the eastern end of the Pyrenees into what was then Roman Gaul. Since no attack was ordinarily to be envisaged from the sea, this linking of the major seaports of the perimeter must largely have served to facilitate the shuttling of troops between them when it could not be done more expeditiously by boat, that is, in winter. It is significant that the one coast not included in this network was that of Cantabria. Romanization among the tribes of the north there was so slight that it could not produce even this basic index of empire.

Seville was the southern center of this network. Not only did the coastal road from Galicia and Portugal touch there before continuing on around the peninsula to Barcelona and Narbonne but one great interior artery ran diagonally and northeast from it to Toledo, Saragossa, and then on to Barcelona. This most strategic route linked the valley of the Guadalquivir, the Tajo basin, and the Ebro valley. To hold it was to dominate the richest and most cultivated half of Iberia.

Second only to it was the system that emanated from Mérida, after coming east from Santarém and Lisbon. From this second hub of the south, one branch ran up the valley of the Guadiana to unite with the road from Seville. Yet another crossed the mountains of Toledo by Trujillo and then passed through Talavera de la Reina to join the Seville road at Toledo. Between the two the valley of the Guadiana was joined firmly to that of the Guadalquivir and that of the Tajo.

Of course a road ran south from Mérida to Seville but yet another ran north to fork off to the northwest to Braga and to the northeast through Salamanca and Zamora to Astorga. At Zamora it was joined by a spur of the Toledo–Saragossa road that crossed the Guadarrama by way of the pass of Navacerrada and Segovia. At Astorga (Asturicas Augustae) both of these north–south routes joined the east–west road that led from Padrón (Iria Flavia) in Galicia through Lugo, then Astorga and León, and on to Pamplona and to Gaul by way of the pass at Roncesvalles. This road was to become the *Camino de Santiago* when that pilgrimage came to be established after the ninth century. For the Romans, however, it tied the northern plateau and the valley of the Duero to the Atlantic coast and to the Guadiana and Guadalquivir basins. Since a spur of it also led east to Saragossa and Tarragona, the Duero basin was connected with that of the Ebro as well.

This brief sketch of the road network of imperial Rome in Iberia illustrates well the pervasive character of its civilization in the peninsula. But even the most casual contemporary traveler will be struck by the extent and the monumental character of Roman building there as it endures down to the present. However, perhaps the most impressive testimony to the attraction of things Roman are the Iberian idioms, Catalan, Gallego, Portuguese and Spanish. As early as the first century AD the Greek geographer Strabo asserted that the inhabitants of Baetica had forgotten their own language. While that appears to have contained some literary exaggeration, four centuries later they, along with the other inhabitants of the peninsula, would indeed have done so. The one certain exception is the Basques. There was no system of Roman roads in Guipúzcoa, Vizcaya, and Alava. Nor do they appear in High Aragon or the Pyrenaen valleys of Catalonia. Likely, the indigenous idiom lingered on there as well as in northern Galicia and Asturias. One might say that the Romans subdued the tribes of the Cantabrians and the Pyrenees but hardly that they conquered them.

Rome found Iberia a world of villages and made it a world of cities. Again that is true except in the mountains of the north. Everywhere else four centuries of Roman administration seems fairly to have dissolved the old tribal structures and to have replaced them with civil and economic ones. When, in turn, that Roman order should have collapsed, the old tribalism proved to have no power to regenerate itself. The new order of the Suevi and the Visigoths, fragile as it was, would instead triumph.

Now it is true that the Roman cities in Iberia were largely political and administrative devices. As generally elsewhere in the world of the western Mediterranean, those cities seldom had any important industry and often not even a commerce beyond that of victualing the government and its garrisons. The major ports are an obvious exception. The ordinary city was populated by officials, civil servants, soldiers, small merchants, artisans, and slaves, and their families. In addition they boasted a number of elite families, possessed of a city dwelling as well as of a rural *villa*, but whose agricultural estates furnished their essential source of wealth. Such cities could, then, support a polite society which could in turn patronize literary and artistic expression and see to the education of its own members. This social world was nurtured by Roman government and law and Iberian products of it, such as Seneca and Marcial, Trajan and Hadrian, moved easily in the higher circles of the imperial Mediterranean.

Nevertheless the massive reality which supported it was the world of agriculture and the countryside. The population of Roman Iberia at its height is ordinarily estimated at 6,000,000. Cádiz, its largest city boasted but 65,000 and Tarragona, the next largest, only 27,000. The total population of its ten largest cities would aggregate but 175,000. That is, roughly ninety-six percent of its inhabitants were rural.

Now both the Roman conquest and the Roman market had reoriented significant portions of that agriculture from a subsistence to a cash-crop basis. The *villa* had become the most important form of agricultural organization and a few material remains of those rural institutions have even been discovered in central Asturias beyond the Cantabrians. As never before, Iberian wheat, olive oil, and wine, in addition to its wool, fish oil, and livestock, moved in the Mediterranean market. Mining was similarly affected as Iberian gold, silver, iron, copper, and lead, were worked for shipment over long distances. To both the former and the latter, new Roman techniques had been applied and worked major expansion and improvement. These innovations were especially notable in the realm of irrigation in agriculture and mechanics in mining. Generally speaking, Iberia benefited materially and socially from the imposition of the Roman order. However, it would also suffer from Rome's decline.

Yet, before that decline became critical, Rome provided the highway for the dissemination of the Christian religion to Iberia. Probably arriving in the peninsula before the end of the first century, Christianity there had become widely enough diffused to produce authentic martyrs by the times of Decius, Valerian, and finally Diocletian (AD 285–305). When the first visible council of the Spanish church was celebrated at Elvira before AD 313, no less than nineteen bishops attended to represent their diocese. If most of these units were clustered in Baetica, nevertheless diocese already existed at Braga, León, Saragossa, and Barcelona. But like the cities, their invariable habitat, none were found in the mountains of the Cantabrian chain or in the high valleys of the Pyrenees.

THE TIME OF TROUBLES

The larger aspects of the decline of the Late Roman Empire are well known and the developments in Iberia were not particularly distinctive. From AD 250 plague was endemic for about fifteen years. Beginning roughly about AD 260 the collapse of the imperial frontier on the Rhine resulted in the penetration of Germanic tribesmen even into Iberia. The major invasion route was around the eastern end of the Pyrenees and the valley of the Ebro was the region which suffered most. Tarragona, Lérida, Saragossa, and Pamplona were attacked. Other groups of invaders may have entered by way of Roncesvalles and pillaged their way down the valley of the Duero, visiting their wrath in turn upon Palencia, Valladolid, León, and Astorga. Lusitania and Baetica suffered less severely but Coimbra and Mérida were also attacked. Curiously in all this, there is no record of organized resistance. In all probability the invaders were able to recruit in the peninsula among the margins of the rural population, from decaying tribal groups, and even disaffected regular troops.

When this storm had worn itself out and order had been restored, here as throughout the empire after AD 286 under Emperor Diocletian, the population of the peninsula had clearly begun to shrink to an estimated size of about 4,000,000 on the eve of the fifth-century invasions. A concomitant decline of commerce can be best measured in the physical shrinkage evident in the acreage of port cities. In general, the political and economic preeminence of cities over the country districts so typical of the classical world was failing as well. Both cause and effect of this phenomenon was the growth of the *villa* into great *latifundia* in the more favored agricultural regions of the river valleys and the reduction of small proprietors to economic and legal, even military, dependence on the Late Roman magnate class which owned the former.

As with the invasions of the third century, those of the fifth century were prepared by the decrepitude of the imperial government itself. But this time they were visited upon an Iberia with less power of absorption and assimilation. The story of the failure of imperial government upon the death of Emperor Theodosius the Great (379–395), the rivalry of eastern and western portions, the revolt of the Visigoths in the Danube provinces, the ineffectuality of Honorius in the west, and finally the ultimate collapse of the Rhine frontier in 407 is too familiar to need much telling here. By the summer of 409 the first contingents of Vandals, Suevi, and Alans, had threaded their way through the pass at Roncevalles and a German future was in the making for Iberia.

Notwithstanding, the peninsula would long continue to be involved with the death throes of the Roman Empire in the west. In fact, at the time of this invasion that empire was hopelessly divided. The Emperor Honorius in Ravenna was confronted by a former general of Roman Britain, Constantine, who had been proclaimed emperor and had subsequently made himself master of Gaul and Iberia. The latter's own general, Gerontius, had broken the power of the Roman troops loyal to Honorius in the peninsula but had then, in turn, revolted against Constantine and set up his own puppet emperor in Iberia. Gerontius concentrated his forces in the valley of the Ebro to defend against an attack by his previous master whose capital was at Arles in Provence. He also invited the Vandals, Alans, and Suevi, then concentrated in Aquitaine, into western Iberia as his allies. They entered unopposed by the pass at Roncesvalles. Avoiding the valley of the Ebro, the Germans took possession first of the valley of the Duero, then of Galicia, and finally of Lusitania and Baetica. There was only scattered opposition and within two years they were settling as garrisons in and about the larger cities. There, under a long familiar political and legal device, they kept their own identity intact under their kings but as *foederati*, i.e., allied peoples settled on Roman territory, were able to draw upon the resources of the Roman administration for maintenance and support.

Meanwhile the Emperor Honorius had watched helplessly from Ravenna while the Visigoths, having broken through the defenses of the Upper Adriatic from the Balkans, swept the length of Italy itself, sacking Rome in 410. These circumstances encouraged Gerontius to march against Constantine at Arles but his ambitions came to an abrupt end in 411. Following the death of Alaric in southern Italy the Emperor Honorius had come to terms with the Visigoths and despatched them as allies, together with troops of his own, to the south of Gaul. Faced by these forces, Gerontius' army revolted and he was killed. Honorius' forces then forced the surrender of Constantine at Arles. In Iberia the troops of Maximus, the puppet emperor set up by Gerontius, mutinied at the news, returning to their loyalty to Ravenna. Maximus fled to find refuge and obscurity among the Germans of the peninsula. For the moment, the integrity of the Western Empire had been restored.

For Rome, the question now became how to reassert its control in more than nominal fashion. To this end the Visigoths, now quarrelling among themselves and desperate for supplies, could be utilized. Under their king, Walia, they had already ventured into Iberia once in 414 without great result. Now as *foederati* of the empire they were despatched into the peninsula in 416 in order to reclaim it for Rome. Walia's campaign succeeded brilliantly and, in a climactic battle not far north of Algeciras, he destroyed the armies of both the Alans and the Siling Vandals. Bereft of their kings and most of their military effectives, those two federations disintegrated and their surviving members were absorbed by the still potent Hasding Vandals under King Gunderic and the Suevi.

Fearing too complete a success of Walia, Rome now recalled him and, by virtue of a new pact or *foedus*, settled their allies permanently in the south of Gaul in the valleys of the Garonne and the region about Toulouse. There was a redistribution of lands in these areas in favor of the Visigothic king and his nobles and their followers. Gallo-Roman *latifundists* were compelled to part with a portion of their holdings in return for the protection afforded by their new Visigothic neighbors. For a century yet, the Visigothic kingdom centered on the south of France.

In Iberia, Rome had recovered the basin of the Ebro and the coast of the Levant as far south as Cartagena as a result of their efforts. A new Roman force of about 4,500 was now despatched under the command of a "Count of Spain" who took up residence at Tarragona. Imperial authority had been restored to the Tarraconensis and the coastal area of the old Cartaginensis but Baetica, Lusitania, Galicia, and the inland reaches of the Cartaginensis, remained in the hands of the Suevi and the Hasding Vandals. These tribes ruled with the more or less reluctant cooperation of the great Hispano-Roman *latifundists* who were the other real power in the occupied areas. So Rome seemed disposed to leave matters until Gunderic of the Vandals undertook a war against the Suevi in 420 which might have ended in the conquest of the latter. This was not desirable from the Roman point of view and the troops from Tarragona marched west and forced the Vandals to conclude the struggle.

In the following year a potentially more serious event occurred. With the acquiescence of Gunderic the old pretender to the purple, Maximus, emerged from obscurity and reasserted his imperial dignity. Once again the army of the Ebro, this time heavily reinforced with Visigothic auxiliaries, marched into Baetica and scored initial victories over Maximus who was captured and sent to Ravenna to be executed by Honorius in 422.

Subsequently, however, the Vandal Gunderic scored a crushing victory and immediately went over to the offensive against the empire. While the Tarraconensis was to be held, the losses of men in 422 could not be made good and the death of Honorius in 423 further complicated defensive efforts. Cartagena fell in 424 and, having seized the makings of a fleet there, Gunderic even raided the Balearics in 425. In 428 it appears that he had wrested both Seville and Cordova from those elements of the population still loyal to Rome there. When Gunderic died in 428 he had become master of all Iberia but for Galicia held by the Suevi and the Tarraconensis. However, his brother Genseric, who succeeded, was to organize the successful invasion of the province of Africa in 429 and the Vandals crossed the straits of Gibraltar and disappeared from Iberian history.

The resulting vacuum in the peninsula could not be filled by Rome. The province of Africa, the granary of Rome, at all costs must be protected from Genseric. Simultaneously servile revolts erupted in Gaul and the Visigoths threatened to move south into the Narbonensis and Provence. All these problems left free rein to the Suevi in Iberia even though the total numbers of the tribe did not exceed 25,000 souls. Reinforced by recruits from among the depressed lower orders of Hispano-Roman society, they carried on a war of attrition against the Hispano-Roman nobility and bureaucracy. Under their king, Rechila, the Suevi gradually expanded from their strongholds in Astorga, Lugo, Oporto, and Braga, from Galicia south into Lusitania and even Baetica. In 439 Rechila took Mérida and by 441 Seville as well. At precisely this juncture new and most serious slave revolts broke out in Gaul but this time also in the Tarraconensis. It was another five years before a *magister militum*, one Vitus, could be spared for Iberia. At the head of an army composed largely of Visigoth allies, he marched south into the valley of the Guadalquivir only to meet defeat there at the hands of Rechila in 446.

That victorious king of the Suevi died in 448 having achieved control of the entire peninsula except for the valley of the Ebro. Rome and Rome's Iberian allies and sympathizers must have now despaired of any full restoration of imperial power there. The former sought ways to hold the Ebro basin, the latter the best accommodation possible with the new masters. The new king of the Suevi, Recharius, almost immediately sought an alliance with the Visigoths. In 449 he journeyed by the pass at Roncesvalles to the court of Theodoric I, whose daughter he married. The trip to Gaul was marked by Suevic pillaging of much of the northern Tarraconensis and the return around the eastern end of the Pyrenees was accompanied by the sack of Lérida and the environs of Saragossa. The resulting confusion encouraged a new servile revolt in the valley whose highpoint was the capture of Tarazona and the execution of its bishop by the rebels. At this juncture, the defeat of the Huns at Chalons in 451, the death in that battle of the Visigothic Theodoric I, and the death of Attila himself in 453, all combined to momentarily restore the imperial position in Gaul. In Iberia, however, the best terms that a formal Roman embassy of the latter year could extract from the Suevi was an agreement to respect continued imperial rule in the Tarraconensis.

But the final ruin of imperial authority in Iberia was the work of Rome itself. In 454 the general, Aetius, who had restored Roman authority in Gaul was assassinated by the directive of the Emperor Valentinian III, who feared the former's ambitions. Scarcely six months later Valentinian was himself assassinated by disgruntled associates of Aetius. Thus perished the last member of the house of Theodosius the Great and with him any last hopes for the restoration of imperial power in the west generally.

In Iberia the inheritors of that mantle were to be the Visigoths. The new Visigothic king, Theodoric II (453–466), would support the Gallo-Roman Avitus, a new pretender to the imperial dignity, and invade the peninsula in his name in 456. At a great battle near Astorga he crushingly defeated the Suevi, occupied that city, Braga, and Oporto, and captured and executed Recharius, the Suevic king. When Avitus was defeated and killed in Italy, Theodoric had to return to Gaul but the army left behind consolidated Visigothic control in Baetica, Lusitania, and Cartaginensis. That force comprised a series of garrisons whose commanders shared power with the Hispano-Roman nobility and bishops. These local troops mounted campaigns almost yearly against the Suevi who, under their new king Remismundus, were able to reconstitute their old kingdom in the province of Galicia and later in the north of Lusitania. In 468 the Suevi even held Lisbon. Nevertheless, Remismundus recognized a vague over-lordship of the Visigoths.

In 466 Theodoric II was murdered in Toulouse by his brother, Euric (466–484), who succeeded to both the throne and the ambitions of the former. In Italy the imperial dignity had become a trifle, awarded by the barbarian *magister militum* Ricimer to the currently most useful Roman noble. Those circumstances allowed the Visigoths in Gaul to impose their own authority, first in the Narbonensis and then in Provence. That done, they controlled the access to Iberia completely. On the death of Ricimer in 472, Euric took advantage of the compounded confusion in Italy to despatch two armies into the Tarraconensis. When the *Dux Tarraconensis* there, Vincencius, joined himself and his few remaining troops to the Visigoths, Roman authority vanished finally from the peninsula. Then in 476 another barbarian *magister militum*, Odoacer, formally abolished the imperial dignity in the west and any likelihood of its return disappeared. Iberia was now very unequally divided between Suevi and Visigoth but the Hispano-Roman magnates were necessary to each and increasing cooperation between Roman and Germans must be assumed.

This state of affairs continued until the very end of the reign of Alaric II (484–507), son of Euric. There was lingering rebellion against the new Visigothic rule in Tarraconensis but, without any clear alternative, that initiative never had any real chance of success. On the other hand,

Alaric II mounted an energetic program of rule. His advisers and judges prepared a simplified code of Roman law, the famous *Breviarium*, which was promulgated in 506 for the better governance of his kingdom. A general council of the Catholic bishops of the realm took up the matters of reform and reorganization at Agde in 506. It is important to notice that none of the thirty-four bishops in attendance held sees in Iberia. The kingdom of the Visigoths was still very much a Gallic entity with a peninsular appendage.

To protect his realm against the increasingly aggressive Franks to the north, Alaric mounted an extensive policy of alliances. He himself married a daughter of the Ostrogothic Theodoric the Great. He also sought the support of the Burgundian kingdom. Then, in 507, disaster struck. The Visigothic army was roundly defeated at Vouillé in the northern Aquitaine by the Franks under Clovis and Alaric II himself died on the field. Simultaneously, the Burgundians reversed their attitude and invaded the Visigothic realm. In short order, Aquitaine, Gascony, and the Auvergne, were absorbed into the Frankish kingdom, whose armies went on to besiege Carcassonne. The Burgundians held Arles under siege and took Narbonne. All of Provence and the Narbonensis seemed about to fall and the Visigoths to become another of those Germanic tribal confederations that would vanish from sight after a resounding military defeat.

A SECOND VISIGOTHIC KINGDOM

In fact, what was to emerge gradually over the next eight decades was a new kingdom of the Visigoths; this time an Iberian entity with a Gallic appendage. That this should have happened at all was the result of the intervention of the new master of Ostrogothic Italy, Theodoric the Great (493–526). With the blessing of the Eastern Roman Emperor, Zeno, Theodoric had led his people out of the Balkans and wrested control of Italy away from the German Odoacer. For more than a quarter of a century his was to be one of the wealthiest and most solidly based of the Germanic kingdoms of the west. Ruling as the nominal agent of the Roman emperors of Constantinople, he had some appeal for the old Romanized population in Italy, Gaul, and Iberia. In 508 he sent an Ostrogothic army into Gaul, forcing the Burgundians to raise the siege of Arles and the Franks that of Carcassonne. Narbonne was recovered and the Narbonensis and Provence liberated. For the next eighteen years the real ruler of the Visigothic realm was Theodoric. This has been done in the name of his grandson, Amalaric, born of Alaric II's marriage to his daughter.

What was important for its effects was his policy of administering his Visigothic possessions. Military affairs were vested in an Ostrogothic client of his own, Teudis by name. Civil administration was placed under a new "Prefect of the Spains." The control of the estates of the royal fisc, remnants of the former imperial fisc lands, came under a separate set of administrators. This division of authority delayed for decades the need for Hispano-Roman and Visigothic nobles to assimilate or at least reach some sort of lasting accommodation. Meanwhile Visigothic settlement in the peninsula was swollen by refugees from the south of Gaul.

These tumultuous changes of the late fifth and the early sixth century had no discernable effect upon that other Iberian world of the Cantabrian and Pyrenaen regions, long peripheral to even a healthy, Roman provincial world. Doubtless the generalized melee offered opportunities to those tribal societies to plunder selectively or to join and change sides as auxiliaries but their homelands continued unchanged by that world of war.

The very ability of the new Visigothic realm to survive was called into question by the death of its initial protector, Theodoric the Great, in 526. His grandson, Amalaric (526–531), who then succeeded to the crown, clearly had ambitions to rebuild the realm, even in its former Gallic extension, for he fixed his residence in Narbonne and married a Frankish princess. Nevertheless, the Frankish King Childebert coveted the remaining Visigothic provinces of Septimania. In 531 he invaded them and defeated Amalaric near Narbonne, whereupon the young king fled south to Barcelona. There he was murdered by a member of his own entourage and with him ended the Visigothic royal line descended from the great Alaric I, sacker of Rome itself.

The new king, Teudis (531–548), was that Ostrogothic general appointed to command the military of the peninsula by Theodoric and the former guardian of Amalaric. The former's accession was probably accompanied by some distribution of royal fisc lands to both the Visigothic nobility and the Ostrogothic warriors who had bolstered the Iberian garrisons during the latter's minority. Teudis also had previously taken a wife from the family of the Hispano-Roman nobility and that faction of the kingdom too likely shared in the distribution of fisc lands. If the royal authority suffered from all of this, at the same time it advanced the cohesion and mutual interest of the political classes of the new realm.

Teudis was unable to limit entirely the Frankish advance consequent on the rout of Amalaric. Visigothic Septimania became, more than ever, a narrow coastal strip along the Mediterranean. Still, that much was held and, when the Franks invaded the Ebro valley in 541 and held Saragossa to a siege for more than a month, the invaders were themselves crushingly defeated as they sought to withdraw to the north. The accelerating decline of the power of the descendants of Clovis now began to make the power of the Franks less threatening. Still, Teudis established his ordinary residence at Toledo in the center of the peninsula and turned his attention to bringing former Roman Baetica and Lusitania under control. He had progressed substantially in this aim when he was murdered by someone of his own court in 548. He was succeeded briefly by another Ostrogothic general, Teudiselo, in turn murdered in a palace conspiracy at the end of the following year. The conspirators proceeded to the election of the Visigothic noble, Agila (549–554), to the rickety throne.

The realm now threatened to dissolve in bloody anarchy. Baetican Cordova rose in revolt and routed Agila when he attempted to crush it in 551. Then the garrison of Seville also rebelled and chose the Visigothic noble, Athanagild, as new king. But Agila retained Mérida and contained both groups of rebels in the environs of Cordova and Seville.

Simultaneously a new threat to the struggling Visigothic realm had appeared on the scene. The death of the Ostrogothic Theodoric in Italy had closely been followed by the accession in Constantinople of Justinian the Great (527–565) and this emperor hoped to reclaim the west for the imperial authority from the various ramshackle Germanic principalities there. Justinian had begun with the assault on the Vandals in the old province of Africa and within a year of the first invasion in 533 had utterly destroyed that enemy. Bereft of their power, the Vandals were absorbed with scarcely a ripple into the general population of a restored Roman province.

The victorious army of the new Rome on the Bosphorus under the general Belisarius next undertook the reconquest of Italy. There the kingdom of the Ostrogoths offered stronger resistance. Not until 554 were the armies of Justinian finally victorious.

In 551, during the climactic period of that struggle, Justinian had received a tempting offer from the pretender, Athanagild. In exchange for military assistance against Agila, the Visigoth was willing to cede that coastal fringe of the peninsula reaching from Cádiz in the south to Valencia in the east. Little could be done just then except for the despatch of a minuscule force in the spring of 552. Still, with its aid Athanagild was able to score a victory that summer over Agila in the valley of the Guadalquivir. Yet the struggle dragged on in a series of skirmishes. Then in 554, with the Ostrogothic War concluded, a much larger Byzantine force was sent to Iberia and landed at Cartagena, which port effectively became the capital of the restored Roman province.

The clear intention of Justinian's generals to rebuild Roman authority caused grave concern among the Visigothic nobility. The result was their assassination of Agila in Mérida in 555 and the subsequent recognition of the rebel Athanagild as lawful king (555–567). Even so, no expulsion of the Byzantines was possible but rather a new treaty seems to have been reached with them which kept the valley of the Guadalquivir in Visigothic hands. For the next dozen years the new king kept Suevi, Byzantines, and Franks, at bay but when he died in Toledo in 567 his power was so insecure that the rebel city of Cordova was still independent.

This weakness was aggravated by the failure to choose his successor for almost six months after his death. Then the lead was taken by the Visigoths of Narbonne who chose Liuva I (568–573) because their concern about pressure from the Franks left no more time for hesitation. The brief reign of this monarch is chiefly to be remembered for his association in power with himself of his brother and successor, Leovigild (569–586).

Leovigild quickly made Toledo his usual residence and married the widow of Athanagild as a step to consolidate his power in the south. After the death of Liuva he became the monarch who secured the fortunes of the Visigothic realm. Already before that date he had taken the offensive against the Byzantines in 570 and had expelled them from the upper reaches of the Guadalquivir Basin. The following year he took Medina Sidonia which impeded Roman communication and mutual supply between Cádiz and Málaga. One year later, in 572 he had reduced rebel Cordova to submission. The next six years were spent in a variety of local actions along the borders of the Suevic kingdom in the lower valley of the Duero and Galicia, in the upper reaches of the Ebro on the margins of Basque country, and again in the highlands of the eastern Guadalquivir.

This process of consolidation was interrupted abruptly by the revolt of his oldest son, Hermenengild, in 580. Leovigild had associated both Hermenengild and his second son, Recared, with him in the royal dignity on the death of Liuva. In 579 he had sent the former south to Seville to assume the government of Visigothic Baetica and Lusitania and the result was Hermenengild's revolt less than a year later. The rebel son's cause was adopted more or less enthusiastically in Seville, Mérida, and Cordova, and found support also from the Suevic kingdom and the Byzantine governor. Clearly, the challenge was serious and Leovigild took care to consolidate his own position before responding. Not until 582 did he begin a counteroffensive which saw the fall of Mérida to him within the year and allowed him to begin a siege of Seville in 583. When Hermenengild attempted to break the siege he was soundly defeated and his father then turned on the Suevi who had come south and forced them to retire precipitately into Galicia.

Seville surrendered soon after and Hermenengild retreated upon
Cordova, trusting in his allies in that city and in Byzantine assistance. But
Leovigild offered a large bribe to the latter if they would desert his son's
cause. When they accepted, Hermenengild had no recourse but to throw
himself upon his father's mercy in 584, while his wife and children were
spirited off to Constantinople by his erstwhile allies for such use as future
Roman diplomacy might have for them. The hapless prince was sent
in captivity to Tarragona where he was subsequently and conveniently
murdered in 585.

With all elements in his own realm now thoroughly cowed and
Byzantine ambitions at their lowest point in thirty years, Leovigild
decided simply to make an end of the Suevic kingdom in Iberia. Of late
it had been particularly active and might become more formidable if
neglected. At some point in the last quarter of a century, we cannot be
positive of the date or even the particular monarch involved, the Suevic
royal house had eschewed its traditional Arian Christianity and converted
to the Catholic faith. That step removed an obstacle which had impeded
their full acceptance by their Hispano-Roman subjects for the last one
hundred and fifty-odd years. Moreover, they had begun an aggressive
cooperation with the united Christian church of their realm, holding two
councils at Braga in 561 and 572 to round off and improve its organization. Finally, they had begun to press against the independent tribes of
northern Galicia in a bid to expand their realm.

Unfortunately for the Suevi, their own dynasty was divided and
quarreling when Leovigild struck in 585, captured and deposed the last of
their kings, placed permanent Visigothic garrisons in Lugo, Braga, and
Oporto, and incorporated the kingdom into his own. When he died in
586 Leovigild was master of a Visigothic realm which comprised all of
Iberia, except for the Cantabrian and the Mediterranean littorals, and of
Septimania beyond the Pyrenees.

2

THE GERMANIC KINGDOM IN IBERIA,
569–711

With the accession of Leovigild in 569 the Iberian kingdom of the Visigoths was to become the vehicle for the creation of a new society during the next century and a half. In its course the distinction between Roman and German would disappear as conquerors and conquered insensibly became one people. Germanic kingship and the Germanic conception of nobility would gradually replace the institutions and offices of empire and would inaugurate a reign over the western political and social imagination which still has not entirely lost its power. Yet the most profound transformation in process during that 150 years was the Christianization of the Iberian population. That conversion was, of course, intimately related to the emergence of a stable monarchy and a stable nobility as institutions which could survive the eighth-century collapse of the Visigothic realm itself and emerge, phoenix-like, in the new Christian world of Asturias. More significantly still, that newly achieved Christianity would furnish an alternative, a counter-, identity to an Iberian population submerged beneath the tide of Islam. As Mozarabic Christians they would endure. As Asturian Christians they would resist. Finally, after almost 800 years, the Iberian kingdoms would have reclaimed the entire peninsula for a social order which was formally Christian, monarchical, and hierarchical.

The origins of Christianity in Iberia date from the Roman era, of course, and well before the fall of Roman authority in the peninsula there were already a body of Christian martyrs, an organized diocesan structure, and even a fair number of monasteries. Its Bishop Hosius of Cordova had been the major advisor of Constantine the Great at the Ecumenical

Council of Nicea in 325 and Bishop Priscillian of Ávila (d. 385) had been, perhaps, its first influential heretic. Nonetheless, as everywhere else in the west when the Roman Empire perished in the fifth century, Christianity in Iberia was still largely an urban phenomenon. Bishop Martin of Braga (d. 580) would fulminate against the paganism of the *rustici* and the Sixteenth Council of Toledo in 693 would still legislate against those of the countryside who worshipped trees and stones rather than the Christian God.

Yet the archeological evidence demonstrates clearly that the situation had changed drastically by that time. Excavation of sixth-century *villae* reveals that within them, unlike their precursors, the chapel or oratory has become a regular part of estate architecture. But not only have the rural nobility become Christian and patrons of Christianity. By the seventh century excavation of adjacent rural hamlets, *aldeas*, demonstrates these settlements as well often boast small churches. If it would be premature to speak of a parochial system in the countryside, it seems incontrovertible that the rural population had largely been converted.

If it were needed, this same evidence would indicate the conversion of the nobility as well. The conversion of the Emperor Constantine himself in the fourth century had of course removed any legal inhibition to the conversion of the Roman senatorial and knightly classes but the entire thrust of their cultural inheritance as well as their solidarity as an elite continued to work against such a departure. The dynamic of their conversion in Iberia remains impossible to follow with any precision but the ordinary inclusion of a Christian chapel on their estates signals that it has transpired. It is also noteworthy that certainly by the time of Leovigild those bishops who are identifiable by reason of their prominence in the Christian church are already drawn almost invariably from the ranks of the old Hispano-Roman elite. Indeed, it is not too much to say that the episcopal dignity has itself, for better or worse, been assimilated to the noble order.

The situation was far other for the Visigothic nobility. By reason of the conversion of their people to Christianity by the followers of Arius of Alexandria in the mid-fourth century, the Visigoths had found themselves regarded as heretics by the orthodox Christians of the west whom they had conquered. Nevertheless, with some individual exceptions, they had retained their Arianism and its peculiar, tribal organization as had Vandals, Ostrogoths, and Suevi, under the same circumstances. This had entailed an ecclesiastical division and duplication in the kingdom which was a fertile source of social division and strife as well. As late as the time of Leovigild one can identify no fewer than ten cities in Iberia which boasted an Arian bishop and that king in his later years seems to have attempted an offensive against the orthodox church to weaken its majority position. It was to be this religious division and barrier to full integration which King Recared, son of Leovigild, would so dramatically abolish in the course of the Third Council of Toledo in 589.

That ecclesiastical council followed hard upon the annexation of the kingdom of the Suevi who had themselves abjured Arianism for orthodoxy shortly before conquest. It was preceded by the death of the old king Leovigild in 586 and the succession of his son Recared (586–601). Within a few months of his father's death, the new king himself decided upon the adoption of the orthodox faith and, after a period of preparation which had to contend with some objection and even conspiracies against the projected new order of things, summoned a council of the realm to formalize and promulgate the adhesion of both the king and the "gentis gothorum" to the traditional faith. The surviving acts of the council reveal to us a Christian church in the Visigothic kingdom organized into some sixty dioceses grouped into five metropolitan provinces, Seville, Lusitania, Toledo, Braga, and Narbonne. Eight Arian bishops signed the profession of faith contained therein as well as the orthodox bishops, the king, queen, and some of the Visigothic notables of the realm. With that action the Christianity of the kingdom became one and, precisely as one, practically irresistible.

The reader will understand, of course, that to speak of the Visigoths, or any other society, as Christian here implies merely a formal and legal adhesion. It prescinds entirely from a judgment on the spiritual or intellectual character of any individual's religious assent. But in the former sense, the Third Council of Toledo enhanced the already burgeoning process by which the Christian church was becoming the fundamental social institution in the peninsula. With the possible exception of the crown itself, the church had become the greatest landowner in the realm. The acts of the council reaffirmed that the bishop was the sole legal proprietor of all church property of the diocese but also that even the bishop was rarely at liberty to alienate the property of that church. Under such circumstances the church would continue to accumulate property and the bishop to evolve into the director of a great landed patrimony which would place him automatically among the magnates of the realm.

But with the dominium over land went a large measure of dominion over the people living on it. The council mandated that even freedmen, formerly slaves of the church, should continue subject to its legal tutelage (*patrocinium*). The regular civil jurisdiction over the dwellers on its lands was increasingly in the hands of its proprietor. This same process was at work on the lands of lay magnates as well, of course. But, to our knowledge, no lay magnates could summon agents of the royal fisc and local judges to their presence as the acts of this council provided for them to attend and be accountable to the projected semi-annual meetings of the provincial ecclesiastical synods. The council further reaffirmed that clerics were not to resort to secular tribunals for judgment in clerical matters. Nor were the public authorities to exact services from clerics or subjects of the church. On the other hand, bishops were to sit with the secular justices to punish the crime of infanticide. To the authority of religion the church was rapidly reinforcing and adding those of wealth and legal jurisdiction.

While this development went forward with increasing speed in the countryside its analogue was noticeable in the cities as well. There the old civic council of curiales was virtually extinct. At least in all but the most important cities it had been replaced by an urban official, *comes civitatis*, named by the crown but this worthy lived increasingly in the shadow of a bishop. After all the bishop was always there, indeed was becoming the greatest urban landholder, had his own court and his own legal jurisdiction, and being a royal appointee could be presumed to have the king's ear should a conflict occur. The magnate family from which the bishop was drawn appears often to have had long association with and influence in the episcopal city while the *comes* seemingly did not. One can watch the architecture of the city becoming steadily more Christian as first amphitheatres, then theatres, circus, and temples lost their original function and fell into disuse. Very frequently, they were then transformed into new urban Christian churches or monasteries or became the quarries from which the former were constructed. The old urban center of classical antiquity was evolving rapidly in the direction of the medieval episcopal *castrum*.

THE COUNTRYSIDE AND THE MAGNATES

The establishment of a single Christian religious authority and its expansion in city and country reacted strongly with other contemporary developments in the countryside to produce a new social order there. In the first place there was a sharp contraction of the total area devoted to *villa* agriculture. That regime had always had its limits, of course, being suited primarily to the most fertile, largely lowland soils with access to a stream or river for either or both irrigation and transportation of bulk goods to market. Moreover, it had grown in response to the opportunities of a cash-crop agriculture offered by an imperial market. Much has been written to prove the continuance of trade in the western Mediterranean after the fifth century but none of it has established the perdurance of the flourishing imperial trade in staples which was the foundation of the prosperity of the *villa* system.

Bereft of its *raison d'être*, that system could not but contract. It would also metamorphose from *villa* to estate, from market production to autarchy. That meant its practical disappearance from less favored or developed regions of the peninsula such as Asturias, Galicia, High Aragon and the very extensive foothill areas generally. In such places authority other than local vanished and the life based on a simpler level of herding and subsistence farming by individual families expanded. Where it had once entirely yielded to the pressure of Romanization, tribal life did not resume but even there an animosity towards former masters seems to have remained among rural peoples of this fringe, freed by default and neglect from old authorities. Fueled by poverty as well, it expressed itself in banditry, theft, and raids where it bordered the remaining estate culture. The acts of Visigothic councils and the texts of Visigothic legal codes are full of proscriptions against those people who harbor runaway slaves and who are themselves obviously only marginally within the orbit of the law.

This situation is reflected in the architecture of the later Visigothic estates. These are simply smaller in compass and ruder in construction. Above all, they are almost without exception fortified. The countryside about them has become latently hostile. However, in such of them as continued to exist, the authority of the Hispano-Gothic magnate had been markedly reinforced. The acceptance of Christianity, signaled by the appearance on the premises of a chapel, had also placed the magnate in a privileged position in the religious order. He selected the priest who ministered therein, not only to him but to the slaves of his household and likely the tenant-farmers of the environs as well. Where the latter had managed to procure a church in their own *aldea*, the magnate selected its priest as well. If the locale boasted a monastery, it was likely to be of his foundation, peopled by his relatives and dependants, and its properties administered in the furtherance of his, as well as its, interests.

The legal literature of the times reflects almost constant quarrels between these rural magnates and the bishop of the diocese over the actual collection and enjoyment of the rural rents, of rural taxes, of rural judicial fines, and even of rural tithes. Doubtless the bishop did rather better at asserting his rights to the first and the last of these, although even then with real difficulty. Nevertheless, quarrels over the division of the spoils should not distract us from the more usual reality of a cooperation between noble bishop and Christian noble to control, direct, and profit from the countryside and its peasantry. For most purposes, seen from the perspective of the farmer, lay magnate and bishop were but two, mutually reinforcing aspects of that authority which was the context of his life. To the extent that the peasantry had actually internalized Christianity they were now assured that the universe was indeed rational, that it was ultimately friendly if mysterious. They understood that it was the creation of a loving God who had sent His own Son to redeem them. They themselves were thus assured of their own individual worth and eventual immortality. Meanwhile, however, they lived in a sinful world where the power of the divine was mediated through the hierarchy of king, noble, and bishop and their role in it was work and obedience.

That labor and its conditions does not seem to have altered very much as a result of the disappearance of the empire within what remained of the estate culture. Agricultural techniques and tools continued to be quite the same. Irrigation was still practiced wherever it had been feasible. The use of iron to edge farming tools remained widespread. Simple smithing may even have become more common since dependence on local resources increased. The same necessity probably made animal husbandry increasingly important in relation to farming within this local economy.

Legally, rural slavery was widespread and the central portions of the noble estate appear to have been worked by slave gangs which could number in the hundreds. Still, outlying portions were worked by semi-free peasants who enjoyed what a later age would call a *tenement*. That is, they were ordinarily entitled to the continued use of a hut, of a portion of the tillable, of access for their domestic animals to common pasture, and, for their animals and themselves, the rights to utilize the edible wild foods and timber of the woodlands adjoining the estate. In return, they owed deference and a share of their product as quitrent to the master of the estate and another share of both as tithe to the local church. In other words, it would take a delicate pair of calipers indeed to measure the difference between the material and social lot of this peasantry and that of its predecessors of the past 7,000 years and its descendants of the next 1,000.

In this local world the proprietor was king, for practical purposes. He might in many instances actually be the king himself, or a bishop, or an abbot, but usually he was the Hispano-Gothic magnate. Variations within this class itself were wide but it can be safely be asserted that the members of it were themselves poor and rude by comparison with the old Roman senatorial class. That is, they disposed of very little income in money and less as the sixth century turned into the seventh. They might be given it by the crown occasionally and othertimes could collect some in the form of fines. But increasingly royal gifts were in the form of jewels and objects of gold and silver and the liquid wealth of the magnate himself was largely kept in that form. Except for bishops and abbots, formal education was ever more rare. The real education of the magnate was in the military arts, hunting, and husbandry, i.e., the practical masculine virtues. Travel outside the immediate province, except sometimes to the royal court or council, was unusual, outside the peninsula almost unknown save for fisher-folk or the very great.

Overwhelmingly the magnates were local figures. Their horizons were almost as limited as that of their peasantry. Their own income was largely in rents and services, collected in kind and in labor. They did not want for food, or wine, or horses, or weapons, or servants, but it was increasingly difficult to turn these solid assets into the more civilized forms of wealth. Perhaps the greatest luxury of the class lay in its power. More and more the magnate ruled his little world without hindrance or let. That was a function of the progressive weakness of the crown and its inability to project its power far beyond the royal presence itself. Royal resources were becoming similarly inflexible, composed of rents and fines rather more than taxes, which latter were becoming more and more difficult to assess and to collect. The very royal coinage seems to have been struck largely to mark solemn occasions and to distribute to a mustered army.

That army consisted of the magnates gathered with their retainers. Except when the royal host was mustered, the army of the realm shrank to the royal bodyguard. Frontier districts such as Septimania had their *dux* and many of the provinces and cities their *comes* but already by the mid-sixth century these officials seem to be drawn from one or the other magnate family of that particular district. Rather than garrisons one should see them commanding their own bodyguards and retainers, swollen by the general levy of the district in cases of invasion, war, or rebellion. Under such circumstances the king must rule by the force of his personality, the excess of his talent, the diplomatic skill to divide his opponents, and the charisma of his office. He could hardly compel obedience against the magnates and was hard put to purchase it.

The history and the legal sources of the sixth and seventh centuries combine to provide a picture in which the Visigothic kings are increasingly driven to resort to confiscation of land to restore their fortunes. Such extreme measures testify to the underlying condition in which the crown had to alienate land from the royal fisc as the ordinary means of purchasing support. But such alienations more and more reduced the king to merely the greatest noble of the realm. Ambitious rulers could only increase their resources by reclaiming the land by one device or another. In the meanwhile, the local magnates augmented their estates out of neighboring royal fisc lands, sought to promote their relatives and friends to the local bishopric, church, or abbey, and exercised an authority based simply on superior power where a royal office could not be purchased to legitimate it. The history of the Visigothic kingdom is one of the progressive decline of royal power and the increasing autonomy of the local magnate. In that regard, its evolution is quite like that of the Germanic monarchy everywhere in the post-Roman west.

COMMERCE AND CITY

The reduction of the imperial world to a collection of provinces, or even locales, bound tenuously by a kinship in religion and language was in good part the result of the failure of commerce as well as of politics. Yet sixth-century Iberia was participant in a shrunken Mediterranean trade which did continue to bring to it some luxuries and some styles. The attested presence of Syrian traders in ports from Lisbon to Tarragona, for instance, provides evidence for such a continuity. But yet more eloquent is the dominance of first Italian Ostrogothic and later Byzantine motifs in jewelry and of North African patterns in pottery. Such peoples were sufficiently familiar for their styles to be influential rather than merely outlandish. Moreover, the long coast of the peninsula continued to offer opportunity to a fishing community. That of Catalonia interacted certainly with that of southern France. That of Algeciras and Malaga could hardly avoid contact with that of Ceuta just across the straits. Even the fishing community of the Cantabrian coast made contact fairly regularly, it seems, with its counterparts in western France, Brittany, and far Ireland. The fact that various of the works of Bishop Isidore of Seville (600–636) were known in the latter in the second half of the seventh century reminds us that, if few people traveled, some traveled very widely.

But if casual trade in more than seafoods could result from such regular contacts, the disappearance of the old fish oil (*garum*) manufactories in Lusitania and Baetica illustrates the failure of that imperial trade which formerly supported a major commerce. The basin of the Guadalquivir saw some manufacture of pottery distinctive for its North African motifs but it does not seem to have been widely distributed even in the peninsula. So too, the mining industry which had moved Iberian iron, copper, and lead, throughout the Mediterranean disappears. Mining on the Roman scale was pointless for a purely local market. The widespread use of iron to edge agricultural tools proves that some mining continues but, like almost everything else, on a suitably reduced scale. Copper too was still mined and there is evidence of some substantial production of bronze jewelry in the western basin of the Duero but its products are found only in the peninsula.

Clearly the only flourishing international trade was that in slaves from Slavic territories beyond the Elbe which found its way through Frankish Gaul to the Mediterranean. Gregory of Tours gives even literary evidence of that and, significantly, the most numerous finds of Visigothic coins outside of the realm itself have been in the Rhineland. But perhaps the best commentary on the general question of the survival of trade is precisely that of the coinage. The Visigothic kings accepted and continued the coinage of Rome. But with them the gold *solidus* became merely a money of account. It was no longer minted. Only the gold *tremisses*, that is, "thirds," were struck and these were more and more adulterated with base metals in the seventh century. In other words, on the one hand the government of the realm found it increasingly difficult to claim the sort of revenue which would allow it to maintain its coinage and on the other a volume of trade which would have demanded such a coinage had dwindled away. Still more striking is the disappearance of the Roman bronze coinage. That is the starkest sort of testimony to the contraction as well of local trade in humble objects. Even peasants do not ordinarily make their own dishes, shoes, or sickles, of course, but we must be prepared to think of a commerce so limited that eggs, cabbages, and sheep, can be pressed into service as media of exchange.

Now such a major contraction of commerce must, in turn, result in a contraction of the cities which depended upon it for their very existence. We do well to remember, in the first place, that no city so much as maintained its population on the basis of its own natural increase until after the arrival of modern medicine in the nineteenth century. All urban centers before that time depended upon continuous immigration from the countryside simply to achieve stability in this respect. Now it is commonly predicated that the total population of the peninsula shrank from 6,000,000 at its height in the early imperial age to less than 4,000,000 by the seventh century. One should expect that the cities shared in this phenomenon and disproportionately so. Roman cities were always rather more centers of government and administration than of trade. But as the Roman government decayed and disappeared, its host of officials, bureaucrats, and functionaries, were in no measure compensated by the agents or retinues of the Visigothic kings. At the same time, the shrinkage of the merchant community, its families, and servants, also sharply restricted those opportunities which had tended to attract the more adventurous of the countryside in an earlier age.

As a result of all three factors we should expect the population of Cádiz to have dropped from 65,000 to 20,000 at most and that of Tarragona from 27,000 to perhaps 8,000. Smaller cities may even have fared a bit better as they were not so dependent upon extra-peninsular trade. Archeology demonstrates that as the gross area of cities declined, like the *villae* of the countryside, they also grew walls to protect themselves against the harsher circumstances now obtaining. In addition, this smaller, walled area not infrequently had substantial open garden spaces within it. Yet, with the exception of Cartagena destroyed by the Visigothic kings as an act of policy and of Lusitanian *Conimbriga* transferred to a more easily defensible site, few of the old Roman urban centers disappeared entirely during this period. They were, in fact, taking on a new orientation and function which was to help to maintain them.

Where these cities had been primarily centers for Roman secular administration, they now were invariably becoming centers for the administration of the Christian church. That church tended to ape the empire in many fashions and its bishop therefore was to be quintessentially an urban administrator. Whether or not the times were propitious for such practice, he would rule the area of the Late Roman diocese as the area now of the episcopal diocese, and that from the old capital of the former.

That practice could not even proximately compensate for the losses which the Iberian cities were otherwise experiencing, of course. Nonetheless, in the northwest and in the case of what had probably never been more than glorified garrisons such as Viesu, Lamego, even Braga or Astorga, such new episcopal cities may well have represented positive growth. By contrast, new cities of royal foundation such as Recopolis, Victoriacum, and Ologicus, proved to have no future at all. Elsewhere, though the city might be shrinking about them, the bishops assembled their episcopal *familias*, raised new subordinate churches within the limits and, in some favored suburbs, patronized the establishment of urban and suburban monasteries, even a hospital separately endowed in seventh-century Mérida. Such nuclei, together with assistants, subordinates, slaves, and families could satisfy the need for employment of fair numbers of artisans and craftsmen as well as simple purveyors. Contemporary literature and scattered archeological remains speak of quite large episcopal and monastic building campaigns in places such as sixth-century Mérida and seventh-century Toledo. Some of these seem to have enjoyed royal and noble patronage and others not. Surviving remains, largely in the countryside, indicate a fairly high level of competence in architecture and architectural decoration supported by such activity and the same must have been true of the manual trades generally.

But the crown and the magnate class had not yet entirely deserted the city for the countryside. The Visigothic kings seem to have moved often from city to city, although Toledo was a preferred site. Up to the beginning of the seventh century some faint traces, at least, remained of the old urban *curial* class in the major cities and even magnates who had evaded that onerous distinction sometimes maintained an urban dwelling and from it strove to control or even dominate the new episcopal power there. Nevertheless, it is likely that most cities continued to experience the decline of both their population and their economic life down to the appearance of Islam in the peninsula.

INTELLECTUAL LIFE IN A NEW WORLD

Though we have been concentrating thus far upon decline, and properly so, in the economic and political institutions and life of the Iberian world, we should distance ourselves somewhat from that pejorative notion in examining other changes which were occurring at the same time. In terms of thought and political ideology what takes place is simply a profound alteration in the conceptions with which Iberian society addressed reality. To speak of an intellectual revolution is strictly correct if one does not understand thereby a rapid and a total adhesion to it of all sectors of the society.

This remarkable cultural alteration, which will involve the blending of classical, Germanic, and Christian elements in uneven proportions, was not unique to Iberia in the post-Roman west. Yet that common development would take particular form subsequently in Iberia as a function of its most particular history. From the outset, Christianity was the controlling strain in that dynamic.

While the Visigoths came to the peninsula as conquerors, at most levels the remarkable fact is just how little influence they were destined to enjoy. At the fundamental level of language one can almost say that the Germanic invasion of Iberia might well never have occurred. That is, Latin there will continue its slow evolution towards Castilian, Catalan, Gallegan, or Portuguese, largely unscathed. In the vocabulary of any of those idioms it is difficult to find as many as three hundred words of Germanic root. Their grammar was to continue more massively Latin still.

This slightness of impact was in part a result of their relative paucity of numbers. Combining the best estimates of the numbers of all of the German tribes who invaded the peninsula during the fifth and sixth centuries would not yield a total of more than 500,000 persons as against an indigenous population of perhaps 5,000,000, depending upon the time of their entry. Even in those areas where the invaders seemed predominantly to have settled, for the Suevi the north of Portugal and Galicia and for the Visigoths the eastern plain of the Duero, it is impossible to detect a peculiarity of language pattern that results – much less a change in agricultural practice, a difference of domestic architecture, a new pattern of land settlement, or of burial custom. One must understand that the striation of Visigothic society already into noble, freeman, and slave, would necessarily have limited their influence but that, above all, their relative backwardness in most respects in contrast to the peoples whom they overran would lead them simply to adopt the practices of the more civilized majority. In all matters, including those so fundamental as language and religion, they ultimately conformed, except in the realm of political life as we shall see.

The language of thought in Iberia, like the language of daily speech, was to be Latin. There is simply no piece of literature written in Gothic there of which we have record. Even though the Gothic language was employed in the liturgy of the Arian church down to 589, we must assume that by such time it had already become a sacred, cultic tongue, increasingly unintelligible to its ordinary auditors. At the same time, for quite different reasons, Greek was ceasing to be known in the peninsula. Of that second language, the theoretical adornment of the complete Roman gentleman, one can find but a single competent native practitioner. Abbot John of Biclarum, born somewhere about Santarém and remarkably of Gothic descent, is the only sixth- or seventh-century figure of the Visigothic kingdom whom we can confidently assert to have had a good working knowledge of Greek. There were, of course, Greek-speaking merchants in some of the ports and Greek-born individuals who sometimes even achieved high office in the peninsular church, but they had no impact upon the literary or intellectual evolution. But if the language of thought was to be that of Rome its content was to be everywhere reworked by Christianity.

That would be so largely because education was in the process of becoming a clerical phenomenon, and so it would be a professional education which would produce a professional literature. Among the casualties of the new, ruder, and rural society which was emerging were the ubiquitous lay teachers of antiquity, the *grammaticus* and the *rhetor.* Since education in the classical period rarely had an institutional form but was instead a matter of individual mentors and their pupils, we are unable to trace its decline closely anywhere in the old western Empire. But just because its medieval replacement typically took institutional shape, we can follow its development at least in a very general way. Already in 527 the Second Council of Toledo provided that children pledged to a life of religion by their parents should be educated under the direction of the local bishop. But before that time, at the end of the fifth century, there was an established monastic school in Valencia which had trained Bishop Justinian of that city and perhaps three of his brothers who also became bishops. In that Christianity was a religion of *The Book*, the church must undertake to produce literate recruits for its clergy if society did not. Clearly, by the end of the troubled fifth century an education was increasingly difficult to obtain in Iberia.

How soon schools became a practical clerical monopoly one cannot say. Among the Visigothic kings Sisebut (612–621) was not only literate but apparently an author of some ability. There is testimony at least to the existence of a royal library and the seventh-century *comes civitatis* of Toledo, Laurentius, also had one. It is likely then that some of the greatest secular figures of the realm still resisted the total identification of "nobleman" with "warrior" and were able to find tutors for their children. But Sisebut is the sole layman and author of whom we are aware and he may well have been educated by monks. Bishop Isidore of Seville, the most famous Latin author of seventh-century western Europe, was a product of monastic education and certainly a majority of the bishops of the Visigothic kingdom were. Despite the exhortations of councils, in Iberia as everywhere in the west, bishops had so many other responsibilities that they were happy to pass off that of educating the clergy to the monasteries.

If education in the peninsula was becoming increasingly clerical that does not mean that the interests of its sons were entirely private ones. The new religion of society was dependent upon the written Scriptures and Isidore of Seville was not alone in Iberia in producing a renewed text of the Bible based upon the now two-hundred-year-old Vulgate of Saint Jerome. While it might be that only the clergy were able to read that text, yet all preaching and teaching were to be based upon it and one says without fear of contradiction that the Christian Bible was to become the fundamental common cultural, literary, and religious source of the society of the West for the next 1,300 years.

Most intimately related to the role of Scripture in Christianity were the mass and the sacraments. These elements of a sacred liturgy were to achieve a fixed form during the Visigothic period which was to endure in the Iberian church for the next 500 years. One ordinarily calls it the Mozarabic liturgy because it was the service, in the first instance, of those Christians living subject to Muslim dominion, or "Mozarabs." It was embodied in a *Liber Ordinum*, a *Liber Sacramentorum*, a *Liber Comicus* of movable Gospels and Epistles, and an *Antifonarium* of sung portions. To these were joined a hymnal and a prayer book. All in all, the form of worship of the Iberian Christian church took on its classical form during this period but we are ignorant of the individuals to whom it was due.

The concentration upon Scripture and liturgy was, however, accompanied by the composition of ancillary works in other genres, professional in a stricter sense because not directed to Christians generally as were the former. That is, the age produced its share of Scriptural commentary, ever the first work of the educated cleric. In volume it was closely followed by polemical literature directed against Arianism,

Priscillianism, and Judaism and by a considerable body of dogmatic work, most of this latter being Christological in theme. Bishops Isidore of Seville and Fructuosus of Braga also authored monastic rules which were to have currency in the peninsula for a long time. None of these works became classics and we have little interest in them today but they did respond to the intellectual concerns of their own times.

The classical genre of the *De Viris Illustribus* was employed by Isidore of Seville among others but the content largely changes from the emperors, philosophers, and men of letters of classical times to bishops and saints. A related form is the *vita* of the saints which we read for the historical information they contain but the age read for edification. Bishop Braulius of Saragossa in the seventh century did a life of Saint Aemelianus (San Millán) which tells us something of the attempt to convert the pagan in the mountains between Burgos and Logroño. Valerius of Astorga wrote a life of Saint Fructuosus of Braga which treats the missionary endeavors of the latter in the northwest. On the other hand, the *Lives of the Fathers of Mérida* is valuable for its revelations of the political and social life of that city in the sixth century. King Sisebut made his contribution with a *vita* of Bishop Desiderius of Vienne (595–606).

That king also composed, if we can believe the attribution, an *Astronomicon*, or astrological poem. Indeed the age had something of that peculiar passion for Latin poetry written for generally didactic and educational purposes which reminds one of similar Carolingian output later. The rather sophisticated and classical practice of publishing a collection of one's own or another's letters was also fairly commonplace. In the late seventh century Bishop Julian of Toledo wrote a commentary on the *Grammar* of Donatus and some others authored grammatical works. There are also some historical works. Isidore of Seville composed a *History of the Kings of the Goths, Vandals, and Suevi*. Bishop Julian of Toledo did a *History of King Wamba*. But the most important historical work of the period, and that which supplied the general framework within which the whole understanding of human society and history were subsumed, was Paulus Orosius' *Seven Books of History against the Pagans*, written at the beginning of the age.

In the second century BC the Greek Historian Polybius had constructed a history in which the central theme had been the gradual growing into unity of humankind, with the Roman Empire seen as the culmination and realization of that universal striving. During the fourth century AD Bishop Eusebius of Caesarea had composed a chronicle which adapted Polybius' schema so that the Empire became the providential instrument of human unity which prepared the conditions for human Redemption and the transmission of the faith to the entire human community. Henceforth the essence of human history was to be understood as the interaction of the Christian church and the Roman Empire in the proselytization and salvation of humanity.

Now the very completeness of this schema, which started with creation as recounted in the Old Testament and combined the history of Israel and the secular history of Polybius to produce one sweeping whole which made all of the human experience intelligible, proved to have enormous appeal to a newly Christian Roman Empire. Eusebius wrote in Greek, of course, and the genre of universal history was to become fundamental to the perception of the Greek world. But his *Chronicle* was to be quickly translated into Latin and continued by no lesser personages than Saint Jerome and Rufinus. It also basically conditioned the form of Saint Augustine of Hippo's *City of God*. In the western Latin world, too, the universal chronicle would become the essential framework within which history was conceptualized.

There it was to be the Iberian presbyter Orosius who supplied its classical form. Born somewhere near Braga about 380, Orosius became a refugee when the Suevi invaded Galicia and Lusitania about 410. His travels took him to Hippo in North Africa where he met Saint Augustine who later suggested that Orosius compose such a history to complement Augustine's *City of God*. The Iberian continued on to Palestine where he met Saint Jerome as well. Eventually he returned to Iberia and completed his history down to the year AD 417 but after that time we hear no more of him. In his *History* Orosius had drawn not only on Eusebius but Livy, Caesar, Suetonius, Tacitus, Florus, Rufinus, and Eutropius. It would become the history book to the western Middle Ages. Hundreds of manuscripts of it still survive for it became basic to the sound monastic or episcopal library and hundreds of other manuscripts either based upon it or simply continuing it also still exist.

In Visigothic Iberia the universal history thus begun was continued by Bishop Hidatius of Galicia, on the basis of Saint Jerome, up to 468. Subsequently, it was probably one Bishop Justus of Urgel who carried the former's account up to 567. The Goth of Santarém, John of Biclarum, and later bishop of Gerona brought matters up to 590. Then Isidore of Seville's universal history, or *Chronicon*, related further happenings up until AD 616.

Bishop Isidore also composed the other most influential work of this period, the *Etymologies*, in twenty books. The first four books of this opus dealt with the various disciplines of education comprised by the *trivium* and the *quadrivium*. The next two with medicine and law. Books Seven and Eight treat theology, Nine and Ten government. The four following cover human anatomy, animals, geography, and cosmology. The remaining six books describe what may be called the practical arts from building, through agriculture, metals, coinage, foods, clothing, implements, even games and war. The *Etymologies* was to become the great encyclopedia of the Early Middle Ages. Until outdated by the recovery in the twelfth century of the original texts of Greek science and philosophy, on which it was based, it was to be the indispensable text for the instruction of the young, especially in the subjects of the *quadrivium*, i.e., mathematics, geometry, astronomy, and music. Throughout western Europe it was found in episcopal and monastic libraries and the first four books were often copied and circulated independently as educational manuals.

Bishop Isidore, whom we have had occasion to mention so often, came from an important Hispano-Roman family of Cartagena that fled to Seville on the latter's occupation by the Byzantines in the mid-sixth century. His brother, Leander, was bishop of Seville (578–599) before him, had visited Constantinople, authored a number of polemical works, and had figured largely in the affairs of the kingdom. Isidore, a product of a monastic school in Seville like Leander, also visited Byzantium, and eventually succeeded his brother as bishop (600–630), becoming similarly prominent in political affairs. Under their leadership Seville became a culture center through which knowledge of the corpus of the Western Latin Fathers of the church and of the secular classical Latin authors would be transmitted to succeeding generations.

Almost all that we know of education and the educated during this time points to their being domiciled about the episcopal city. Beyond Seville, there are the notable bishops of Saragossa, John (620–631), Braulius (631–651), and Taius (651–644). Later still there are the bishops of Toledo, Justus (633–636), Eugenius I (636–646), Eugenius II (646–657), and Alfonsus (657–667). In addition, the episcopal centers of Gerona, Urgel, Valencia, Palencia, Astorga, and Braga, were all represented in the surviving notices of contemporary scholars. But where we have biographical data it appears that they were the products of an urban monastic school rather than a strictly episcopal one. In a tradition which went back formally to the sixth-century Cassiodorus, the monks pursued that Christian wisdom which was enshrined in Scripture and the commentaries and treatises of the Latin Fathers but only after they had mastered the seven liberal arts which defined the basic education of the Late Roman world. In pursuit of the latter, they perused not simply Donatus and Priscian but Virgil, Caesar, Cicero, and most of the Roman authors who are still known to us.

The influence of Cassiodorus illustrates the fact that Visigothic Iberia was yet a part of the post-Roman Mediterranean society. So too, Bishop

Martin of Braga (569–579) derived ultimately from Pannonia and Bishops Paul (530–560) and Fidelis (560–571) of Mérida came from the Greek east. Both Leander and Isidore of Seville spent considerable time in Constantinople. For almost a century the southern and southeastern coast was a Byzantine province. In the sixth century the monk Nanctus fled Africa for Lusitania and in the same period one Donatus led a group of African monks, who brought their own library, to found the new monastery of Servitanum in the peninsula.

These events and their like found their reflection not only in literary borrowing and imitation but in the jewelry and pottery styles of the times. Perhaps their most spectacular influences are still visible in the structures of those Visigothic churches which survive. These are largely rural monastic ones for city churches were subsequently rebuilt many times. Structures such as Quintanilla de la Viñas outside of Burgos and San Fructuoso near Braga feature the Byzantine and North African horseshoe arch and the square apse, for instance. Such elements too will find perpetuation and elaboration in the subsequent Mozarabic style.

LAW AND INSTITUTIONS

Yet another testimony to the receptivity of Visigothic Iberia to wider influences is the altogether remarkable collection of the *acta* of ecclesiastical councils known as the *Hispana*. The earliest manuscript is of the ninth century but its composition dates from the mid-seventh and it may ultimately derive from a collection begun by Isidore of Seville. It includes the texts and some associated documents of 37 Iberian councils, 10 Greek, 9 African, and 17 Gallic ones, in addition to some 103 papal decretals. Our immediate interest in it derives from the view it gives of the Visigothic monarchy and monarchical institutions.

Beginning with the Third Council of Toledo in 589, that ecclesiastical device was to be gradually transformed into the central institution of the realm, after the monarchy itself. In that council of bishops it is already clear that the king has convened it and that he will confirm its actions. But if Recared gave a decisive turn to its formation, the council will not become crucial to the kingdom until the very weakness of the crown demands it. With Toledo IV in 633, the presence of the great palatine nobles in the assembly is first noted. Toledo VIII furnishes initial proof that the kings have begun to submit their agenda to the council in written form, a *tomus*, Toledo XII in 681 supplies the first explicit evidence of the customary departure of the king after his presentation of the *tomus* so as to allow freedom of discussion to the group. Between

Toledo IV in 633 and Toledo XVII in 694, fifteen general councils of the realm will meet, an average of one every four years.

Beyond the form and history of the general council itself, this series portrays the essential characteristics of the Visigothic monarchy. What is most remarkable from the standpoint of later western monarchy is the absence of a ruling dynasty, the central prop of the crown's authority. Moreover, while accident plays its part, it emerges as a matter of policy that Visigothic monarchy will remain elective rather than hereditary. The old regnal line of the Visigoths had perished with the murder of Amalric in 531. After the Ostrogothic hegemony and a time of troubles, the monarchy under Leovigild and his son Recared had recovered and adopted the practice of associating its heirs with the reigning king in an effort to establish a dynasty. However, the murder of Recared's young son, Liuva II (601–603), put an end to such plans and opened up a new period in which only one of four kings, none related to his predecessor, left the throne by natural means.

In 633, Toledo IV set some essential rules. The preceding monarch, Swintila (621–631), was alleged to have abdicated by reason of his crimes. His brother, wife, and sons were barred from succession and their possessions were forfeit. Future kings must rule under the law or face excommunication. Ordinarily, on the death of a king, the clergy and the magnates will select a new one. Presumably, some process of this sort had been followed in the installation of the then ruler, Sisnandus (631–636). The council also legislated that anyone who conspired for the deposition or murder of a legitimate monarch would suffer excommunication.

A few years later, under the rule of Sisnandus' successor, Chintila (636–642) who was no relative of the former, Toledo V in 636 recognized the new ruler but asserted as well that only election, not lineage, makes a king. However, in an apparent effort to strengthen the authority of such elective kings, the council also legislated that those who planned for the succession during the lifetime of the existing ruler were excommunicate. At the same time, it reinforced the position of the nobility by stipulating that the *fideles* of a monarch could not, after the king's death, be deprived of his rewards for their services by anyone, presumably his successor as well.

In 638 Toledo VI restated and broadened that provision by extending it to the goods granted the church as well. It also made explicit that only a Goth of good character could be elected king while it explicitly ruled out persons of unfree ancestry and those who had received tonsure. Further stipulations followed in Toledo VIII in 653. The election must take place either in Toledo or on the site of the prior king's death and by vote of the bishops and palatine nobles. The elect must be Catholic, unassuming, just, and dedicated to the good of the realm. Before his accession he must swear to uphold its laws. For violation of his oath he may be deposed.

All of these cumulative stipulations reflect the intent of the bishops and palatine nobles to monopolize the selection of the Visigothic monarch and to control the conditions under which he could act. Despite their legislation, however, it is clear that violence and the threat of it continued to make monarchs and that their pretensions were not accepted by the nobility at large. Yet attempts to reinforce the power of the crown by making it hereditary proved to have insufficient backing.

The last of these followed the curious abdication of Wamba (672–680). Toledo XII in 681 recognized Ervig as his successor because he had been designated by Wamba and subsequently had been anointed. There was no mention of his election. In addition it recognized his right to appoint a bishop to any of the sees of the realm and to have the bishop of Toledo install them. Two years later Toledo XIII legislated that Ervig's queen might not be remarried or forced into concubinage after his death nor could she or his sons, daughters, or relatives be killed, mutilated, deprived of their possessions, exiled, or forced into the religious life. On the other hand, a general pardon was extended to all those who had been condemned for rebellion over the last forty years and their confiscated property was to be restored. There was to be an amnesty for all unpaid sums owed to the fisc and palatine nobles and bishops were not henceforth to be degraded without the public judgment of their peers. All of this looks very much like an attempt at a general political settlement in which the Ervig's family is given dynastic status in all but name.

In 687 Ervig abdicated in favor of his son-in-law, Egica (688–702), and Toledo XV of that year specifically upheld the legality of the oath which had been exacted by Ervig from all of his subjects to support the provisions of Toledo XIII in favor of his descendants. In 693 Toledo XVI would extend those same protections to the progeny of Egica and would also take the highly significant step of requiring a mass to be said daily in every church of the realm for the safety and wellbeing of the king and his family. At his death in 702 there seems to have been little or no opposition to the succession of his son, Witiza (702–710), and a dynasty was finally in the making, perhaps. However, a revolt against that prospect was associated with the death of Witiza and a disputed succession produced two claimants, Rodrigo (710–711) and Agila II (710–714). The latter was likely related in some degree to Witiza although he was probably not his son. This final breakdown of the Visigothic monarchy helped to facilitate the Muslim invasion of the following year.

But if the Visigothic monarchy and kingdom were to perish their traditions would survive, preserved in the *Hispana* and in the *Liber Judiciorum*, to supply the intellectual justification and inspiration for their reincarnation in the Asturian monarchy of the Cantabrians. This latter volume was another of the remarkable and precocious achievements of the Visigothic kingdom. Its written legal traditions had begun with the promulgation by Alaric II of the *Breviarum* in 506. This was a much simplified form of Roman law promulgated for the benefit of his non-Gothic subjects. The *Breviarum* was to remain in force in the Visigothic kingdom for 150 years thereafter and was to have even more lasting influence in the later Frankish world of former Gaul. But in 506 it was issued to complement that reworked Roman and customary law which had already been devised by Alaric's father, Euric, some thirty years earlier for the government of his Gothic subjects. It was this latter collection which was eventually to issue in the *Liber Judiciorum*.

The development of a largely Iberian kingdom after the debacle of 507, the abolition of the legal prohibition of intermarriage of Goths and Romans by Leovigild in the middle of that century, and the conversion of the Goths to orthodox Christianity under his son Recared shortly thereafter, combined to remove much of the rationale for separate laws. Nevertheless, the distinctions were not formally abolished until Chindaswinth had the old code of Euric reworked into a single legal system which applied to the entire territory of the realm and all of its inhabitants, Goth or Roman, about the middle of the seventh century. This code no longer survives except as incorporated into the revision made by his son, Receswinth, around 654. This revision, in turn revised by Ervig in 681 and with some additions by Egica and Witiza, is what we know as the *Liber Judiciorum*. Its manuscript tradition is ancient, reaching back to the eighth century, which testifies to its continuous influence despite the disappearance of the political world which had produced it.

The *Liber* is composed of 559 *capitula* divided into twelve books. After the introductory book which dealt with the nature of law and the duties of the legislator, the remaining ones treat of the jurisdiction of various judges, judicial procedures, witnesses, documents, marriage, sales, inheritance, church property, crime, and a variety of other topics. This combination of civil, commercial, and criminal code, must have been relatively all-encompassing for the needs of a society as simple as the Visigothic kingdom had become by the end of the seventh century. Still, by that time one must have grave reservations about the ability of the kings to enforce the uniform application of its provisions in any given instance. Yet its mere existence must have furnished a norm from which all exceptions, except those of pure violence, must be somehow justified.

Moreover, since the *Liber* was not a political code in any thorough-going sense, it could and did become the basis of the law which was later adjudicated in the Christian Mozarab communities by their own judges and counts when they had passed under the political dominion of the Muslim. Its very survival in those societies would also make it susceptible of transmission to those Christian kingdoms of the north of the peninsula when these later had achieved such size and stability as to require a legal frame.

Once one passes from the description of things that should be, as contained in the canon and civil law, to a consideration of the actual state of the royal administration of the realm an extreme caution is in order. The former sources speak of a palatine nobility which clearly existed, divided sometimes into *seniores*, *fideles*, and *gardingi*. Presumably the latter are relatively humble members of the royal bodyguard, the *fideles* perhaps those tied to the crown primarily by gifts of fisc lands, the first, members of the best families of the kingdom who monopolize the major court offices. However, we know nothing of the way in which they were chosen. One suspects that a de facto hereditary right already inhered in certain families. It is unlikely that they were paid, except for members of the guard. Likely they all served at the good pleasure of the king but we have noticed the conciliar legislation introduced to make it impossible for a king to dismiss the appointees of his predecessor. In brief, probably the most realistic way to describe them is that they are the most powerful current supporters of the king among the great nobility. That is, they owe their place more to family wealth and power than to royal selection.

Clearly there was some division of responsibility among the nobility. A count of the stables likely commanded the bodyguard, another count the notaries, yet another the royal chamber and hence the fisc. Did those divisions extend to the countryside in more than legal intent? Again documents sometimes speak of a "duke" of the province who seems to be a military figure as against the provincial "rector" who is a civil one. At a lower level, this distinction appears to reoccur between the count of the district and the count of the city. Again there are clearly judges for the courts and collectors of taxes. But the same problems of ignorance bedevil any attempt to discern who they really are and how they function as besets the character of the court.

In general, local divisions seem to follow old Roman ones. We hear, sometimes, of a duke of Lusitania or the Narbonensis. So too the countship likely followed the late imperial divisions. But there are no records which would indicate that such clear divisions were continuous, that they extended to the entire realm, or whether their holders were simply the local magnates writ large, unpaid and essentially irreplaceable except by royal support of a local rival. I, for one, suspect that it was just so.

The crown did attempt to maintain the tax system which they had inherited from Rome, at least insofar as it applied to the real property of all free men. At the same time, they kept up the port tolls on commerce. But such evidence as does exist demonstrates amply that real property was progressively escaping taxation as the best of it gravitated to the hands of the church or the magnates and as small freeholders sought the patronage of one or the other of those privileged orders. Moreover, the decline of commerce must have sharply reduced the income from tolls. In 653 the Eighth Council of Toledo legislated the difference between the familial and the public resources of the king. Surely they were not establishing a distinction but attempting to maintain one which was daily more unrealistic. Given that local taxes were not collected but farmed, are we involved here with more than the sale of offices? More and more, the only real royal officials would have been estate officials. Since there was no dynasty to husband the royal fisc lands, even this resource must have been increasingly precarious.

The condition of that Christian church so closely associated with the monarchy is rather clearer. The *Hispana* collection makes it obvious that ecclesiastical divisions followed the old Roman imperial ones, continuously and almost without change down to the great watershed which was the Muslim conquest. The six great metropolitan sees, Toledo, Mérida, Seville, Tarragona, Braga, and Narbonne, presided over what had been the Carthagenensis, Lusitania, Baetica, Galletia, and the Narbonensis. Another sixty or so bishoprics occupied those cities which had been the center of Roman districts. These bishoprics were filled with royal appointees, consecrated by their respective metropolitan, who ordinarily served for life.

Now it is certainly true that extraneous factors operated to condition that clearly defined process. Episcopal families were far from uncommon, where we can follow the succession, in sees such as Seville, Saragossa, Valencia, and Toledo, for instance. Social and political considerations obviously influenced the operation of the royal choice. That is reflected also in the change of the bishopric from an almost exclusively Hispano-Roman preserve in the early sixth century to the Hispano-Gothic representation in that office of something like three times their incidence in the general population in the seventh century. Still an ecclesiastical administration survived in a way that the civil administration did not.

This Visigothic church was in only the most sporadic contact with Rome. For the century and a half following the death of Pope Gregory I the Great (590–604), only eight papal letters addressed to it survive. Still, one should take into account as well the substantial collection of papal decretals included in the *Hispana*. The prestige of the bishop of Rome was accorded consideration although his advice was sought but rarely. One should also note that the coast of Cantabria, the Basque country, and High Aragon remained beyond the Christian pale.

THE CLASSIC VISIGOTHIC KINGDOM

The reigns of Leovigild (569–586) and his son Recared (586–601) mark the apogee of the Visigothic monarchy. Their policies were at once both ambitious and imaginative and their execution of them was in good measure successful. It is not too much to say that they refounded the kingdom.

One great part of Leovigild's plan was to alter the character of the monarchy itself by surrounding it with the charisma of the most success-ful and prestigious government that age, the restored Roman Empire of Justinian I the Great (527–565). In his lifetime, Leovigild had witnessed the Byzantine destruction of the kingdom of the Vandals and its recovery of North Africa. That had been followed by its reconquest of Italy and the eradication of the Ostrogothic kingdom there. Uncomfortably, it had reached even into Iberia where it held the entire coastline from south of Valencia on the Mediterranean to just south of Cádiz on the Atlantic. If further Byzantine progress was to be forestalled perhaps imitation was the best weapon.

In any event, though he was able to do little more than prevent Roman advance into the basin of the Guadalquivir, Leovigild chose to assert his own separate dignity by dropping any pretence of willing subordination. For the first time, between 575 and 577, a Visigothic gold coinage was issued which bore not the likeness of the emperor but that of their own king. Toledo was chosen to become the *urbs regia* and in it he built a palace with a royal chapel dedicated to Saints Peter and Paul. There the king wore the royal diadem and sat upon a throne, in obvious imitation of Byzantine ceremonial for previous Germanic kings had not employed such trappings. He also took for himself the imperial prerogative of founding new cities: Recopolis in Guadalajara and Victoriacum in the Rioja. To these symbolic gestures he added the substantial reality of an Iberia in which all revolt had been crushed, the kingdom of the Suevi annexed, and the Byzantine confined to half of the coastline. He also early associated his sons with himself in the royal dignity in a clear bid to create a dynasty.

His son Recared built upon this considerable foundation. For his father's doomed attempt to secure religious unity in the realm on the basis of a modified Arianism, in the Third Council of Toledo of 589 the son united the realm around the orthodox faith and an orthodox church firmly subordinated to the crown. The king was now *orthodoxus rex* and the vicar of the Almighty for the governance of the realm. Moreover, Recared had proved his mettle by snuffing out three plots against this development and a Frankish invasion of Septimania to boot in 588–589.

Though the king had no need to call a new council of the magnitude of Toledo III, his legislative activity outside such means is reflected in the *Liber Judiciorum*. He seems as well to have sought to build a following by the return of some property confiscated in his father's reign and by the promotion of a favored palatine nobility. His leadership as warchief, always important to that class, was suitably active with repeated if inconclusive victories over those old threats, the Byzantines and the Basques. Though he first sought a Frankish wife, on being rebuffed he married one Baddo, probably a member of the Visigothic nobility. In fact, his marriage diplomacy proved to be the shipwreck of the grand design.

It appeared that Recared had no son by his wife. It would be his bastard son, Liuva II (601–603), who briefly succeeded him with all of the weakness which that background implied. Despite the fact that Recared died still king and that his son acceded without difficulty, by the summer of 603 Liuva II was deposed in a palace coup and subsequently murdered. So ended perhaps the best opportunity to strengthen the Visigothic crown by the creation of a new dynasty.

Despite that central failure, the Visigothic monarchy still possessed two immediate advantages. One was the momentum it had inherited and the other was the rapidly accelerating weakness of its strongest rival, Byzantium. Following the death of Justinian in 565, Constantinople dealt with increasing difficulty with the irruption of Lombards into Italy, Slavs and Avars into the Lower Balkans, and Persians into Syria down through the reign of Maurice (582–602). The reign of his successor, the usurper Phocas (602–610), was an utter disaster and the fall of the imperial city itself was threatened. That meant opportunity in Iberia since the Byzantine province could expect little help against attack. King Witeric (603–610), a former Gothic noble of Lusitania, campaigned actively against it but without major success in his brief reign. He seems to have been ambitious and sought a Burgundian wife only to be rebuffed as Recared had been. He was assassinated at a banquet in his own palace in April, 610. The very brief reign of Gundemar (610–612) who followed him on the throne is also quite obscure, although marked as well by campaigns against the Byzantines and Basques. It also ended from natural causes.

The major gains remained to the successors of these ephemeral kings.

Sisebut (612–621), that curiously learned monarch who composed poetry and a saint's *vita*, also overran the whole of Constantinople's possessions on the southwestern and southern coasts before being poisoned. He carried on a very active diplomacy with both Franks and Lombards and, latterly, with Constantinople. He promoted the theocratic idea of kingship begun by Recared and dedicated a church in Toledo to Saint Leocadia whom he possibly saw as patroness of the kingdom. He also associated his son on the throne with himself in a clear bid to establish a dynasty. The young Recared II perished within a few days of his father.

After some hesitation, the conspirators who had assassinated Sisebut and his son decided to advance the *dux* Swintila (621–631) to the throne. This was the general who had defeated the Byzantines in the south under Sisebut. He was now to be the king who brought to a definitive end their presence in Spain. He reconquered the remainder of their territories on the east coast, seizing Cartagena in 625 and razing it completely. Like his predecessors Swintila thus displayed the contemporary weakness of Constantinople rather than the power of the Visigoths. In 628 the Byzantine monarch penetrated the Persian highlands where he won a crushing victory over Rome's old foe. Obviously, he had little aid to spare for Iberia. Moreover, the utter destruction of Cartagena should be read less as a sign of vengeance than as evidence of Swintila's doubts that the distant seaport could be held permanently against Byzantine seapower.

Swintila's earlier victories (621–622) over the Basques are best viewed in the same light. Visigothic kings had been recording victories over the Basques for the last half century but we are told that Swintila operated from Calahorra and established a base at Olite in Navarra after his success. Despite occasional punitive, more or less successful, expeditions, the Basques appear to have been expanding steadily from Guipuzcoa and Vizcaya. Alava was incontestably theirs, Navarra and High Aragon at least cultural provinces, and they were ready to contest for Upper Rioja with the Toledan kings. At the same time they were expanding northward in the Frankish realm, occupying what we now call Gascony and threatening Aquitaine itself.

In any event, Swintila certainly believed that the crown must be strengthened. He carried out some confiscations of both noble and church properties in order to build up the royal fisc. He associated his son, Ricimer, with him on the throne in a bid to create a dynasty. Indeed he seems to have proceeded so actively as to alarm his original supporters who wanted a victorious warchief but hardly so powerful a king. In 631 a revolt broke out against him led by Sisenand, possibly another *dux*, in Septimania and the resources of that province together with a large assemblage of Frankish mercenaries prevailed and Swintila agreed to abdicate in 631 on condition that his and his family's lives be spared. Nevertheless, what was basically a civil war continued into 633 in the south of the peninsula under the leadership of his brother, Geila, and another claimant to the throne.

All of this disorder so alarmed even the successful rebels and their new king, Sisenand (631–636), that they resorted to the first great church council since 589. In 633, Toledo IV legislated an elective kingship but attempted to establish rules which would permit an effective reign and an orderly succession. Still, in this one case we can see rather more about the nature of the rebels and thus the problem. Sisenand was of a magnate family of the Narbonensis. He may have been *dux* there. Certainly another member of his family was then *dux* in Galletia and, once the revolt carried, two other members of it became bishops of Beziers and of Narbonne. It would take more than legislated ground rules to restrain such potential conspirators. It should be noted that the Frankish mercenaries who guaranteed the success of the rebellion had to be purchased not with coin of the realm but rather with a large piece of worked gold said to weigh some 500 librae. Things had come to such a pass that even high treason was conducted by barter. In all events, Sisenand himself seems to have adhered to the bargain struck at Toledo IV for he died peacefully in that *urbs regia* in March of 636.

He was succeeded for another brief period by Chintila (636–639) about whom we know very little. He was remarkable certainly for having held two general councils during that short time, Toledo V (636) and Toledo VI (638). Both moved to reinforce the character of kingship as it had been defined in 633, insisting that election rather than lineage made a king, and that only a Goth of modest ambitions might be elected, specifically ruling out anyone of servile ancestry or anyone who had been a tonsured religious. After the death of such a king, his family, his retainers, and the church should all retain their property and offices. Taken together both the pace and the provisions indicate a sense of urgency and concern for the good order of the realm. Well they might. Like most Visigothic kings before him Chintila had used his power to secure the succession of his son, Tulga (639–642). In this case also the arrangement did not long survive his own death. His heir was too young to cope with the violent politics of the realm and was swept aside, tonsured, and thrust into a monastery.

His successor was again a *dux* but one of more than mature years, said to be aged seventy-nine when he seized power, and one certainly convinced that drastic measures had to be taken to preserve the realm. The reigns of Chindaswinth (642–653) and his son Receswinth (653–672) were to provide some three decades of vigorous rule, reminiscent of the reigns of Leovigild and Recared in the sixth century. The old king began by striking against the seat of rebellion, the Gothic nobility. While he may not have executed the 700 of them credited by the Frankish chronicle, his proscription of them was drastic enough to leave a vivid historic memory, carried beyond the Pyrenees by those who fled his wrath. Their goods went to strengthen not just the royal fisc but also those nobles who would adhere to the royal program and person. There was also a notable reclamation of lands from the church whose bishops were inextricably bound up with the families and therefore the ambitions of the nobility. Part of the effectiveness of these measures is to be seen in the notable increase in weight and quality of the coins issued during his and his son's reign.

But the true extent of his daring was to be found in his total disregard of the law enacted by the last three councils of Toledo about the royal succession. On January 20, 649, his son Receswinth was associated with him on the throne, apparently at the request of Bishop Braulius of Saragossa, another bishop, and a member of the nobility. Now Braulius was the most influential churchman of the peninsula at the time. Despite his troubles with the church in general, Chindaswinth had cultivated the Saragossan by appointing his friend and associate, Eugenius, bishop of Toledo less than three years earlier. Such objection as would arise to this constitutional coup only occurred shortly before the old man's death on September 30, 653. It took the form of a revolt in the valley of the Ebro which sought the aid of the Basques against whom, like virtually every other Visigothic king, Chindaswinth had campaigned. The revolt rolled up to the very walls of Saragossa but failed there despite a two-month siege and subsequently was suppressed and its Gothic leader executed.

Receswinth would continue the work of his father in the most obvious fashion by issuing a new law code, which had long been in preparation, in 654. The tome represented not simply a reissuance of a traditional Visigothic code but, of its more than 500 chapters, some 98 derive from Chindaswinth alone and another 111 from Receswinth. The two monarchs made a major attempt to refashion the law of the realm and clearly abolished any lingering distinction between their Gothic and Roman subjects. Not in a hundred years had Visigothic rulers displayed so much political imagination and daring.

Only against this background may the legislation of the Eighth Council of Toledo in 653 be properly appreciated. In it Receswinth agreed to a restatement of the elective character of the kingship and of a king who would rule according to law or face legal deposition, a restatement of the distinction between the personal and the official possessions of the monarch, and a general amnesty for all rebels of the last thirty years.

There were grounds here for a general political settlement and it should be remarked that the reign of Receswinth would go down in future chronicles as precisely one of peace and order. Modern historians have tended to see in the council a retreat forced on the king from the aggressive rule of his father. Perhaps, but one can afford to be magnanimous from a position of strength. The councils which were to meet during the remainder of his reign, Toledo IX (655), Toledo X (656), and Mérida (666), busied themselves largely with the proper order of things within the church and the dimensions of the powers of that ecclesiastical magnate, the bishop. The king, on the other hand, went on legislating for the entire realm. Finally, Receswinth must have found it possible to rule within the confines of the settlement of 653 for he died peacefully and full of years on September 1, 672.

The major failure of his reign lies in that he left no heir, so far as we can determine. He had been married at least as early as 650 but his young wife had died at twenty-two after but seven years of marriage. There are no notices either of children from that marriage or of any subsequent marriage of the king in the fifteen years or so of his reign. Such a lapse was crucial to the hopes of dynasty and scarcely less so to the newfound strength of the monarchy. Under such circumstances the crown passed to one of the palatine nobility, a Gothic noble and warrior by the name of Wamba (672–680). He was accepted by the church of the kingdom and is the first Visigothic king whom we know with certainty to have been anointed as well as crowned.

It is common with modern historians to see a decline of the Visigothic kingdom, beginning with Wamba, which will eventuate in the conquest of the Iberian peninsula by the Muslim only forty years later. Still, the assumption that a more or less lengthy decline must precede a fall, though tempting, is neither a metaphysical nor a historical necessity. We are fairly well informed about the reign of Wamba because the contemporary Bishop Julian of Toledo wrote a history of its beginnings. From this and other sources, it appears that the new strengths deriving from the long and strong reigns of Chindaswinth and Receswinth carried over into that of Wamba. As we shall see, it is questionable to what extent the model of decline can be applied to that of his successors as well.

Of course the Visigothic kingdom continued to be subject to those stresses from which, one thinks, no king in the Germanic west was exempt during the Early Middle Ages. The attempt to rule any considerable area almost without an administrative structure placed most of the advantages in the hands of local forces, especially when these local forces were essentially warrior in nature and autarchic economically. As early as the spring of 673 Wamba was leading a punitive expedition against that stubborn and expanding people, the Basques, when he received notice of a revolt against him in Septimania led by the count of Nimes and the bishop of Maguelonne. The king's first response was to detach part of his army under a Goth named Paul to quell that rebellion.

As that general hastened eastward through the Tarraconensis, however, he conceived the idea of putting himself at the head of the rebellion rather than crushing it. The *dux* of the Tarraconensis joined him. At Narbonne he was indeed elected king. The rebels of Nimes and Maguelonne embraced his cause and two of the six provinces of the kingdom were in open revolt. Nevertheless, the essentially regional character of the rising is evident in that it failed to secure any support in the remainder of the kingdom. As in the earlier rebellion of Sisenand against Chintila, the northeast of the peninsula and Septimania were demonstrating that special character for which geography predisposed them. Unlike the revolt of Sisenand, this one found no assistance from the Franks to the north and so failed in short order. When he received the news of Paul's treason, Wamba made a forced march on the Tarraconensis and quickly reduced Barcelona and Gerona to obedience. His army then advanced in three columns into the Narbonensis, taking Narbonne, Beziers, and Maguelonne. Nimes was last to fall in the beginning of September and the revolt was over.

Of the remainder of the reign of Wamba, we know little but that little does suggest a strong king. The two councils held in his time, Toledo XI (675) and Braga III (675), both continued to concentrate on ecclesiastical matters, in particular the definition of episcopal powers. It is possible to suspect a royal intent to reform the church with considerable clerical support. That suspicion is reinforced by the royal creation of two new bishoprics, one of the royal chapel itself and another of the monastery of Aquis in Lusitania, both suppressed in the following reign. Wamba would also be recalled fondly in the eighth century as the author of much new construction, in Toledo in particular. But he also legislated new norms for the mobilization of the royal host which reveal the practical weakness rather than the strength of the contemporary monarchy.

The reign of Wamba ended in one of the more bizarre and visible episodes of Visigothic history. In October, 680, the king either fell ill, became convinced he was dying, abdicated and assumed the religious habit, and designated the palatine noble, Ervig (680–687), as his successor or a drug was administered to him which left him unable to prevent these things from being accomplished while he was unconscious. We are furnished the first explanation by the testimony presented to Toledo XII (681) by Ervig in order to justify his accession. The second explanation derives from eighth- and ninth-century sources.

Aside from the succession of Ervig itself, a number of important facts need to be noted about the event. First, Ervig was related by marriage to King Chindaswinth and it seems obvious that the number of lineages held capable of producing a royal candidate were narrowing. Second, Wamba was forced into retirement in a monastery but not killed. He even continued to have some influence from that retreat. Evidently his own lineage was not rendered powerless by his fall although we hear nothing of a direct line of sons and daughters. Third, Toledo XII was publicly willing to accept designation by Wamba and unction by Bishop Julian as sufficient to make a king irrespective of the matter of election. All of these point to a general strengthening of the hereditary principle in the peninsula.

Despite the peculiar circumstances of his ascent, Ervig clearly continued the general policy of his predecessors. The *Liber Judiciorum* was issued during his reign in 681. Although in all probability the code was being reworked in the reign of Wamba, it was Ervig who saw the work carried through. Moreover, the same Toledo XII which recognized his right to rule also publicly acknowledged the right of the crown to name every bishop of the realm, although the language presumed the cooperation of the bishop of Toledo with the king.

Yet another general council was held during Ervig's relatively brief reign, Toledo XIII (683). There the conciliatory policy of recent kings was again reflected in a general amnesty of all rebels back to the time of Chintila. In addition, it was mandated that palatine nobles and bishops might not be deprived of their office or rank without the public judgment of their peers. For the population at large, a cancellation of all prior debts to the royal fisc was enacted. Finally, the rights of the royal family were guaranteed in important detail. On the death of the king, neither the queen, her children, nor relatives by marriage, could be forced into religion, killed, mutilated, deprived of their property, or exiled. Any of these things, of course, would have either prevented or reacted severely on their ability to succeed their father on the throne. In addition, it was specifically prohibited that the widowed queen should be remarried or forced into concubinage. This latter, then, barred the most obvious route to the throne for those outside the royal family at the time of the king's death. Later evidence informs that Ervig was to require a general oath of his subjects to uphold these guarantees to his family.

The death of the king came peacefully on November 14, 687, and he was able to designate his own successor. This was Egica (687–702), a *dux* but of what province we cannot say, a relation in some degree of the lineage of Wamba, and a son-in-law of the deceased Ervig. Once again the principle of heredity seems to have prevailed over that of election for no challenge to his accession is recorded directly. Some opinion has seen Egica a noble of a rival lineage forced on Ervig at the expense of his own direct line but such an interpretation is difficult to defend. Less than six months after his recognition, Egica called a general council, Toledo XV (688), in which the oath required by his predecessor of all subjects to protect the persons, properties, and rights of his family was upheld at the same time that Egica himself was held blameless of violation of that oath by reason of his ascent to the throne. At the same time the king was held to be free to remedy such wrongs as his father-in-law may have worked.

Doubtless there had been maneuvering and muttering at the fashion in which Egica had become king. It may well have included the children of Ervig who would not necessarily have assented readily to even a completely free judgment of their father that the political situation made the selection of a son-in-law rather than a son preferable. There also seems to have been some subsequent friction which, at one point, led to a break between the king and his queen, Ervig's daughter. There certainly was a major conspiracy, whether or not it involved the family or Ervig, at some point during the next four years.

By Toledo XVI in May of 693 Egica had triumphed over all obstacles. There he was able to secure the assent of the church to his deposition of the very metropolitan of Toledo, Sisibert, who had been involved in the plot, and of the reshuffling of the bishops of Seville, Braga, and Oporto. Not since Recared had there been such a dramatic demonstration of regalian authority over the church. In addition, Egica exacted the protection of the law for his children after his own death such as had been extended to those of Ervig by Toledo XIII. The queen was not specifically mentioned, however, so that the estrangement of the two continued for a time. Finally, the council also decreed daily mass to be offered in every church of the realm for the king and his family. The religious and political significance of this last is hard to overestimate. Taken together, it is difficult to read these provisions as less than the tacit recognition of Egica's lineage as the royal dynasty. In any event, no Visigothic king of Toledo or his family ever came so close to realizing that aim.

A year later the family guarantees were reenacted by Toledo XVII (694) and this time they specifically included Queen Cixila so that the dynastic rift had been healed. The provision of the same council that the first three days of such meetings would be reserved for ecclesiastical business during which no laymen would be present sounds positively defensive in this context. At this time, or shortly thereafter, Egica followed out the logic of what he had done to date by associating his son, Witiza, on the throne with himself.

Egica is also credited with the continuation of the perennial regalian policy of persecution of the more dangerous nobles, although the sources are later. Certainly, under Egica, the anti-Semitic policy of the Visigothic kings and church reached its height. According to the king's testimony at Toledo XVII the Jews of the kingdom had been involved in the plot against him and therefore the council legislated that they were, collectively, to be enslaved and their property confiscated. These provisions were themselves an extension from others of Toledo XVI which had prohibited their activity in commerce and severely penalized Christians who dealt with them.

Now this legislation was new only in its extent for anti-Semitic measures went back to Recared and, indeed, to Alaric II. Scholars have attempted to account for its especial virulence in the Visigothic kingdom on a variety of grounds. One of them must be the relatively important numbers and the wealth of the Jewish community in both the southern parts of the Iberian peninsula and in Septimania. That is, they were a particular target in the Visigothic kingdom because they were highly visible. Another likely factor was that the church generally at the time was engaged in an almost endless series of Christological controversies as it sought to find a way to combine trinitarian beliefs with the emerging theological vehicle of Greek philosophy. The Eastern Empire had been rent for three centuries with Arianism, Nestorianism, and Monophysitism, this latter still most active in the seventh century.

Now the western church had largely escaped the troublesome effects of these "Greek" heresies which had relatively few adherents in the west except, of course, precisely in the Visigothic kingdom which had been officially Arian until the late sixth century. One suspects that the Jews drew such unfavorable attention in part because of the resulting peculiar sensitivity to the full divinity of Christ in the Visigothic church, which is proclaimed in council after council and creed after creed, and the Jewish flat denial of any such attribute. The particular political difficulties of the Visigothic kings also certainly came into play for the Jewish communities of the realm were numerous and wealthy enough for them to be important and sometimes influential factors in political matters, at least in the cities. The activities of the Jewish community of Narbonne at the time of the revolt of Duke Paul is only the best documented instance.

At the same time, it must be noted that this legislation, and one suspects just as much of the rest of the *Liber Judiciorum* and the conciliar *acta*, was utterly ineffective. Despite all paper restrictions, the Jewish community of the realm continued to thrive. Pope Gregory I will write at the end of the sixth century to protest the fact and Pope Honorius I (625–638) will do the same in the seventh. At the end of the Visigothic kingdom itself kings still find it necessary to legislate against them. Yet, all such legislation to the contrary, bishops, nobles, ordinary Christians, and even kings one suspects, found it useful to deal otherwise with them in practice and the Jewish community will continue apparently unreduced in numbers or influence into the succeeding Muslim period.

It is likely that there was yet another serious rebellion against Egica in late 702 but again he weathered it and managed to die peacefully in 703 still king. He was succeeded by his son, Witiza (703–710), of whose reign we know very little. A half century later he was held to be generous to the nobility prosecuted by his father but that would seem to be a feature of the beginning of every reign and naturally so. His times were also said to be marked by famine and plague in the peninsula. We do know that the weight of the coinage declined sharply. There was a council, Toledo XVIII, held during the reign but its acts have been lost.

Witiza died a natural death in 710, having designated his son Agila (710–714) as his successor. This was the fourth king in succession to be chosen by his predecessor and drawn from the same family. One thinks that if a hereditary monarchy were to be prevented the nobility had to react, particularly since the new king was quite youthful and might be expected to have a long reign. A portion of the nobility did just that and chose Rodrigo (710–711), who had probably been *dux* of Baetica, as their king. Agila managed to retain the loyalty of Septimania and the Tarraconensis but Rodrigo was recognized in the remainder of the king-dom despite the presence in Seville of Bishop Oppa, brother of Witiza. Both claimants were in fact dethroned by the Muslim invasion of the following year which toppled Rodrigo immediately and Agila somewhat later when they had penetrated to the north.

The fall of the Visigothic kingdom was certainly dramatic and has encouraged a variety of attempts to account for it over the centuries since. By and large these have varied from treachery to sinfulness, from political faction to loss of primitive Germanic vigor. Simply put, however, the event hardly warrants extended pondering. The conquest of the Roman Empire in the west by the Germanic tribes two centuries earlier is a real conundrum in that a more primitive people conquered the more advanced one and it is precisely the condition of civilization that ordinarily confers an insuperable advantage in such contests. But at the beginning of the eighth century in Iberia two relatively backward peoples met and one of them was vanquished. Unless one posits a much higher degree of sophistication for the Visigoths than the observable facts warrant, no greater crisis or decline need be descried than the one which had been gradually turning Roman society into a Germanic one for the past three centuries.

Contemporaries, of course, saw it differently. If the Muslim invasion had not taken place, it is quite likely that the Visigoths would have achieved a hereditary kingship eventually; but it is unlikely that it would have been more impressive than early medieval Saxon, or Merovingian, or Lombard kingship. The ferment in post-Roman society in the west was too profound for that and the emergence of a form of political rule of a legitimacy sufficiently strong to master the ground on which it stood seems inherently unlikely.

As it was, the Straits of Gibraltar were but fourteen kilometers across and the Iberian peninsula was uniquely open, in Europe, to invasion by a people able to be continuously reinforced from North Africa and inspired, in some measure, by a new vision of society whose warlike aspirations matched well their own desires and aptitudes. When they had managed to defeat a king whose real importance lay in his own estates and personal following together with some control over a tiny noble and clerical elite as scantily based as he himself, the lands before them were unable to find a further principle of resistance. Even so the Muslim were unable to conquer the peninsula, less able than the Visigoths for that matter. The Basque country remained beyond their world. Asturias they penetrated but briefly. Galicia and northern Lusitania they occupied for perhaps forty years. The basin of the Duero they were to abandon almost as quickly. But for four centuries they were to hold its coasts and the river basins of the Guadalquivir, the Guadiana, the Tajo, and the Ebro. The Iberia that had always mattered was theirs.

3

IBERIA AND THE DĀR-AL-ISLAM
711–1009

No feature of the history of the eighth century is so remarkable as the genesis and explosive growth of the world of Islam. There was literally no precedent for it in antiquity and no reason why a reasonable, contemporary observer should have expected it. In scarcely two decades from the death of Muhammad in 632 a newly united Arab world had swept away the Persian Empire of the Sassanids and was probing the valley of the Indus in the east. The same period had seen it tear the provinces of Syria, Palestine, and Egypt, from the Byzantine Empire and for more than a century yet the ultimate survival of the Eastern Roman Empire was open to serious doubt.

That the initial energies of Islam were far from spent meant that expansion to the west in Africa after the fall of Egypt in 642 was in the natural order of things. That northern coast had long been an important part of the Roman world, the Byzantine enemy was still entrenched there, and the climate and geography were congenial to the Arab. After a series of exploratory thrusts and counterthrusts, the great Byzantine capital and base at Carthage fell definitively in 698. The major problem to Arab rule in the African northwest now became the resistance of the native Berber peoples of the region. But in fairly short order there, Islam was to demonstrate its remarkable absorptive power for unsophisticated peoples.

Nevertheless, the process of pacification and conversion was hardly underway in the Magrib before the invasion of Iberia was essayed. That undertaking was unremarkable given the long established relationships between North Africa and Iberia in the political, commercial, and cultural orders. After an initial probe of the southern coast of Iberia in 710, an outright invasion was mounted in 711 by Tāriq, commander and freedman of the Arab governor of the province of Africa, Mūsā ibn Nasayr. When Tāriq disembarked at that Gib al-Tāriq, which has ever since commemorated him in late April, the Visigothic kingdom was divided between Rodrigo and Agila. Rodrigo was apparently engaged in one of those punitive expeditions against the Basques of the north which had been the periodic necessity of every Visigothic monarch since the sixth century. He now hastened south only to meet crushing defeat at Guadalete on July 19. With that event he vanished from historic record.

After defeating another Gothic army near Ecija east of Seville, Tāriq sent light forces to see what they might effect at Málaga in the southern littoral while he proceeded north against Toledo. It was a daring but logical move if he wished to paralyze further resistance and to seize the royal treasury which might make such struggle possible. On his march he found Cordova undefended and took it; arriving thence in Toledo he found that city also in disorder and similarly at his mercy. He then seems to have undertaken a major reconnaissance in force across the Guadarrama. There, in the valley of the Duero during 712 he broke up attempts to organize further resistance at Amaya in the foothills of the Cantabrians and at Astorga. Tāriq returned to Toledo only in 713 to meet Mūsā ibn Nasayr.

The governor of North Africa, having word of his lieutenant's triumphs, himself had landed at Algeciras in the summer of 712. Mūsā moved north taking Carmona by treachery and then Seville from a dispirited garrison. From there he marched north to lay siege to Mérida where a defense had formed which would detain him until June 30, 713, before it was broken. While besieging that city he despatched his son, Abd al-Azīz, to pacify the upper reaches of the Guadalquivir basin. This latter expedition produced the famous text of capitulation of the Gothic noble Teodemir in Murcia of April 5, 713. The forces of Tāriq and Mūsā then joining in Toledo, a yet more extended reconnaissance of the north was undertaken. Tāriq may have gotten so far as Tarragona and Barcelona while Mūsā, after taking Saragossa, struck west even to Lugo in Galicia before returning south.

Now this campaign and its chronology are confused but at least by 714 Mūsā and Tāriq had been recalled to Damascus by the Umayyad Caliph Walid I, who apparently had not authorized the invasion of Iberia and who retained serious doubts as to its advisability. Neither ever returned. Instead, for the next forty-five years the new Islamic domain in Iberia was to see the rule of a series of governors, sometimes appointed from Africa or Damascus and sometimes merely recognized by one or the other after they had intrigued or fought their way to command in Iberia. Some ruled for as little as six months. That any permanent structure emerged from this welter of faction and confusion at the antipodes of the dār-al-Islam must be credited to largely local initiatives of a loose coalition of clans and tribes and the attractive power of Islam itself. As it eventuated Andalusia, or al-Andalus, which was the preferred Muslim name for all of the territories in Iberia controlled for Islam, would be considerably less than the peninsula.

During that tumultuous half-century, the attempt was made to push al-Andalus beyond the Pyrenees. This involved the conquest of modern Catalonia and then Septimania. We hear no more of Agila, who presumably ruled the Tarraconensis and Septimania from 710 to 713. An even more shadowy Ardo I disappears in 720 when Barcelona and Narbonne were overrun from the south. In the succeeding decade Muslim forces fanned out as far as Arles in Provence and Poitiers in the Aquitaine. The Frankish reaction there under Charles Martel led to their defeat and repulse at Poitiers in 732. From that point, a Frankish counter-offensive under Pepin I would gradually expel the Muslim from Provence and Septimania, taking Narbonne itself in 759. The rising power of the Carolingian dynasty would put a term to the western advance of Islam just as the contemporary Isaurian dynasty of Byzantium was to proceed from the victory of Leo III (717–741) at Acroinon in 739 to reclaim Asia Minor in the east. The last vestiges of a Visigothic kingdom had disappeared but its inheritor in the northeast was to be Frankish rather than Muslim.

For the next four centuries, however, the old Roman Tarraconensis was to be an integral part of al-Andalus. On the other hand, the Muslims seem to no more have controlled the Basque territories than did their Roman or Visigothic predecessors. Farther west, at some time between 711 and 722, there was briefly a Muslim garrison at Gijón in Asturias on the far side of the Cantabrians. With that exception, the Asturian world never came under their control. In the extreme northwest, old Roman Gallaecia was briefly held by Islam although it is impossible to determine just how thoroughly that land of mountain valleys and coastal fringe was ever subjugated. In any event, the beginnings of the Berber revolt against Arab domination about 740 led to the evacuation of that province. At least north of the valley of the Miño River, today the effective border between Spain and Portugal, the domination of Islam had been ephemeral and insignificant.

The Berber revolt in Iberia was significant because it coincided with a general convulsion of the dār-al-Islam at the end of its first century of existence which had much to do with the end of that great period of expansion. We shall return to the general development but here we should attend first to the problem of the nature of the old Roman province of the Carthaginensis which had never been a geographic unit in the sense of the great river basins of the peninsula. During the Visigothic period its administrative unity had disappeared as first the Byzantine occupied, and then the Visigoth destroyed, the seaport of Cartagena itself. The old metropolitan ecclesiastical status of that church, with its jurisdiction over the Mediterranean littoral, Murcia, La Mancha, the valley of the Tajo, and that of the Duero, was then assumed by Toledo. But Toledo would retain control of all but the last, for that city and jurisdiction would be incorporated within al-Andalus. The Duero River basin would not.

The central valley of the Duero had had something of the character of a frontier even in late imperial times. There had apparently been some substantial settlement there later by the Visigoths, particularly in its eastern reaches about Segovia and Palencia. Nevertheless, it did not have the richness of a Baetica or a Lusitania to attract the Muslim invader. Along with the other relatively more barren areas it seems to have fallen to the lot of their Berber allies. Now the revolt of 740 and the great famine of the years between 748 and 754 combined to lead to the latters' widespread withdrawal from that area as well. In brief, the Muslim occupation of the Duero River basin was never more than very thin and soon became largely confined to the northern fringes of the Guadarrama. Already in the middle of the eighth century it had become a world of war between Christians of the north and Muslims of the south, which further lessened its attractiveness. Consequently, this basin never did become a part of al-Andalus but rather it will be against a threat from this direction that the marches of al-Andalus around Badajoz, Toledo, and Saragossa, will be organized.

The Berber rebellion which contributed to the virtual absence of Muslims in the northwestern fifth of the peninsula is usually seen as a protest against the lack of that fundamental equality of believers mandated by the Koran but only slowly accorded to the newly converted non-Arab. In part it doubtless was but, since many of the Berbers were still pagan or Christian, its very dimensions indicate that it was an ethnic phenomenon as well. While it eventually failed in Africa and Iberia, large numbers of troops from the Syrian regiments had to be despatched by Damascus to quell it.

Also contributing to the seriousness of the conflict was the struggle which had been in preparation between the various Arab factions. In Iberia this is generally associated with the tribal rivalry between Qays and Yemeni. At any event, that was the most legitimate face which could be put on what was occurring by either contemporaries or later historians.

Also involved was that assertion of variant local interests which Arab masters soon began to reflect, once settled in the peninsula. These differences were doubtless exacerbated by others which the participants had brought with them, that is, the gap that had appeared between the views of Arabs settled in the sophisticated former areas of the Roman or Persian Empires and the more fundamentalist views of those who continued to reside in the Arabian homeland. But even more grave was the glaring lack of any generally accepted religious or political legitimacy in the new dār-al-Islam. That absence bedeviled Iberian Islam as it has every Islamic society down to the present.

At the death of Muhammad in AD 632, the Prophet left the community of Islam without a political theory or even a religious succession. There was only his personal example of the combination of both powers in one figure. At first, the succession of those associated with Muhammad himself provided an uncontroversial solution but that device could hardly outlast a generation. After the reigns of the first four, "rightly guided caliphs," in 661, this matter became critical. The question became, as it would usually remain, whether the leader of the community would be selected on political criteria or religious ones. At that point, the political principal triumphed in the person of Muawiyah, then governor of Damascus, and the caliphate became frankly hereditary, the Ummayad dynasty ruling until AD 750 when it perished in a torrent of blood.

However, the religious principle originally represented by Alī, the son-in-law of the prophet, gradually found embodiment in what will become Shiite Islam. That is, the proponents of the theory that the dār-al-Islam ought to be ruled by a prophetic figure, an *imām*, usually with claims to be somehow descended from Muhammad but also essentially designated by Allah for the guidance of his followers. Thus a revolutionary principle found embodiment in a sectarian movement which could challenge the now hereditary caliphate, or any political authority, at any moment.

On the other hand, the caliphate itself was never purely political. Rather, it relied on religious rule based upon the Koran, which itself was being formed into a written canonical text during the seventh century, and also upon the *hadīth*, sayings and practices of Muhammad, of which collections were also being made during that time. Such a body of law, at once religious and secular, was to be interpreted by judges (*qādīs*) and by legal scholars (*faqīhs*) for the guidance of the entire community of Islam, including the caliph himself. Of course, the caliph ultimately appointed to both positions. In brief, this is the system which is identified with what we call Sunnite Islam.

To this permanent difference of theory and principle the times would occasionally add the grievances of ethnicity, class, and family ambition to supply an explosive mixture. In the mid-eighth century precisely that happened in the Near East when the Abbāsid dynasty (750–1055) overthrew the Ummayads. Abū al-Abbās claimed descent from the Prophet. He was supported initially by the Shiites and by Persian and Mesopotamian elements against the Syrian base of his opponents. After he had triumphed, he moved the center of government of the dār-al-Islam from Syrian Damascus, to a new caliphal city constructed on the Tigris, Baghdad, and remodeled his administration along Persian imperial lines. He also carried out a wholesale slaughter of the Ummayads and their supporters. It was fateful for Iberian Islam, however, that one of the Ummayads escaped and fled west.

This was Abd al-Rahmān I (756–788) who was to become the first Ummayad emir of al-Andalus and who established the dynasty which was to rule there until 1031. After some time as a refugee among the Berbers of the Magrib, he may himself have had a Berber mother, the fugitive manipulated all elements in the ongoing civil war in Iberia and finally emerged victorious over the last governor there. For almost two centuries thereafter, the Iberian Ummayads were careful not to challenge directly the legitimacy of the Abbāsid caliph in Baghdad, taking for themselves only the titles of *mālik*, or king, and *amīr al-muminūn*, or commander of the faithful. But they effectively ignored it and defeated all Abbāsid conspiracies to overthrow them. They were fortunate in their location at the far edge of the dār-al-Islam to which caliphal power had never extended very consistently. They were also fortunate in that Abbāsid control was never effectively established in Morocco to their south and that one Idris, claiming descent from Alī, established himself as Shiite caliph among the Berbers there after 789. Moreover, farther east, the Shiite regime of the Aghlabids came to power in Tunisia and Algeria from AD 800, insulating the Iberian Ummayads even more effectively.

GOVERNMENT AND SOCIETY IN AL–ANDALUS

Under the early Ummayads the government of al-Andalus was gradually regularized. Local control was much more decentralized than under Romans or Visigoths. The provinces, or *quras*, were smaller: Málaga, Medina–Sidonia, Morón, Jaén, Elvira, Talavera, Tarragona, and Barcelona seem to have been organized very early. The three marches, Badajoz, Toledo, and Saragossa, feature essentially the same organization but their governor was likely to enjoy greater independence of action. Obviously all were based upon a fortified city of some importance and the *walī*, or governor, was invariably an urban figure. Each was assisted by a *qāḍī*, or judge, and a *muhtasib*, or market supervisor. The province thus precisely mirrored the organization of Cordova itself under the central government. In theory, the governor was appointed by the Ummayad emir and removable by him at will. In fact, government remained highly personal and a *wālī* was chosen from among one's kin, or at least one's clients, whenever possible. In addition, the farther the province from Cordova the more likely that the governor was a member of the most important local Muslim family or clan. For the ruler not to appoint such a man was often to invite revolt. In this respect, little had changed from the Visigothic period except the identities and the religions of the major figures.

By way of contrast, the figure of the emir differed profoundly from that of Visigothic king. The former literally embodied the religion of the community, a fact that gave him a more effective claim on the loyalty of his subjects. From the time of the emir al-Hakam I (796–822) the rulers of al-Andalus enforced a uniform jurisprudence based upon the teaching of Mālik ibn Anas (d. 796) of Medina to the exclusion of the other three leading schools of Islamic law. They appointed *qāḍīs* of that persuasion without exception and received the support of those judges in return. They also enjoyed from the first a regular money economy based both upon rents from the confiscated royal fisc and upon the tithes levied upon believers and the taxes assessed upon unbelievers. This income was signalized by the regular issuance of a stable silver coinage, the *dirhem*. It also permitted the maintenance of a standing, mercenary army already from the time of Abd al-Rahmān I. Formidable in itself, this army was made even more so by the practice of recruiting it from among the Berbers of North Africa or among slaves of Christian origin. Being loyal to none but its paymaster, it was thus susceptible of use against the fractious Muslim aristocracy of Iberia. Rebellions remained frequent in the period of the Ummayads but success was never more than an episode.

This government protected and dominated a society most imperfectly Muslim. The armies of conquest were made up of Berber and Arab in numbers whose proportion is impossible to determine. Probably all of the Berber troops were not Muslim at the outset but the likelihood is that they swiftly became so. Their desire for military and political solidarity with the Arabs would have made it imperative. The combined number of these troops who entered the peninsula at one time or another during the eighth century is now believed to be about 50,000. If we allow for casualties, the number who most likely survived to become permanent inhabitants may approximate 40,000. If one accepts the total population of Iberia about this time as about 4,000,000, then they were initially a minority of some 1 percent.

After a brief period when the conquerors' presence consisted of little but garrisons in the most important towns, a land distribution was carried out on principles of which we are ignorant. In conformity with Arab practice grown up in a century of conquest, the lands of those who resisted were confiscated by the caliphal government. Subsequently these lands, less the caliphal fifth, were distributed to the army. The lands of those who submitted according to treaty were guaranteed to them on condition of an annual payment. However, since the treaty with the Visigothic magnate, Teodemir, in April of 713 set that payment at one dinar per person per year in addition to payments in kind, the opportunities for further acquisitions of land must have been numerous. If the terms recorded in this treaty are taken as the norm, given the poverty of Visigothic Iberia at the outset of the eighth century, default must have been more common than payment.

Whatever the particulars, it is clear that the conquerors became the landed aristocracy of al-Andalus, though doubtless their ranks included a few of the Visigothic nobility who had had the presence of mind to switch allegiances promptly and enthusiastically. Equally few Muslims would become either peasant proprietors or country gentlemen. The agricultural system which they had appropriated was based almost exclusively upon a combination of slave labor and a dependent peasantry. Like sensible victors, they became landowners but largely as urban-dwelling collectors of rents. Since until the time of Abd al-Rahmān I they continued to be obligated to military service, they must have appeared till then still very much an urban garrison, though now a wealthy one, congregated about the courts of their traditional tribal leaders. One measure would make the Muslim community of Cordova itself scarcely 4,000 souls seventy-five years after the landing of Tāriq. Yet that probably made their numbers roughly one in ten in urban centers there or ten times higher than the initial ratio in al-Andalus as a whole.

Nevertheless, what strikes one is the enormous difference in effects between the Germanic invasions of the fifth century and the Muslim invasions of the eighth. Inevitably the difference must be explained largely in religious terms. The Arian Christianity of the Germanic conquerors proved to be too diluted a variant of the orthodox faith of the conquered ultimately to preserve the former's identity. The Islam of the Arabs was rather a vigorous and distinctive creed which constituted its adherents at once a religious, political, and social community united against the non-believer. Closely allied to the religious factor was that of language. In fifth-century Iberia the Gothic of the tribes yielded to that Vulgar Latin which was the language of the orthodox faith as well as of the conquered majority. But the conception of Arabic as the language chosen by Allah to be the vehicle of his final, perfect Revelation, guaranteed that tongue would survive as not simply a sacred language but as the *lingua franca* of politics, high culture, and even commerce. It would thus reinforce the integrity of that community already defined by religion.

Given those permanent conditions, the initial circumstances of the conquest must have made for a rapid increase of Muslim numbers. Unlike the Germans the Muslims came as an army, not a migration of peoples. But, remaining in the peninsula for many years they must have formed liaisons with native women which would have brought the latter and their children into the community of Islam, at least quadrupling its numbers within the first generation. Indeed, given the permissiveness of Islam towards polygamy and the new-found wealth of the conquerors, the ratio may have been even more impressive. In addition, the sudden creation of a new political and social world, where all advantages lay with those of the new faith, may probably be held to have led to conversions to the new creed at least approximating the numbers of the invaders themselves in the first generation. We have no data, as such, for the phenomenon but the known instance of the adoption of such a course by that important clan of the Visigothic nobility which subsequently became the powerful Banū Qāsi of the Middle Ebro is suggestive. The action of the heads of that house must have been followed by the clients, dependents, and even slaves, of the house and amounted thus to the Islamization of perhaps several thousand people in but one case. All in all, it seems quite reasonable to postulate that, by the time two generations had elapsed, the Muslim community of the al-Andalus had grown from 1 percent to something like 10 percent of the total.

This despite the fact that, although there must have been some proselytization by individuals, Islam guaranteed the integrity of the religions of the other "peoples of the Book." One of these was, of course, the Jewish community who were protected in their right to worship in the traditional faith, to be ruled by their own law in concerns internal to their community, to retain their property, and to be governed by officials chosen by their community and approved by the emir or his agents. This was the emerging regime of *dhimmi*, or subject peoples in the dār-al-Islam. So long as such recognized religious communities accepted subjection to the rule of Islam and paid the special taxes concomitant with such status, they were at least tolerated. They were, however, subject to the most severe penalties should they attempt to proselytize among the Muslim community or to prevent sincere conversions to it from among their own numbers. Relations between Muslim and Jew were regulated by Muslim law.

The numbers of the Jews in early Islamic al-Andalus is as impossible to calculate as their number in Roman or Visigothic Iberia. When some estimates do become possible, about AD 1000, the figure of 60,000 has been suggested. Given the general population increase in the peninsula of those three centuries intervening and the generally favorable attitude towards them evidenced in that period, one might hazard an estimate of perhaps 25,000 souls in 711. In numbers it was a tiny community but a variety of factors contributed to give it an influence and importance far beyond its numbers. The emphasis within Judaism on the Bible and the Torah and the importance to the adult, male believer of being able to read them, assured that literacy would be much more common among Jews than among either Muslims or Christians. As a predominantly urban and literate community in a dār-al-Islam which concentrated all political and economic direction in the city, the Jewish community was uniquely fitted to provide intellectual and commercial, sometimes even political, leadership.

Sometimes it is alleged that the Jewish community also profited from major assistance given to the invaders in the process of the eighth-century conquest. One thinks that the ferocious legislation against Jews of the late Visigothic monarchy would have predisposed them to such a course even if, as it appears, that legislation was singularly ineffective. Still, concrete details as to exactly what constituted the aid given to Tāriq or Mūsā by Jews in the eighth century are conspicuously absent. Nevertheless, what will gradually take shape in al-Andalus between AD 711 and 1100 is certainly a golden age of Iberian Jewry.

The great mass of the population of al-Andalus, perhaps a majority as late as the eleventh century, were the other *dhimmi*, the Mozarabs. This Christian population came to be so-called because they gradually adopted the dress, some of the diet of the Muslims, and even achieved some degree of bi-lingualism in Arabic. They retained their distinctive religion and the Vulgar Latin which would slowly evolve into the Romance tongues. So far as it related to its working, the land was overwhelmingly theirs. Slave or peasant, they labored under the direction of a master alien in religion and language. Nonetheless, they had their own social organization with whole villages having their own headman as well as priest. Initially most of them may even have served the same Visigothic Christian master who had signed a privileged capitulation with the Muslims. Such a situation is difficult to find after the first century of the conquest however. In fact, there was a gradual breakup of the great Visigothic *latifundia* after the conquest, the disappearance of the domainal unit and the slave labor that had worked it, and the commutation of labor dues into simple rents, so that the Mozarab farmer seems to have become a tenant almost without exception.

Yet in the church they continued to have a wider organization as well. Such Mozarabs as were urban dwellers, slaves, laborers, artisans, and small shopkeepers, one suspects, would be united in the major towns under a bishop as well as a secular officer sometimes called a *comes*. Especially if one accepts at face value the existence of some sixty bishoprics in the late Visigothic kingdom, there was a major attrition or consolidation among the Christian bishoprics of the area then comprising al-Andalus. If we eliminate the rough third of those which lay in territories beyond Muslim control by the end of the eighth century, we can still find but eighteen of the remaining forty which have continued to function. The gap might also suggest a far greater rate of early conversion to Islam than we dare to postulate. On the other hand, the Christian church structure was ripe for rationalization even in the late Visigothic period and the disorder of the conquest may have stimulated such a process.

However that may be, the fact is that the Mozarabic Christian church of al-Andalus continued to possess a substantial episcopate each of whose members was the leader and spokesman for not just the Mozarabic community of his city but of the entire surrounding diocese. Although the regular meeting of great national councils to coordinate and regulate their activities was past, they continued to consult with one another in less formal and probably less frequent fashion. They were sporadically in touch with the Roman church. Pope Hadrian I (772–795) complained in letters of some of their irregularities. The fact is clear as well that, as literate men of property and power in their own right, they were regularly consulted by the emirs or wālīs whose desires for orderly administration depended in some degree on the cooperation of these most visible and enduring leaders of the Mozarabic population. Even in diplomatic contacts with the Christian powers north of the Pyrenees, these bishops could often function as the most suitable representatives.

"THE COURSE OF CIVILIZATION IS FROM EAST TO WEST."
PAULUS OROSIUS

In material terms the most important fact about al-Andalus, religiously divided and not infrequently rent by revolt, is that it presided over the greatest increase in human prosperity that the peninsula had seen to that date. It is beyond dispute that the Muslims carried the development of Iberia far past what had been achieved in Roman times and yet more strikingly beyond the decline which had marked the Visigothic period. By AD 1000 the population of al-Andalus itself may have equalled the Late Roman population of 4,000,000 for the entire peninsula. The pattern of population of the cities had changed notably with Muslim Cordova at

90,000 inhabitants replacing Roman Cádiz which had boasted 65,000 as the largest city in the peninsula. Tarragona gradually declined until it became an entirely depopulated border district, but Seville with 52,000 and Toledo with 28,000 people had grown far beyond anything previously known.

The economic basis for this growth was an extended and flourishing new agriculture in the countryside, gradually being developed in the whole of the dār-al-Islam in these years and sparking a general rise of population throughout. The typical course of development was from east to west and new crops and new techniques found their way to Iberia throughout the period. In the ninth century the cultivation of the banana and cotton can already be detected. They were followed by hard wheat, rice, sugar cane, eggplant, and watermelon, in the tenth. The eleventh century records the arrival of sorghum and spinach.

Now all of these foodstuffs represented a major diversification and improvement in diet of course. But they also increased the quantity of food available in two fashions. Some of them, such as sugar cane and rice, gave a much larger yield per acre than any existing crop. Others, such as sorghum, hard wheat, and cotton, were much more resistant to near-drought and so allowed land marginal for want of sufficient rainfall to be brought under cultivation for the first time in the peninsula. Moreover, many of these new species were useful not only for human sustenance but also for livestock fodder and agricultural compost. Sorghum canes could even be used for thatch, fencing, and baskets, while its seeds could be fermented into a beer.

Some of the hardiness of the new crops could be combined with new techniques and practices which must have had the effect of virtually tripling the amount of land available for cultivation in Iberia. For one, the Muslim world early had broken from the standard of antiquity that a field could only be cultivated once in two years. Fields will now routinely be put under the plow every year. Almost as significant, the new agriculture will also add, in many places and with many more drought-resistant crops, an entire additional growing season when the Mediterranean summer begins to be first utilized as a possible period of cultivation rather than being treated as an agricultural "dead time" as in antiquity. There seems, as well, to have been a marked extension of land devoted to the cultivation of crops long familiar such as the olive and the grape, the latter despite the Koranic prohibition of spirits. Of course these innovations had to be bolstered by a much more active regime of fertilizing and crop alternation, to which the agricultural manuals of the time give much attention.

Combined with these new crops and techniques was the more

aggressive employment of old technologies. Roman Spain had clearly relied upon irrigation but almost solely of a gravity flow type which drastically limited the amount of land which could be so treated. They understood the water-raising techniques embodied in the *noria*, the wheel fitted with buckets, but they seem to have used it only to clear mines. In al-Andalus there was to be an enormous spread of this device using alternatively the power of men, animals, or the water itself to propel it. At the same time, the greater utilization of groundwater through cisterns, piping, and above all the *qanat* or underground canal long familiar to the farmers of the Middle East. Again, these technologies increased both the area of land which could now be used and the variety of crops which could be grown on it.

Finally, cultural factors seem also to have played a part in this remarkable improvement in the world of agriculture. Under Islamic law it appears that land had fewer familial or customary restrictions upon its transfer and moved more easily into the market. Land left uncultivated for more than three years could be confiscated and resold. Irrigated lands, devoted to the raising of fruits and vegetables, were more lightly taxed. Although the practices had been inherited by Islam at the conquest, widespread agricultural slavery and a peasantry which owed labor dues seem largely to have died out. Moreover, the emirs, the caliphs of Cordova, and many of their courtiers appear to have been fascinated by the riches of the soil of the Guadalquivir valley and its possibilities. Abd al-Rahmān I is reported to have imported trees from all over the Mediterranean to grace the gardens of his *alcázar* and given credit for the introduction of a variety of the pomegranate and another of the date palm to Iberia. Just so, Abd al-Rahmān II (822–852) is said to have introduced a new and better variety of fig. Such amenities as the lemon, lime, and sour orange, may also have been first introduced by such royal patronage.

All in all, there was a gradual but startling recovery of the countryside of al-Andalus from the poverty of Visigothic times and even of Roman. Not only did the population which it could support increase but the evidence is that this same higher population was better nourished even though most land was worked by a Mozarabic peasantry subject to a much higher rate of taxation due to their religious status. Relatively speaking, agricultural prosperity was fairly general also despite the fact that so large a percentage of the land was held by a rent-collecting, urban aristocracy most often differing in religion from its agricultural tenants. In part, this must be explained by the new participation of al-Andalus in a revitalized Mediterranean trade which increasingly marked the dār-al-Islam as the age progressed.

This new trading community would superficially resemble the classical Mediterranean under Rome. In Arabic it had a *lingua franca* which more than overmatched the old Greek *koine*. For a single Roman commercial law it had the ubiquitous Koran and the jurisprudence flowing from it. For the kinship of Christianity it substituted the community of Islam. What it did lack was a Mediterranean Sea policed by a single government. Indeed, during the eighth century and into the first quarter of the ninth, warfare and piracy were endemic at sea when that great highway was not, in fact, controlled by an actively hostile Byzantium. Under these circumstances, the caravan routes along the North African coast from Morocco to Cairo assumed a new commercial importance.

In common with the remainder of Islam in the west, Iberia possessed no real naval force, which in this period means relatively little commerce for the same ships could be utilized for either purpose. A local fleet which operated out of Tortosa and Tarragona harassed the Carolingians along the southern French coast in the late eighth century and into the ninth. Its highpoint came with the Balearics were finally overrun in 902. Doubtless when these ships were not busy with piracy and raids they carried a local trade along the coast of the Iberian Levant, the Gulf of Lyons, and the southern French coast. Farther south, a then much more modest center of shipping existed at Almeria.

The great blossoming of Iberian overseas trade, however, still must wait. The key proved to be in North African Tunisia where during the independent reigns of the Aghlabids and then the Fatimids, first Pantelleria, then Malta, and finally Sicily itself fell into Muslim hands in the course of the ninth century. Together with the fall of Crete to Islam in 827 these successes created a string of buffer islands south of which Muslim commerce at sea could flow from west to east and back again in greater safety and hence volume. In Iberia the changed conditions are reflected in the fact that Abd al-Rahmān III (912–961) was the first Ummayad there to adopt the title of caliph, the first to organize a truly peninsular fleet, and the first to issue a gold coinage.

While the full flowering of the trade of al-Andalus arrives only in the tenth and even eleventh centuries, the features it displayed were largely permanent ones present on a smaller scale in earlier, less prosperous times. Despite the religious and political schism between Ummayad Iberia and the Abbāsid Near East, religious, cultural, and economic contacts remained close. Most obvious in this regard is the pilgrimage to Mecca which could not, in the nature of things, cease and supplied a certain volume of travelers to fill enterprising Muslim craft, and so support trade, with predictable regularity. Such travel also kept the west in touch with the styles, products, and technology of the eastern Mediterranean and created a taste there for the same. Travel also developed for other purposes, notably study. These factors combined to make quite usual the acquisition of the silks, paper, glassware, and fine metalware of the Near East by the wealthier classes of al-Andalus before the techniques of their production were themselves imported.

But the trade with the Near East was never so important in either volume or value as that with the North African coast. Tunisia, Algeria, and Morocco to a lesser extent, were major centers of exchange between the Near East and Iberia, of course, but they were the exchange point for goods of that caravan trade which crossed the Sahara from the Sudan and the headwaters of the Niger and the Senegal too. These routes had been pioneered during the early ninth century and after that time reached the northern coast regularly with their cargoes of gold, ivory, and slaves. According to a geographer of the time, ibn Hawkal, the westernmost route alone provided Abd al-Rahmān III with an income of 500,000 gold dinars per year, when that caliph was able to control it. Wealth on this scale would do much to explain why the Shiite Fatimids of Kairouan made such strenuous efforts to wrest it away from the Iberians despite the fact that they had conquered and built Cairo for their new capital in 973, and that they would be increasingly preoccupied in Egypt and the Levantine coast.

Whoever its masters, from the late eighth century Tunisia in particular had prospered as the mosques and aqueducts built then to adorn its cities well illustrate. It was noted for its wheat and olive oil but became a center for the manufacture of fine glasswares, enameled pottery, and carpets as well. None of these could not be had farther east but it would be at greater cost. All of them were produced somewhere in Iberia. But, in a place like Almeria with no hinterland to speak of and kilometers of rough travel to reach the valley of the Upper Guadalquivir, it was often cheaper or more convenient to obtain them by sea from North Africa, and then too the style might be different. In the tenth and eleventh centuries al-Andalus imported even wheat from North Africa but surely it went to similar coastal areas which the plentiful wheat of the *mesetas* reached only with extreme difficulty.

With few exceptions the products which Iberia contributed to this busy trade were homely ones. Timber from the delta of the Ebro at Tortosa, for general building purposes but above all for ships. There were shipyards along the east coast from Denia, through Alicante, to Almeria in the time of al-Idrīsī. Surely ships were sold, as well as sailed, to the timber-poor African coast farther east. On the other side of the peninsula in the Algarve, Alcácer do Sal exported timber as well as beef. More to the south, Silves exported its figs, and Niebla mined marble and iron. From the plain about Seville olive oil and figs were consigned for the east. Málaga, al-Idrīsī says, sent its figs to Egypt, Syria, Iraq, and India. Now figs were hardly rare in any of those places but apparently a thriving entrepreneur could sell an exotic variety there at a good price so long as the sea freights were cheap. From Guadalajara came saffron, a bit farther north the Guadarrama provided copper and iron ores, and somewhat to the south in the basin of the Guadiana the mines around Almaden furnished mercury.

Now only the first and last of these were material for export in the raw form but the new abundance of the agriculture of al-Andalus permitted the greater proliferation of secondary occupations as well. Some of these sent their product abroad too. The steel of Toledo, especially worked into swords, became famous. So did the leathers of Cordova, the linen of Saragossa and of Elvira, and the cottons of Seville. By the tenth century Cordova had become famous for its silks and its crystal as well and the new papermaking industry centered around Játiva on the east coast was already supplying its product to the Christian community which sometimes employed that material to make new copies of their liturgical books.

If activity in the fields of Iberia under the Ummayads surpassed that of Roman times, so did that of the artisan in the tannery, the forge, and at the loom. In the larger towns, the artisan population was so numerous that it was organized by the government into corporate structures under an official, an *amīn*, who was responsible for their maintaining standards of quality in production. After all, in marked contrast with the Visigothic monarchy, the market or sales tax, *qabala*, was a major item in the government's income. In such towns or cities one found streets and sometimes even sections whose name indicated both the trade and the numbers of those engaged in it. Cordova was said to have no less than 13,000 workers in the textile industry alone.

By the tenth century Almeria, on the southeastern coast, had become the greatest port of the peninsula for the traffic in fine goods and textiles with Africa and the east. Moreover, abroad should not be simply construed as the Near East or even Tunisia and Sicily. From the ninth century onward Berber Morocco was increasingly becoming Muslim, Arabized, and relatively prosperous. At the same time it was turning into a market for Iberian products and would become a student of Andalusian techniques in the near future. Then too there was the backward Christian north. Poor as it might be its kings had funds for the purchase of rich Andalusian fabrics, at least they were sometimes wrapped in them for burial. Worked ivory caskets were purchased to hold the remains of Christian saints and fine Andalusian linens sometimes covered the altars.

North of that line in which the grape would grow, those with the money and the taste also made a market for the wines of the south.

Nonetheless the greatest market for the artisanry of al-Andalus was the internal one. The richness of its new agriculture produced a more general prosperity in which farmers could buy as well as sell. Most of the products of which al-Idrīsī spoke were those destined for an internal market, whether they were copper, iron, marble, wood, raisins, cottons or pottery. Most of these things were destined for the inhabitants of those 8,000 flourishing villages on the plain about Seville which he mentioned, perhaps with some hyperbole. But if these products were destined for them they were also to be represented, in one way or another, in the mosques, *alcázars*, the town walls, the country castles, being erected by the emirs, later the caliphs, and even by the *wālīs* of the more important provincial towns. These would be raised on a truly lavish, not to say monumental, scale in and around the capital at Cordova.

The mosque of Cordova may be taken as the positive extreme to which the new wealth of the peninsula might be poured into major construction. The historians of al-Andalus assert that the first mosque there was merely half of the extant Christian church of St. Vincent. But what sufficed for the time of the governors was inappropriate for the emirate. Under Abd al-Rahmān I (756–788), the other half of the church was taken and, apparently, all structures on the site razed. Then an entirely new mosque was constructed, much of which still exists. Subsequent rulers, including Abd al-Rahmān II (822–852), added to the building to accommodate a growing Muslim population. But, with the establishment of the caliphate, the building was still too modest and the present structure which overwhelms the tourist of today illustrates well the power and wealth of al-Andalus during the time of Caliph al-Hakam II (961–976).

THE HIGH CULTURES OF AL-ANDALUS

The communities of al-Andalus were, like all of their contemporary counterparts, societies whose cohesive principle was religious. The ultimate knowledge for all of them was religious. Since all of them were, moreover, relatively simple communities in which agriculture was the most familiar feature of everyone's life, their intellectual tradition revolved around the mosque, the synagogue, and the church. For the farmer, the artisan, and their families, education was a family matter. Daughters and sons were taught to cook, spin, nurture children, to plow, care for domestic animals, bake, forge, or make paper, by their mothers and fathers or by their master in the shop who might well be their father.

For the overwhelming majority of them that was the substance of what we, awkwardly, call education. What more they might or might not learn of the world, aside from personal experience, was imparted by a religious figure, *imām*, rabbi, or priest, and was fundamentally religious in content and context.

For most, this education was implicit in their very worship and their religious instruction and would become education in the formal sense only very occasionally and haphazardly. Its transmission was exclusively oral. Only for a small elite, destined for the religious life as such, would it become a matter of literacy. Since Islam, Judaism, and Christianity, were all religions of a "Book of Revelation" the ability to read and write were critical for their religious leadership and recruitment to their ranks therefore implied formal education in our sense of the term. True, ideally all believers, or at least all adult male believers, should be able to consult the sacred text themselves but in actual practice the memorization of a greater or lesser number of important passages seems to have sufficed even there.

The structures which imparted formal education in al-Andalus were parallel for all three communities. Traditionally in antiquity learning was imparted by an already learned person who attracted pupils, disciples, by very reason of that fact. The pupil learned in the home of his master, and might well live there for a time. In the case of the very wealthy, the pupil might be instructed in his own home by a master become "tutor" who might sometimes live there instead. This very simple practice only rarely had given rise to a more formal organization for the transmission of learning. Now it would begin to so develop but only quite slowly and very unevenly among the three religious communities. Formal education would coalesce, in some degree, about the mosque, synagogue, or episcopal palace and monastery, which could become recognized centers for more advanced instruction under favorable circumstances. Nevertheless, it would be a long time before any one of these seems regularly to have boasted a "faculty," i.e., more than one learned person who taught.

In this context, then, what must be taught was similar for each of the faiths. Education was, above all, education in letters. The neophyte must learn a sacred language. Learning was primarily grammar, orthography, philology, initially. After it became logic and rhetoric, the ability to speak and write cogently and with a certain appeal to one's audience. These were the tools for understanding and then disseminating the content of Revelation. But of course, in the developing of such skills, the use of past literature beyond simply Revelation itself was a necessary device and the student ordinarily studied and absorbed something of a canon of literature, history, law, and philosophy as well, even if by indirection.

Within this context, Islam had the handicap of being the latest of the Revelations. At the death of Muhammad in AD 632, its first task was the very constitution of a canonical text of the Koran itself, for the Prophet had written little or nothing. That done in the seventh century, it must be then supplemented by a collection of *hadīth*, or sayings and practice of Muhammad, for the sacred book itself often supplied little practical guide to the complexities of the society into which the conquests of the early caliphs had carried its followers. Ultimately, the most authoritative collections of *hadīth* were ninth-century products.

Now, at the same time, Arabic itself had to be transformed from a largely oral and customary language into a written and even literary one with an agreed-upon grammar, orthography, and script. While this most basic of tasks was in train, the science of interpreting and applying Islam to create a law of the Muslim community, *fiqh*, must be undertaken as well and the first school of such law, the Mālikite, was the product of the Medinan Mālik ibn Anas (d. 795). But from the last quarter of the seventh century, the establishment of the Ummayad caliphate at Damascus had carried Islam into the cultural world of Greek thought. There Greek philosophy and Greek science would first be translated and then, in some degree, harmonized with Islamic thought and absorbed into it. From the late eighth century under the Abbāsids, at Baghdad, Persian and Indian astronomy and mathematics would require the same sort of intellectual athleticism. Indeed the only thing more impressive than the energies of the early warriors of Islam is that of their scholars.

Under these circumstances one is hardly surprised that the high culture of Muslim al-Andalus during the eighth and ninth centuries was largely derivative. That a society on the far frontier of the dār-al-Islam in a newly conquered land struggling to organize there politically, socially, and economically, would contribute to a religious and intellectual process that complex is scarcely to be expected. The warriors and governors brought the institutional framework with them for that was portable but reflection upon, and further elaboration of, it must needs wait.

The beginnings of that process can be said fairly to have begun with the arrival in al-Andalus of the *Muwatta* of Mālik ibn Abās during the reign of al-Hakam I (796–822). This oldest of the Muslim treatises of jurisprudence, the foundation of the Mālikite school, would lay the continuing basis of the Islamic theology and law in Iberia. Not surprisingly given its early formulation, it tended to be literal and strongly traditional in its treatment of the Koran and the *hadīth*. Down to the disappearance of al-Andalus in the thirteenth century, the caliphs and their successors ordinarily collaborated with the *qādīs* to ensure its predominance against all challengers.

But the concern of the rulers of al-Andalus was not simply with the political order. Indeed, they were themselves at once religious and political figures and would have found a distinction strange. Therefore they maintained a court which was also a focus of religious learning. The first really independent western work in Arabic philology, for instance, seems to have been done by al-Zubaydī (d. 989), a Sevillan who was educated in Cordova and subsequently was patronized by al-Hakam II. Since his knowledge extended to law and poetry, the philologist, grammarian, and author was made the tutor of the future Caliph Hishām II (976–1009, 1010–1013) a judge of the city, and its chief of police.

Indeed the caliphal court in Iberia, as in Kairouan, Cairo, or Baghdad, was the center of another type of learning which predated Islam itself and which formed that tradition in terms of which the Koran and the *hadīth* were themselves defined and taught. This was the tradition of an oral, initially tribal learning which was embodied in poetry. Its themes were war, the hunt, nature, wine, and love, all of them inseparable from court life perhaps in any age. Trained in this poetry to some extent, the religious scholar was equipped to function as courtier as well. In fact, this classical poetry remained rigidly traditional in al-Andalus and was chiefly remarkable to contemporaries for the elegance and intricacy with which it fashioned its celebration of the ruler and his favorites. Even the ruler played this game of exquisite compliment and counter-compliment. Abd al-Rahmān I, al-Hakam I, and Abd al-Rahmān II, are all said to have composed such verse.

But such games were played orally and the increasing literary, sophistication, and learning of the court was being reflected in a new written lore. This was the court genre of *adab*, i.e., the encyclopedia of both the form and the content of worldly wisdom. Its greatest practitioner in the west was ibn Abd Rabbihi (d. 940), a Cordovan and court figure under three rulers, culminating with Abd al-Rahmān III. His *The Unique Necklace* in twenty-five books assembles sermons, histories, biographies, poems, statecraft, proverbs, etiquette, anecdotes, and much more in elegantly contrived language. In addition to being an entertainment in itself, it was the indispensable book of the courtier who wished to achieve the appearance of much education without the drudgery of accumulating it.

Because in the Muslim tradition it is so closely devoted to biography, historical writing often is difficult to separate from the *adab* literature. It too found an important place at court for it sang the praises of the prince. The writing of histories began early but before Abd al-Mālik ibn Habib's (d. 853/4) history of al-Andalus from 711 to 839 none have reached us intact. A *History of the Judges of Cordova* by al-Kushānī (d. 971) is valuable for the account of city life in the tenth century.

But the court could be a patron of learning of the most serious kind. Caliph al-Hakam II was a great collector of manuscripts and his agents sought them out in Cairo, Damascus, and Constantinople. Since he was far from niggardly in the payment of copyists, he managed to amass a staggering library for the times. We are told 400,000 volumes but even one tenth that number of volumes would easily have made it a hundred times larger than the best-stocked contemporary monastic libraries of the Christian west. One of the items in it was a Greek manuscript of Dioscorides *Materia Medica* sent him by the Emperor Constantine VII, which was employed to correct the Arabic text then in use in Iberia. This was the sort of resource which would permit Abū Qasim ibn Abbas Zahrawi (d. 1013) to compose his famous medical and surgical encyclopedia which later found its way into the Christian west through a Latin translation.

In this period as well, the astronomy of Persia and the mathematics of India were finding their way west from Baghdad. Euclid's *Elements* was circulating in Iberia as were the logarithmic tables of al-Khwārismī. A revision of the latter was done by Maslama of Madrid (d. 1007) who also did a commentary on Ptolemy's *Planisphaerium*, and wrote widely on not only astronomy but, alas, astrology as well. One does not exaggerate to say that a solid foundation was being laid in the tenth century for the brilliance to come.

Between the conquest and the end of the caliphate in Iberia, Jewish intellectual life exhibited many of the same characteristics as Islam. In strictly religious matters it was dependent upon the authority and learning of the Near East, especially the rabbis of Mesopotamia, with whom it communicated through Kairouan. Manuscripts from the Levant were sought out for the language of the Talmud, Aramaic, was not widely known in the peninsula. For the related matters of an authoritative statement of the conventions of the Hebrew language, it was to be heavily influenced by the work then being carried out in Arabic philology and grammar.

In part this was a reflection of the more advanced condition of these studies in Arabic but it was also a court phenomenon in some measure. Although their positions there were never secure and the opposition of the *qādīs* was always a danger under a weak ruler, both Jews and Christians were sometimes to enjoy positions of considerable influence in the circles of the prince. Their very vulnerability made them faithful administrators and they were foreign to the ordinary Muslim factions there. Such a man was Hasdai ben Shaprut (c. 910–975), son of a

wealthy Jewish merchant of Jaen who had been educated in Cordova and
early displayed a remarkable variety of aptitudes. About 940 he became a
court physician in the household of Caliph Abd al-Rahmān III because of
his fame in the city as a doctor. That position he would continue to hold
until his death in the reign of al-Hakam. Hasdai also seems to have held
an influential post in the customs department for some little time. Because
of his knowledge of Latin as well as Arabic and Hebrew, the caliph
employed him as an envoy to the Christian Ordoño III of Asturias and a
negotiator in affairs concerning the Emperor Otto I of Germany and the
Byzantine emperor.

Most germane to present purposes, however, Abd al-Rahmān
appointed Hasdai *nāsi*, that is, the legal chief officer of the Jewish community in Iberia and Ummayad North Africa. He was to handle their
internal affairs and liaison between them and the caliph. It was a post of
great influence, not least in intellectual matters because of the interests of
Hasdai himself. He it was who intervened to make Moses ben Hanokah,
an Italian scholar who had first been brought to Iberia as a captive, the
chief rabbi of Cordova. Under Moses that city became the acknowledged
center of the study and interpretation in al-Andalus of the Torah,
breaking the old dependence on Baghdad. Hasdai also brought
Menachem ben Jacob, a Jew from the northeast of the peninsula and a
protégé of his brother, into the court as his secretary.

The new secretary would fulfill the usual chores of composing correspondence of his master, praising him in poetry, and presiding over his
master's schedule. Nevertheless, he found time over the years to write *The
Book of Interpretations*, the first major lexicon of the Hebrew language in
the peninsula. This work was subsequently advanced and corrected by
Dunash ben Labrat ha-levi, a Moroccan-born Jew who had been
educated in Iraq but who settled in Cordova as a cantor. There he became
best known as a poet. He wrote Jewish liturgical poetry but also secular
poetry on themes prominent in Arabic poems and he adapted, as well,
Hebrew poetry to Arabic meter and verse structure. Finally he engaged in
a great controversy with Menachem ben Jacob who had fallen from favor
with Hasdai ben Shaprūt. Menachem had rejected applicability of the
framework of Arabic philology to the construction of a similar one for
Hebrew. Dunash ben Labrat held for the utility of the former and his
views were to triumph, making the future happy and close collaboration
between Arabic and Jewish culture in al-Andalus yet more certain.

The development of high culture among the Mozarabs was neither so
brilliant nor oriented toward the same sort of necessities. Though it shared
the preoccupation with language and grammatical studies, Latin was
mature as a written language and did not present the same sort of

problems as did Arabic or Hebrew. Nor was there an extant but foreign center of learning on the order of Damascus or Baghdad to which it was held in thrall. Indeed, in some degree, Mozarabic al-Andalus was itself the authority for the church and Christians in the remainder of the peninsula. Though administrative control over the churches of the northwest and north was lost, it seems to have continued to supply the Christian communities of those areas with the essential models for their liturgical books or ordinals and with those copies of the *Hispana* and the *Liber Judiciorum* which were to be essential to the self-definition of newly emerging communities of the north. In truth, those magnificent manuscripts still extant are some of the best guides we possess to the culture of the Mozarabs themselves.

But from the main trends of cultural life in al-Andalus itself, the Mozarabic community was alienated in some degree. For one thing, it was much more exclusively agrarian in membership than its two counterparts. For another, portions of it were sometimes actively in opposition to Islamic domination. That opposition might be expressed peacefully as in the public denunciation of Islam and the active courting of martyrdom sought and obtained in mid-ninth-century Cordova. Again, it might be marked by participation in active revolt in the countryside as in that of ibn Hafsūn of the late ninth century, although the leadership in such rebellions generally belonged to the *muwallad*, or converts to Islam. Finally, from the middle years of the ninth century as the more visible emergence of Christian principalities in the north furnished an alternative, emigration from al-Andalus of the more enterprising and uncompromising part of the Mozarab community became more and more common.

Not that the Mozarabs of al-Andalus were totally excluded from its cultural or court life. Indeed, at least one contemporary could complain in the ninth century that young Mozarabs knew their Arabic better than their Latin and affected Muslim clothing and fashions. A rough, working knowledge of spoken Arabic was widespread and Romance popular songs appear to have had a distinct influence on Arabic poetry, for the knowledge of the latter tongue was common among the Muslims. But these must have been largely urban and court phenomena just as was the employment of Bishop Recemund of Elvira by Abd al-Rahmān in a diplomatic mission to Germany.

Still, by and large the Mozarabic communities of al-Andalus continued to look back towards an Isidorean and Visigothic past which had vanished. Such intellectual products as we have are of that sort. Bishop Recemund was the author of a liturgical calendar in both Latin and Arabic. The anonymous *Mozarabic Chronicle of 754* depended upon the Isidorean chronicle although it had much to say of early al-Andalus. Bishop Eulogius of Cordova (d. 859) reintroduced a number of classical texts, including some of Horace and Virgil into his episcopal city, presided over a Latinate literary circle there, and wrote a number of defenses of the Christian martyrs of Cordova before being martyred himself. Most famous of all, Bishops Elipandus of Toledo and Felix of Urgel espoused a doctrine of adoptionism under murky circumstances in the late eighth century which was sufficiently prominent to draw upon them the condemnation of Rome, the Carolingian court, and even of some of the fledgling churches of the Iberian north. Of the new Christian order gradually taking form in that north they had no vision.

THE OTHER IBERIA

Certainly one of the most extraordinary events that occurred in Iberia during the eighth century was the appearance of a Christian kingdom in the north centered on Asturias de Oviedo. By the reign of Alfonso II (791–842) there exists a realm which includes not only Asturias north of the Cantabrian chain but Galicia to its west and Cantabria to its southwest, some portion of the Basque lands to the east, and an indeterminate fringe along the southern slopes of the Cantabrians. These areas had had neither a unity nor a political identity in the time of the Romans or Visigoths. They possessed neither roads, ports, cities, nor bishoprics, of which we are informed. No political leader of the peoples residing therein figures in earlier accounts but they are spoken of as constituted by a variety of tribes. Yet, by the end of the eighth century they have found a single political and social identity which is never thereafter lost. On the contrary it will be extended until they will finally come to dominate the entire peninsula.

The dynamic of this most unlikely event is shrouded in obscurity. The Mozarabic *Chronicle of 754* still knows nothing of such a realm. The first glimpses of the process which created it are contained only in the chronicles of the cycle of Alfonso III of Asturias which are composed up to one hundred and fifty years after the events they describe and which sometimes differ among themselves. Yet those accounts do at least suggest the outlines of the profound cultural and social transformation which had taken place in the northernmost reaches of the peninsula.

The beginning lay in the arrival of Visigothic refugees from the Muslim conquest. All accounts agree that the Pelayo (718–737) who gained the small but all-important victory over a Muslim force at Covadonga in 718/719 was a Visigothic noble. But, like the Romans and Visigoths who preceded them, the Muslims never had a secure grasp of that mountain country. Moreover, although Pelayo himself may have been accompanied by a personal military following, it would have hardly been sufficient to secure more than precarious control in the tiny valley about Cangas de Onis. News of his victory may have attracted more Visigothic refugees and some local support but the whole force of the Visigothic kingdom had never been able to subdue the men of those mountains. Pelayo and his successors must have been even better politicians than they were warriors.

A most important first step was Pelayo's marriage of his daughter to the son of the shadowy "duke" Peter of Cantabria. It clearly sealed a union of the two communities which was further bonded when the latter's son, Alfonso I (739–757), succeeded Pelayo's shortlived heir, Fáfila (737–739). The same sort of union, though less completely successful, took place when Alfonso's son, Fruela I (757–768), married the Basque woman, Munia, who must also have been the daughter of a prominent tribal chieftain in the west of that tribal territory. These two unions created the political nucleus of the new kingdom. The attempts to extend it westward into Galicia began already during the reign of Alfonso I but seem to have been effected by conquest as no marriage from among those peoples was recorded. It is possible though that the mother of Vermudo I (788–791) was Galician.

Alfonso I is also recorded to have taken advantage of the revolt of the Berbers against their Arab co-religionists in 740 and the great famines of the years 748–754, both of which led to widespread withdrawal of the former from Galicia and the Duero valley, to conduct a series of extended raids which are alleged to have resulted in the taking of León, Astorga, Braga, and points as far south even as Salamanca. More importantly, he is also said to have put to the sword the Muslims, read garrisons, of those places and to have carried their Christian residents off to the north. Such a result would have greatly increased the Visigothic presence and influence north of the Cantabrians. The resulting strength made it possible in the reign of Fruela I for that monarch to further extend his power over Galicia and to first defeat, and then negotiate a marriage with the westernmost Basques. But a lengthy reaction against this growing power marked the brief reigns of four of his successors, brothers and cousins, until his son Alfonso II (791–842) was able to return momentum to the growth of the kingdom.

But such tribal alliances and unions are notoriously unstable in themselves and tend to break up with the death of the generation which contrived them. A second element in the fusion that was taking place was the belated conversion of the northern tribes to Christianity. Though we know next to nothing about it, there must have been some small previous penetration of that faith among them simply by virtue of their contact with the Christian communities of the Duero basin. Now the existence of such a minority would have facilitated the foothold gained by the Visigothic refugees and the growth of the Christian church would have thus become intimately linked to the growth of the new kingdom. Both Fáfila I and Alfonso I are credited with the foundation of churches.

More important yet, during his raids to the south, Alfonso I removed the bishop of conquered Braga, the metropolitan see of the old province of Gallaecia, to the city of Lugo in the east of present-day Galicia. It became the first bishopric of the nascent kingdom, gave it claim to independence of the metropolitans of al-Andalus, and solidified both the Christianity of the realm and the latter's hold on Galicia. On the death of Alfonso I the miraculous levitation of his body was reported to have recognized his achievement.

But influence in the westernmost portion of Galicia was greatly advanced by the action of Alfonso II. Sometime about 830 the discovery was made by the bishop of Iria Flavia, Teodemir, of a ruined shrine containing the putative remains of the Apostle, Saint James the Great, in the area to be known as Santiago de Compostela. Informed of the find, Alfonso hastened to pay his respects and to subsidize the construction of a church there. He thus secured a powerful patron for his fledgling kingdom and a new base of power in the west of that stubborn territory. In Asturias the king not only moved the royal residence originally in Cangas de Onis, then in Pravia, a location with easier access over the Cantabrians to the Duero valley, he also had built no fewer than three churches in the new royal city. Of course, this new royal residence needs must have a bishopric of its own and the see of Oviedo, completely without precedent in antiquity, was created during the reign of Alfonso II. The most common appellation for this new political structure in the ninth-century chronicles was the "regnum christianorum."

But the chronicles also tell us of a third ingredient in the fabrication of this new community. Alfonso II, they say, restored "the Visigothic order in church and palace." This enigmatic statement both baffles and enlightens us. For clearly it is not so. Surely nothing in the organization of the Christian church of Asturias over the next three centuries will remotely resemble that of the Visigothic kingdom. As for the new Asturian monarchy, it is fundamentally distinct from that of the Visigoths by reason of the centrality to it of a dynasty and of hereditary transmission. These two crucial political entities the Visigoths had never realized. We call it the kingdom of Asturias, or later of León, because our political thought is incorrigibly territorial. But in no genuine document for the next 250 years does one of these monarchs so identify himself. The kingdom is a people under a monarch who invariably styles himself as king by reason of a particular paternity. But while these people are a "gens" they are not the "gentium gotorum" except at times in the literary conventions of that handful of clerics who would write the chronicles. It should be noted that these same authors ordinarily equate "Spanie" with al-Andalus.

Nevertheless, the statement is true as well. For what it tells us is that the authors and the community are in the possession of the *Hispana* which alone would furnish some sketchy picture of a "Gothic order" to be imitated. And, if in possession of the *Hispana*, they doubtless also possessed copies of the *Liber Judiciorum* which would furnish them with a judicial ideal as well as a political dream. But, in addition to these, surely they had received copies of the ordinals, the mass books, the hymnals, of the Mozarabic liturgy in which truly a "Gothic order" would be literally continued. There had transpired, in other words, a narrow but critical reception of the high culture of the Visigothic and Roman past which would, in a rough way, validate their new political necessities.

Finally, the new regime in the north must credit its survival and remarkable success in part to the disarray of its enemies. From the conquest itself al-Andalus was unable to find a stable political order. Revolts of one sort or another led to an early withdrawal from Galicia and the Duero valley and their continuation into the reign of Abd al-Rahmān I (756–788) meant that the Ummayad emirs did not manage to extend their control, more than sporadically, to all of al-Andalus until virtually the end of the reign of his grandson, al-Hakam I (796–822). With the exception of some serious inroads made during the brief reign of the Emir Hisham I (788–796), the result was almost a century of immunity to serious challenge from the south.

But that same lack of political stability had led to a contraction of al-Andalus in the northeast of the peninsula as well, and the emergence of other, smaller Christian entities in that quarter. In addition, however, these new communities would depend upon the growth of Carolingian power to the north of the Pyrenees. After reacting successfully at Tours in 732, the Franks had gone on to extend their power in Aquitaine and in Septimania, finally taking Narbonne in 759. The old Visigothic Narbonensis now in their hands, they received an invitation from rebels against Abd al-Rahmān to take possession of Barcelona and Saragossa. Charlemagne responded with an expedition in 778 which attempted both and failed at both, its rearguard meeting disaster at Roncesvalles during the withdrawal.

But the Franks continued to extend their control in Aquitaine and in 785 they had taken Gerona. This new gain could not help but incite overtures from rebels against Cordova. New intervention would result in the Frankish conquest of Barcelona in 801 and the erection of a Carolingian march in Catalonia which would define the region north of the Llobregat politically as a province of the Frankish kingdom for the next two centuries. Still, this region had a considerable Visigothic population and religious tradition which had not been overwhelmed either by Muslim conquest or Frankish reconquest. Under Frankish patronage, so to speak, it would slowly evolve an identity as distinct from that of Asturias as its language would also come to be.

About the same time, at the western end of the Pyrenees, a different set of conditions were to produce another community. It appears that the basic strata of population in Navarre, High Aragon, Sobarabe, Ribagorza, Alava, and the Upper Rioja, was Basque as a result of migration from Vizcaya and Guipuzcoa which had been fairly continuous in Late Roman and Visigothic times. Nonetheless, pressures from the latter two powers and contact with the older, Latin population had resulted in some melding of language and some adoption of Christianity, at least in the center of that area comprising the Upper Rioja, Navarra, and perhaps Alava. A bishop at Pamplona seems well attested for a time during the Visigothic period.

Now all of this area was occupied fairly quickly by the Muslims after 711 but their control there was complicated by the rapid assertion of quasi-independence by the *walīs* of Saragossa. After that post became almost hereditary in the house of the Banū Qasī, *muwallads* with a claim to distinction and property in the valley from Visigothic times, the control of Cordova was further endangered by the willingness of its governors to ally with the Basques of Pamplona against them. About 740 Pamplona had driven out its Arab garrison. It may have remained independent then until Charlemagne occupied it in 778 but when the Frankish king retreated he destroyed its walls. By 799 it had as governor one of the Banū Qasī, Mutarrif ibn Mūsā, that family having appeared two decades earlier as contenders for the control of Saragossa. Revolt in that year led to Mūsā's death and Pamplona's renewed independence but the growing strength of al-Hakam of Cordova's power in the valley led the Basques of Pamplona to submit to Frankish authority in 806.

In 813 a Pamplona, now in rebellion against the Carolingians, had to be subdued by a Frankish army and subsequently two Frankish marches were established; one in Navarre around Pamplona and another in High Aragon. Both were governed by Basques however. But a new revolt and the defeat of a Frankish army sent to quell it in 824 established the independence of the two. High Aragon was subordinate to Pamplona, the latter under the Basque family of Jimeno Aritza. The area about the western end of the Pyrenees continued to be highly unstable with tribal and clan loyalties competing with some attempts to create a monarchy based on dynasty. We are almost without information about it for a century except that the Aritzas effected the foundation of the influential monastery of Leyre on the boundary between Navarre and Aragon. Apparently the monarchy, in alliance with a church continuously strengthened by Mozarabic refugees from the south, was gradually able to best clan loyalties. So positioned, it was slowly to assert its political and cultural leadership over the remaining territories of Sobarabe and Ribagorza to the east and of the Upper Rioja to the south. The classic Basque tribal country in Vizcaya and Guipuzcoa remained separate, still pagan, still tribal, still purely Basque. The other territories Pamplona was to launch on a different trajectory.

THE WAXING AND WANING OF AL-ANDALUS

Of course none of these principalities of the Christian north were able to constitute a threat to al-Andalus. Although the former would prove able to maintain themselves, the emirs of Cordova continued in possession of four of the five great river basins of the peninsula. The fifth, the Duero, remained a no-man's-land. The history of al-Andalus over the next two centuries was essentially self-contained politically and culturally. That its fortunes should have been, in some respects, so chequered was a function of its own organization.

Modern historical analysis is hampered by the absence of more than incomplete and literary accounts, for the subsequent reconquest largely swept away state papers and administrative records. Nevertheless, it is clear that one cannot account for the troubles of this theocratic state in terms of schism. The sort of rival Muslim claims of religious legitimacy which were to rend North Africa were totally lacking in Iberia. Abbāsid plots, Fatimid claims, self-proclaimed *mahdīs*: from none of these was there a serious challenge to the Ummayad house of Cordova. The emir, later caliph, was absolute beyond challenge. The depressed and subject Mozarab population, although likely always a numerical majority, was largely helpless for lack of leadership or organization. That provided by its bishops and headmen sufficed to maintain its cultural integrity but offered no political, not to say military, potential. The Jewish *dhimmi* lacked either desire or rationale for an alternative social order.

Similarly, the economy offers no viable explanation for such troubles as occurred. All evidence points to a growing prosperity throughout the period. True, there does seem to have been an end to the demographic growth which had marked the earlier period coming in the latter tenth century but that was characteristic of all Islamic Mediterranean lands. It appears to have been a reaction to the exhaustion of all the possibilities of that agricultural revolution which had accompanied the early expansion of Islam and was marked by a noticeable contraction of marginal lands under cultivation. Still, while the demographic pause would have military implications vis-à-vis other societies, there is no reason to suspect that it occasioned major internal economic problems. In the end, one must account for the tribulations and even final demise of the Cordovan regime in terms of its own internal inflexibilities.

The long and prosperous reign of Abd al-Rahmān II (822–52) began with al-Andalus at peace. Thanks to a virtual reign of terror carried out by his father, rebellion of Berber, *muwallad*, and Mozarab alike, had been discouraged. Mālikite *qādīs* preached the orthodoxy of the dynasty, a mercenary army of 5,000 Berbers and slaves surrounded the person of the emir, and the treasury was full to overflowing. Apparently the worst social discrimination of Arab against Berber and both against *muwallad* was yielding to intermarriage and general prosperity. The latter was based on a recovery of the agriculture of the countryside as the effects of the dissolution of the Visigothic *latifundia* began to make themselves felt and new practices began to be introduced.

The new emir himself was young, about thirty years, experienced, and in good health. He is credited over a long life with forty-five sons and forty-two daughters. If taxes remained heavy, his expenditures were very visible and most proper. A major expansion of the great mosque of Cordova and a new main mosque in Jaén, a new city in Murcia of that name, new walls for Seville, and a new *alcázar* in Mérida and another in Cordova, were the major items. Abd al-Rahmān II was also responsible for the reorganization of the chancery and of the treasury.

Generally speaking, the thirty years of his reign were good. Serious revolts were almost absent except for that at Mérida which was snuffed out finally after great exertions in 838. The Vikings raided the coasts of al-Andalus beginning in 844 but conquest was never a possibility and they were ultimately discouraged. The emir himself took the obligation of the *jihād* seriously and mounted numerous campaigns on the northern marches. Yet the results were far from satisfying. Barcelona and Gerona were both besieged in 828 but neither was taken. Pamplona was taken in 842 but could not be held. The Qasī Mūsā ibn Mūsā allied with the Basques of Pamplona in 843 and both were soundly defeated by the Cordovan but both survived. Indeed Abd al-Rahmān had to recognize Mūsā as governor of Tudela from 844 and the chronicles of Alfonso III refer to Mūsā as "the third king of Spain."

A whole series of campaigns were directed against Alava, for that district was steadily passing into the hands of Basques allied with Oviedo, but those highlands overlooking the Upper Ebro eluded his control. In the west a series of campaigns were mounted against the north of Portugal, Galicia, and the lands to the north of the central Duero. The city of León was overrun in 848 but none of these efforts resulted in a major alteration in the position of the adversaries. Doubtless they contributed to retard somewhat the progressive repopulation of the northern half of the Duero basin by the Asturian kings. But that movement continued and the best efforts of an al-Andalus at peace with itself and prosperous could not marshal the resources necessary to counter it.

At Cordova the succession of his son, Muhammad I (852–886), was peaceful and the peace and prosperity of the realm long continued. Revolt in Toledo was bloodily repressed in 854. But what does seem to have been ominous for the future was a continuing growth about the emir of a bureaucracy of slaves, freedmen, and Berbers, which, together with the mercenary troops of slaves and Berbers, was increasingly regarded by Arab aristocrats and *muwallads* alike as insensitive if not hostile to their interests. From 868, beginning with the *muwallad* revolt in Mérida of ibn Marwān, local interests were legitimized by the rancor against the capital. This was especially virulent when the complaints of the *muwallad* over taxation of their lands as if they were still Christian came into play. Mérida was subdued and ibn Marwān fled but the revolt refused to die. Mérida was more strongly garrisoned, then almost leveled, but the revolt moved to Badajoz, which now began its ascent at the expense of the old Roman Mérida, and the Portuguese Algarve. For a half century old Roman Lusitania would escape the grasp of Cordova.

In the midst of the struggle in the valley of the Guadiana, another *muwallad* rebel appeared in 879 in the Sierra de Ronda to the south of Cordova. This was the famous ibn Hafsūn who from his mountain stronghold of Bobastro would alternatively defy and placate Cordova, and ravage in the *qura* of Málaga and often far beyond until his death in 917. The new emir, al-Mundhir (886–888), was campaigning against ibn Hafsūn when he received news of his father's death. Two years later, al-Mundhir died while engaged in a siege of Bobastro and the courtesy of the rebel had to be sought so that the emir's body could be safely returned to Cordova for interment.

The unfortunate prince was succeeded by his brother, Abd Allah (888–912), under whom it seemed that the utter dissolution of central government in al-Andalus was in train and that the age of the *taifas* had already begun. Muhammad I had brought the Banū Qasī to heel by playing off against them the Arab house of Tuchibi whose power was centered about Calatayud and Daroca. Once in possession of Saragossa, however, the new *walīs* were to prove as independent minded as the old.

But under Abd Allah even such relatively pacific areas as Murcia virtually seceded from the emirate. In Seville and Elvira Arab and *muwallad* fought small civil wars with scarcely even deference to Cordova. Of course, that rebel by profession, ibn Hafsūn, dabbled.in these matters, sometimes being nominally recognized by the local plotters and sometimes not. The emir suppressed those he could, ignored or recognized for the moment those he could not, and fought when there seemed some chance of success. At some points his real realm included not much more than the central portion of the Guadalquivir basin from Cordova east to Jaén.

Still, he profited from the inability of the rebels to find an alternative legitimacy for their behavior. No *imām* or *mahdī* arose to challenge the Ummayad as *amīr al-muminūn*. He did manage to score a surprising victory over ibn Hafsūn at Poley in 891 yet the old rebel more effectively crippled himself when in 899 he announced that he would return to the Christianity of his forebears. No great increase of aid could come from the Mozarab community and now many of his *muwallad* lieutenants deserted him. Through all of this near anarchy Abd Allah perdured, surviving even the palace plots of his own sons who secured only their own execution. At the age of sixty-nine in 912 the old emir died peacefully and handed on his diminished realm to his grandson, Abd al-Rahmān III (912–961).

During the past half century, nevertheless, one of the independent Christian realms of the north had profited greatly. Muhammad I had continued the policy of punitive raids against the north with the usual successes but the extraordinary difficulties of Abd Allah made even those essentially defensive measures impossible. At the same time, in Alfonso III (866–910), Asturias would find an energetic and capable captain. This king would take advantage of the current disarray of al-Andalus to raid deep into its marches. Especially in the west he would push the boundary as far south as Coimbra in Portugal. On the line of the Duero River Zamora and Toro were resettled. To the east the foundation of Burgos (884) is traditionally dated from this time. In fact, these advances, coupled with the simultaneous troubles of al-Andalus would lead the author of the *Prophetic Chronicle* to predict the reconquest of the peninsula from the Muslims in 883.

Yet the most important phenomenon of this time was the virtually unopposed penetration of the excess population of Asturias southward from the southern edge of the Cantabrians, flowing down the northern tributaries of the Duero, appropriating the land for crops, constructing tiny villages, protecting them with modest fortresses, until they finally reached that great river itself. This resettlement of the Duero basin north of that river by Christians proceeded from the south as well as from the north, however. Even during the later years of the great Abd al-Rahmān II who was relatively impartial in his treatment of them, the Mozarabs of al-Andalus were increasingly restive with their lot. At mid-century that had been expressed in the open attacks on Islam and Muhammad by some Cordovan Christians which resulted in their martyrdom and eventually that of their bishop, Eulogius.

But for large numbers of Mozarabs the preferable alternative to quiet submission, active revolt, or religious martyrdom, was to be emigration to the now much more visible and proximate kingdom of Asturias. While it is impossible to speak in absolute numbers, the effect on the toponymy of the region between the Duero and the Cantabrians remains obvious to this day. Yet more obvious is the construction in that region of churches built to accommodate them in the southern, Mozarabic style such as San Miguel de Escalada near León or Santo Tomas de las Ollas at Ponferrada in the Bierzo. In 883 Alfonso III would seek to secure the relics of Bishop Eulogius from Cordova, presumably to encourage such immigration. He succeeded in the sense that such northward movement of Mozarabs, which bolstered the Christian kingdom while weakening al-Andalus demographically, appears to have been continuous from this time into the latter eleventh century.

Such flight was not confined to Asturias among the northern Christian principalities but it had more practical effect there. In Navarre, Aragon, or Catalonia, local Christians remained pinned against the Pyrenees despite the problems of al-Andalus. The power of the Carolingians was in full decline in the late ninth century and could not be relied upon for assistance. Wilfred the Hairy (865–898), generally credited as the first independent count of Barcelona, was killed in battle precisely by a Banū Qasī. In general, the strength of the Tuchibi at Saragossa, Calatayud, and Daroca or of the Banū Qasī at Tudela, Huesca, and Lérida, was more than a match for such resources as the diminutive Christian principalities could muster. At most Mozarab immigration lessened the imbalance but it found there no buffer zone to fill.

The most vigorous son and successor of the fortunate Alfonso III, Ordoño II (910–925), inherited only a portion of the realm, the remainder of which was shared out between his brothers. He moved its royal city from Oviedo beyond the Cantabrians to León, high on the *meseta* north of the Duero. That made sense in terms of the development of what we may now call the kingdom of León. Unfortunately, it was less practical in terms of the remarkable contemporary recovery of al-Andalus under Abd al-Rahmān III (912–961). Even though the realm was to be reunited under Ordoño's sons, it was frightfully exposed to a resurgent Islam.

At his accession, the new emir was scarcely twenty-one years of age. Yet within two months he was already in the field against the long-established enemies of Cordova. What followed was far from easy. The crafty rebel, ibn Hafsūn, died in 917 but his sons fought on and not until 928 did Bobastro itself finally yield. But Guadix, Elvira, and Jaén had been subdued in 913 along with the upper reaches of the Guadiana. In 914 and 915 it was the turn of Málaga and Seville. The year 916 saw his generals extinguishing the independence of Murcia and Valencia in the east and portions of the Algarve in the west. Badajoz itself was not reclaimed until 929 and Toledo held out until 932. Where success had eluded the grandfather, the same combination of war and diplomacy secured it for the grandson. With all allowances made for the particular abilities of the latter, it seems likely that thirty years of strife had prepared most of al-Andalus to accept strong and single rule.

When most of this restoration had already been accomplished, in 929, Abd al-Rahmān took the step that his fathers never had risked. He had himself declared caliph. More than anything else, this action symbolized the resurgence of Cordova and the Ummayad power in al-Andalus. While the caliphal title had some diplomatic value abroad, it added not a whit to his real power in Iberia. As emir his authority had already been absolute. If anything, the assumption of the caliphal dignity emphasized once more what would, in less than a century, again tear al-Andalus apart. It reaffirmed the absolute supremacy and irresponsibility of the government at Cordova and increased yet more the distance between the great Ummayad and his subjects. As if to symbolize that state of affairs, Abd al-Rahmān began the construction of the famed Madinat al-Zahra in 936 some five kilometers outside of Cordova itself. The building of that new caliphal palace of no less than 4,000 columns alone would continue for decades but as early as 945 formal receptions were being held there.

Something of the character of the regime may be gleaned from the report that the royal harem included some 3,600 women. Even if they amounted, in fact, to but ten percent of that number the special tenor of such a life would have been extreme. To this gaggle of dependent women should be added the slave bureaucracy which oversaw them and filled most of the posts of the caliphal government, crowding out the Arab aristocracy. A contemporary estimated their numbers at 3,750. Again, a tenth of that would still have been a world to itself. The vulnerability resulting from the European origin and servile status of these slaves made them ductile instruments. Such slaves, along with Berber mercenaries from North Africa, made up the professional, standing regiments of the caliphal army as well. Obviously, Abd al-Rahmān possessed the ability to make such a system function brilliantly. Nevertheless, to members of the

royal house, heaped with wealth and honors, but firmly excluded from
the government, to the Arab aristocracy of Cordova and Seville, and to
the provincials, *muwallads*, and Mozarabs, the regime might be exotic but
it was also alien.

When Abd al-Rahmān turned his attentions to the Christian realms of
the north he was again victorious. Against Ordoño II (910–925) of León
and Sancho García I (905–926) of Navarre even combined, he raided with
some success deep into Navarre and Alava. On the other hand, Ramiro II
of León (930–951) aided the rebels of Toledo and forced the Tuchibi
governor of Saragossa to recognize his suzerainty. When the caliph
reacted with an attempted invasion of León he suffered a major defeat at
the hands of Ramiro near Simancas in 939. But Ramiro was alternately
hampered and assisted by the growing independence of the count of
Castile, Fernán González (923–970), and was unable to capitalize on his
advantage. After Ramiro's death in 951 the caliph was able to manipulate
the troubled politics of succession in the north and to secure his own
hegemony. Nonetheless, Abd al-Rahmān himself was unable to roll back
the Christian occupation of either the north bank or the Duero, Alava, or
the upper reaches of the Ebro.

It has been argued, with some reason, that the great Ummayad had
assumed the title of caliph as a countermeasure to the growing power of
the Fātimids in North Africa and the assumption of the caliphal title there
by the Shiite Ubayd Allah in 909. That refugee from the Near East had
joined others of like origin who were struggling against the Aghlabid
power in Tunisia. As a putative descendant of Fātimah, daughter of
Muhammad, he claimed to be the *mahdī* and finally triumphed, he and his
followers taking Kairouan in 909. The new caliph there had Egypt as his
major objective from the outset, nevertheless the Fātimids were active in
extending their authority to the west as well.

As they did so, the Ummayad caliph became increasingly concerned
and in 931 occupied Ceuta. Abd al-Rahmān also extended aid, and sometimes asylum, to the petty dynasties of Morocco who struggled to elude
the Fātimid yoke. Moreover as Kairouan courted the assistance of the
Sanhāja Berber coalition so Cordova sought ties with the rival Zanāta
Berbers. In 951 Tangier was annexed by Abd al-Rahmān to provide
additional strength for his North African position. But the Fātimids
answered by taking Fez itself in 959 and there things remained at the death
of Abd al-Rahmān in 961. The most lasting result of the rivalry thus far
had been the impetus it gave to both the spread of the Arabic language
and culture among the Berber peoples of the Maghrib and the deepening
of their understanding of Islam.

The first Ummayad caliph of Iberia had reached the ripe age of seventy at his death and therefore his son and successor, al-Hakam II (961–976), was already a mature forty-six at his accession. Despite his being better known as a patron of scholars and the possessor of a great library, the new caliph was an active and experienced ruler who followed the general lines of his father's policies. Vis-à-vis the Christian north, he benefited from the continuing dynastic embroilments there to remain practical arbitrator of their several fortunes and only in 975 did he have to make a major effort which resulted in the defeat of the new count of Castile, García Fernández (970–995), and his allies with great losses. Meanwhile, in North Africa the Fātimid caliph had finally taken Fustat in Egypt in 969 and began the construction of a new capital at Cairo. He moved his court there in 973. Still, the best diplomacy of al-Hakam accomplished little more than the safeguarding of the Ummayad foothold there and the retention of the alliance with the Zanāta Berbers.

The thirty-two years that followed upon the death of al-Hakam were to be ones of almost unparalleled external brilliance and inexorably developing internal political decay. The new caliph, Hishām II (976–1009), was to reign but never to rule. From the outset the talented and ambitious Abū Amir Muhammad ibn Abī Amir al-Maafiri, to be known as al-Mansūr, sought the reins of government and became virtually omnipotent down until his death in 1002. The fact that Hishām was but eleven years of age at his accession led the commanders of the slave palace guard to decide to offer the caliphal throne to a younger brother of al-Hakam, al-Mugira, who was twenty-seven. The assumption of that dignity by a brother rather than a son would not have been without precedent but Chafar al-Mushafi, who was regent during the last illness of al-Hakam, met secretly instead with the commanders of the Berber garrison of Cordova and al-Mansūr. They agreed to proclaim the accession of Hishām with al-Mushafi to become premier, *hāchib*, and al-Mansūr to become *vizier* and first assistant. The hapless al-Mugira was strangled in his own palace at the direction of al-Mansūr. Scarcely two years later in 978 al-Mushafi was forced out of the government by al-Mansūr and in 983 was strangled in prison at the latter's command.

The new ruler of al-Andalus came from an old Arab family of land-owners in the district of Algeciras. His father had had some fame as a scholar and al-Mansūr himself came to Cordova to study in the house of his uncle. After completing his studies he functioned for a time as a public scribe and, in that capacity, came to the attention of al-Mushafi, then *vizier*. Through the influence of the latter, al-Mansūr entered the court of al-Hakam as tutor of the caliph's son, and soon added the dignities of director of the mint (967), treasurer (968), *qādī* for Seville and Niebla (969), and inspector of the mercenary troops of Cordova (976).

But at some point, perhaps after al-Hakam's death, the young scholar also became the lover of the queen-mother of Hishām II, the Basque concubine Subh.

After arranging the fall of his former patron, al-Mushafi, and now *hāchib* himself, al-Mansūr set about consolidating his power. But for ceremonial occasions Hishām II was confined to the palace and encouraged to busy himself in the harem. The *hāchib* now courted the aid of the most famous of the current Ummayad generals, the *muwallad* Gālib who commanded the central marches from Medinaceli. In 978 al-Mansūr was married to his daughter. He placated the *qādīs* by carrying out the destruction of what those worthies saw as dangerous books in the library of the late al-Hakam. At last, Gālib took alarm at the growing power of al-Mansūr, especially the latter's active recruitment of new regiments of North African Berbers and Christian slaves. The old supporter of the Ummayads was forced to seek the aid of Count García Fernández of Castile and King Sancho García II of Pamplona. The issue came to a head on the field of battle outside Medinaceli in July of 981 and al-Mansūr won, Gālib being killed on the field. For the next twenty-one years the former would have no serious rival in al-Andalus.

During that time it was difficult to oppose the power of the usurper because of the fashion in which he cared for the external fortunes of the caliphate. After defeating Gālib in July of 981, al-Mansūr attacked and defeated Ramiro III of León (966–984) at Simancas. Ramiro's cousin and successor, Vermudo II (984–999), he forced to pay tribute. In 985 the *hāchib* led an expedition to punish Count Borrell II (940–992) of Barcelona, taking and burning that city. When Vermudo II attempted to throw off his control, al-Mansūr took and sacked León itself in 988. The count of Castile, García Fernández, died his prisoner after a defeat in 995. In 997 the Cordovan advanced into the mountains of Galicia and burned Santiago de Compostela itself, carrying off the bells of its church to grace the great mosque of Cordova. When the new count of Castile, Sancho García (995–1017), began to act independently al-Mansūr invaded his lands and took and burned Burgos in AD 1000. In fact, the old scholar–statesman–warrior died in 1002 at Medinaceli while returning from another victorious raid through the territories of Castile.

The policy of the *hāchib* in North Africa had been similarly successful. There he played off the ambitions of the Zanāta and Sanhāja Berber confederations in such a way as to render the influence of the Fātimids in Morocco virtually nil. The latter, since their removal to Cairo, had had to operate through their vassals in Tunisia in any event and these latter were progressively excluded from the west. The important oasis center of Sijilmāsa slipped from their control and with it went the control of the westernmost caravan route from sub-Saharan territories. Increased control over the Berbers also strengthened al-Mansūr's ability to recruit them as mercenaries for service against the Christian princes of northern Iberia. Meanwhile, from 997 Ummayad governors ordered the affairs of all of northern Morocco from their new seat at Fez.

However, the internal activity of al-Mansūr was such as to lead al-Andalus to disaster. Already from 979 he had undertaken the construction of a personal palace complex, *al-Madina al Zahira*, which would rival those of the titular sovereign, Hishām, either in Cordova itself or at the older *madinat al-Zahra*. After his victories over Gālib and the Christians in 981 ibn Abī Amir had taken the title by which he is usually known, al-Mansūr billah, "the victorious one of Allah." In 991 he bestowed the office of *hāchib* on his son Abd al-Mālik, renouncing it for himself. In 996 he began to style himself *mālik karim*, "noble king." This policy logically could lead nowhere but in the final displacement of the caliph himself yet al-Mansūr recognized that such an attempt would result in disaster. Still he could not dismount from the tiger.

When the old intriguer died at Medinaceli in his seventies, his son and successor was an experienced politician and general of a mature twenty-seven years. Abd al-Mālik assumed the reins of government, again in the name of the impotent Hishām II, without serious challenge. Over the next six years, he would recapitulate the career of his father in briefer form. Ummayad dominance in Morocco was maintained. Each year saw new raids against the Christian principalities of the north which carried his arms, and frequently his person, into the very foothills of the Pyrenees, the Cantabrians, and the mountains of Galicia. Ramon Borrell I of Catalonia (992–1018) was forced to sue for a truce. Count Sancho García of Castile was compelled to accompany him on a punitive expedition against León. In the latter kingdom, Abd al-Mālik's *qādī* was to be received as arbiter in a dispute over the proper regent for the young Alfonso V (999–1028). But all of this activity came to an abrupt end when al-Mālik died suddenly of a heart attack in 1008.

He was succeeded even more briefly by his younger half-brother, Abd al-Rahmān ibn Abī Amir (1008–1009), a son born of a Basque concubine who was the granddaughter of Sancho García II of Pamplona, called familiarly "Sanchuelo." Within little more than a month the new dictator had taken the step of persuading the caliph Hishām II to name as his eventual successor and heir no one less than Abd al-Rahmān himself. This final outrage against the proprieties of rule in al-Andalus was to prove fatal at once to the house of al-Mansūr, to the house of the Ummayad, and to the political integrity of al-Andalus. Against a background of plot and counterplot, Abd al-Rahmān departed for a campaign against the

Christian north in January of 1009. He had not gotten beyond Toledo when he was informed that revolt had erupted in Cordova. Rapidly deserted by virtually everyone, he was arrested on the road back to Cordova in March and assassinated soon after. But no group among the conspirators had either the authority or the power to construct an alternative order for it and al-Andalus began a violent slide into anarchy and particularism.

4

CHRISTIAN *RECONQUISTA* AND AFRICAN EMPIRE, 1009–1157

The century and a half which followed the collapse of the caliphate of Cordova was to see a fundamental reorganization of peninsular society. The respective positions of Christianity and Islam would achieve something like an equilibrium. After 711, all of the peninsula and its great river valleys were held by the Muslim and only the mountain country of Asturias was left to the Christian. By 1157, the latter had repossessed the basins of the Ebro, the Duero, and the Tajo as well as the Galician and north Portuguese coast. To al-Andalus was left the basins of the Guadiana and the Guadalquivir, the Levantine coast south of Tortosa and the Portuguese coast south of the Tajo. During the same period, however, Christian Iberia had gradually forged ever closer commercial, religious and cultural ties with western Europe while retaining a vigorous and autonomous political development of its own. Spanish Islam, on the other hand, after suffering political fragmentation was incorporated progressively into one or the other of the rising northern kingdoms or into that Moroccan Berber empire of the Murābit, which latter's culture was but a pale reflection of its own.

This massive reorientation of human society in the peninsula has many causes but one of the basic of them was demography. At some point in the tenth century the population of the northern, mountainous rim of Iberia began to expand sufficiently to enable it to flow southward and, with the aid of the Mozarab current of emigrés flowing northward from al-Andalus, to maintain itself in those new climes. Neither of these two flows is strictly measurable, of course, but in their result. Nonetheless, such growing pressures were capable of destructive as well as of constructive effects without a corresponding political and social growth capable of channeling their energies. Finally, even when the requisite development was achieved, the new Christian reality was fashioned by the character of the geography and of the particular Muslim political power then extant in the path of its expansion.

Already in the tenth century the preeminence in the push southward had been taken by the kingdom of Asturias. By the time of Ordoño II (910–925) it had so far repossessed the northern half of the *meseta* of the Duero that the former had moved its royal city to León, by which name we subsequently know that realm. This early success was due in part to the fact that Muslim Andalusia had never had the demographic numbers sufficient to occupy the northern *meseta*. But it was due, as well, to the presence of the natural pathways south offered by the many small tributaries of the Duero, from the Balimbre in the west to the Pisuerga in the east, rarely more than twenty kilometers apart. Along them, agricultural settlements protected by rude fortresses leapfrogged towards that great river, gradually adapting their agricultural techniques to that dryer world as they went.

By the end of that century, apparently two further agricultural modifications were in train. One was the increasing expansion of a combination of plow culture and transhumance stockraising at the expense of the older, hoe culture in Asturias, Galicia, and Bierzo. That change not only diversified the society and increased the wealth of the older regions but it also aggravated an already present pressure of population upon available land by enlarging the amount of land which could be worked by each farmer. But the resulting southward emigration was aided, in its new environs, by the application of Muslim dryfarming and irrigation techniques, above all those associated with the employment of the waterwheel, or *noria*, and the potchain, or *saqiya*, to raise the level of available water and hence the land area susceptible of irrigation. New crops of Muslim provenance, hard wheat and probably sorghum, also facilitated the change. Introduced by Mozarab emigrés, this new agricultural complex made it increasingly possible to farm at greater distances from the first areas of settlement in the riverbottoms. Moreover, the contemporary growing dispersion of the waterpowered, vertical mill was making the emergence of a cereal culture of ever-larger fields possible in virtue of the reduction of labor necessary for the milling process. The increasing use and availability of iron for at least the edging of agricultural implements also contributed to the greater efficiency of the individual's labor.

Thus there emerged a dense, peasant agricultural world in the valley of the Duero, north of that river, probably for the first time in its history. Its prosperity and numbers were sufficient to allow it to survive and recover from the great raids of Islam under al-Mansūr and his son at the end of the tenth century. However, this same Christian society of the north was also experiencing the formation of more general and complex governmental and social institutions that were soon to enable it to project its own strength against a Muslim al-Andalus in growing disorder.

First and foremost among these was the monarchy, of course. Now for reasons peculiar to the modern political culture of Spain, its historians have tended to idealize the strength and public character of the early kingdoms of Asturias and León. Yet it is more likely that its kings, from Pelayo through Alfonso III, were scarcely more than powerful local magnates and able dynasts, whose power rested upon extensive family possessions and strong alliances with other such families and with the church, and that their rule was that of war chief and religious coordinator where it actually extended beyond the lands of the family patrimony. Certainly that seems to have been the way in which they conceived themselves. We call them kings of Asturias or León but they, themselves, seem never to have styled themselves in territorial fashion at all but solely by patronymic, i.e., *Ordonius rex filius Adefonsi regis*.

While his father, Fernando I (1037–1065), may possibly have occasionally styled himself "king of León," a real turning point was reached with Alfonso VI (1065–1109). After gathering up the authority and lands divided by his father among his three sons, Alfonso initially called himself king of León but by 1077 had begun to employ the title of *totius hispaniae imperator*. Out of the welter of possibilities suggested by the disorder of the past, he settled upon that which implied a clear claim to hegemony in, and the independence of, the Iberian peninsula. Thus he wedded the royalty long inherent in his lineage to a declared, legitimate, territorial basis.

Of course, as a practical politician, his immediate aims and means were much more limited. But within the lands north of the Duero he set in operation the devices by which the Leonese monarchy was to go from strength to strength over the next nine decades. One of these was an alliance with the episcopal office within the church. Bishops became more clearly royal officers and appointees and from their episcopal seats the towns and countryside about them would become a society increasingly ordered into diocese, archdeaconries, and finally parishes. Alfonso bolstered the sees of Palencia, Braga and Coimbra, refounded by his father, and himself saw to the restoration of the episcopal sees of Toledo (1086), Osma (1102), and Salamanca (1102), as his campaign of repopulation and reconquest advanced into the basin south of the Duero and then leapt the Guadarrama range into the basin of the Tajo.

At the same time, he continued and extended the policy of alliance with the great French Benedictine house of Cluny, then achieving European prominence under Abbot Hugh the Great (1049–1109). He doubled the annual gift of 1,000 dinars his father had instituted and began the donation of Leonese and Castilian monasteries which was gradually to cover the north of the peninsula with a network of reformed, Cluniac houses grouped into an Iberian province of that order. The Cluniac monk, Bernard of Sedirac, was installed as archbishop of Toledo (1086–1125) and the new primate and royal confidant would cooperate in placing like-minded French monks in the sees of Santiago de Compostela, Braga, Coimbra, Osma, Salamanca, and later in Segovia and Sigüenza.

Alfonso VI also effected a major extension of the closer ties of the house of León–Castile with Europe north of the Pyrenees. His first wife, Agnes, was daughter of Duke William VIII of Aquitaine, his second, Constance, the sister of Duke Eudes I Borel of Burgundy, his third, Berta, a scion of some north Italian noble house, his fourth, Elizabeth, offspring of some French noble house, as was his sixth, Beatrice. Such marriages were probably arranged with more thought to bolstering the prestige of the crown and dynasty at home than any prospect of foreign assistance for few princes could actually project their power to the limits of their own lands much less beyond. Still, few means were more effective in differentiating the new dynasty from aspiring rival houses within the realm. Alfonso VI also married one daughter, Elvira, to Count Raymond IV of Toulouse and another, to Duke Roger II of Sicily.

Alfonso chose, as well, to cooperate with the new spirit of church reform permeating the entire European west but reflected particularly in the establishment of the reformed papacy. After some initial struggles with Gregory VII (1073–1085), in which that difficult pontiff finally allowed the papal claim of sovereignty over the Iberian peninsula to fade quietly, the Leonese monarch supported the replacement of the Mozarabic liturgy by the Roman, as decreed in his Council of Burgos (1080), welcomed papal legates in his realm, and allowed quarreling churchmen to carry their appeals to Rome so long as his own vital interests were respected.

In addition to the operations of his clerical lieutenants, the king exercised some local control through the medium of the royal *merino*, which office now begins to emerge clearly in the documents. The *merino* was above all an estate officer responsible for the safety and productivity of a block of royal fisc lands in a given area. However, he also functioned as a judicial figure who maintained peace within the royal lands and led their contingent to the gathering of the royal host.

Nevertheless, most other locales were, at best, under only tenuous royal control. Some fisc lands themselves, the *infantaticum*, were entrusted to junior members of the dynasty for their support and, hopefully, their supervision. Other fisc lands, the *comitatum*, were granted to castellans or counts to support their exercise of royal authority in the area. But of course these latter were chosen from the emerging nobility of the period who could be themselves controlled only with great difficulty. In fact, the gradual evolution of the agricultural world had contributed to the formation of a more and more wealthy group of clan chieftains, especially fortunate farmers, and professional warriors, now becoming something like a noble estate, who themselves were directly engaged in extending and rationalizing their economic and political power. This expansion, that of the contemporary crown, the church, and that of the peasant communities, or *aldeas*, themselves, was part of the process of bounding, organizing, and regularizing the relationships which obtained in the countryside for the first time in the north.

Moreover, the development of western military techniques in the direction of the superiority of a mounted, heavy cavalry reinforced the economic and social power of the new nobility in particular. They were willing to cooperate with the new royal power but only if their own desires for legal recognition of their seignorial rights and judicial authority over the peasants of their own dynastic possessions were met. By and large, the crown would accede to these demands. That process has ordinarily been decried as a concession to feudal decentralization and tyranny. Rather, it should be seen as an intrinsic part of the contemporary formation of the new territorial kingdom and, in all likelihood, the only route then possible to create one. It was not the destruction of an older, public order, which had no existence but in myth in the lands north of the Duero, but rather the invention of a territorial order *de novo* there.

To such extent as it functioned as a whole at all, this new kingdom was directed by a royal court almost permanently in motion from district to district. This *curia regis* was made up preeminently by the king himself and the other members of the dynasty. To them were joined ordinarily the great prelates of Toledo, León, Astorga, Palencia, Segovia, Burgos, Salamanca, and Ávila, that is, of the episcopal sees of the heartlands of the kingdom. At court almost as frequently were one or another of the members of the greatest noble houses of the center of the realm, the Ansúrez, the Téllez, the Ordóñez, the Castro, the Lara, the Haro. Already in the late eleventh century the borderlands of Portugal, Galicia, and Asturias were less frequently visited by or represented in the central agency of royal government. Attempts to have them supervised by a cadet member of the dynasty worked awkwardly and, in the case of the first, resulted in the emergence of an independent kingdom there in the first half of the twelfth century.

One can hardly speak of specialization within the royal curia except for the emergence of a group of clerics who form the royal writing office, or chancery, already under Alfonso VI. The latter assumes even more regular practices and hierarchical organization under Alfonso VII (1126–1157) when the title of chancellor itself appears. The offices of *majordomo* and *alférez* also are clearly distinguishable from the period of Alfonso VI. The first presumably saw to the order of the regal household as it circulated through the realm, especially its provisioning. No organization is visible at court and so the likelihood is that the *majordomo* had the active oversight of the various *merinos* of the fisc only when the court was actually in their vicinity. The *alférez* was the leader of the royal bodyguard which formed the nucleus of the royal army when the latter was summoned into being. Both of these posts were monopolized by cadet members of the great noble houses of the kingdom who had probably been trained and educated in the court. From the time of Alfonso VI forward there appears to have been a sort of rough *cursus honorum* in which the young noble served first as *alférez*, then as *majordomo*, and finally left court to take up the countship which was, practically, hereditary in his family. The countship was a dignity rather than an office.

This incipient structure of royal government was supported above all by rents from the fisc and the proceeds of justice done thereon. Its basic needs were also provided in some measure by its wealthier subjects upon whom fell the duty of *yantar*, or that hospitality that accommodated the royal court when the latter was in its vicinity. In addition, the king was entitled to the military service, or *fossatum*, of his nobles, prelates, and peasants, in varying degree, and to the *fossataria*, or shield tax, when his subjects preferred to be quit of that service itself. He was also entitled to a variety of district corvees which helped to maintain, repair, and defend royal property and castles when necessary. The *mercatum* and *portaticum* were levies which fell upon commerce in the various towns and on the roads of the realm. From the utter absence of a machinery to collect them one presumes that such levies were regularly farmed when they were not alienated outright, although bishops, abbots, and *merinos* may have had some responsibility for their collection within their respective jurisdictions.

Certainly the latter was true of the organization of the royal mints. Alfonso VI is the first Leonese monarch known to have issued a coinage. It was a billon penny struck at mints established by the beginning of the twelfth century in Oviedo, León, Palencia, Santiago de Compostela, Lugo, Toledo, and subsequently at Zamora, Segovia, and Sahagún. The bishops of these locales, and the abbot of Sahagún, were entitled to a portion of the proceeds of the mint as they ordinarily were to that of the market tax, the transport tax, and even of the royal rents within the episcopal city. In this symbiotic relationship, the king just as regularly regarded himself as entitled to a share of ecclesiastical revenues, especially the tithe. The crown also levied what was, in effect, a tax on the practice of Judaism in the realm in that all Jews were direct subjects of the king and made regular payments for his protection. This tax was collected by their own officials who were, of course, essentially religious leaders.

To this traditional assortment of revenues, the new, more regular, and more ambitious government would come to add the *petitum*, as its name implies a general request for subsidy to meet special needs. But for the period between the collapse of the caliphate of Cordova in 1009 and the full imposition of Murābit rule in Muslim Iberia in 1110, no source of revenue was more important than the tribute, or *parias*, exacted from the *taifa* kings of al-Andalus. These might amount to an annual payment of 10,000 gold dinars or more from each of the wealthier *taifas*. The first great reconquests against Muslim Iberia were carried out by armies financed by the *taifa* kingdoms themselves.

THE SAVAGING OF AL-ANDALUS

If other Christian princes had occasionally taken advantage of the political fragmentation of Muslim Iberia in the eleventh century, Fernando I of León was the first to make major and permanent territorial encroachments by virtue of it. His activity was limited to two strategic areas. One was Portugal where he cleared the valley of the Duero by the capture of Lamego in 1057. The remainder of his Portuguese campaigns were directed at the successful clearing of the next valley to the south, that of the Mondego River, of Muslim rule. This he did with the conquest first of Viseu, in its upper reaches, in 1058 and then of Coimbra, which dominated the lower basin, in 1064. At the other end of the Duero, Fernando overran San Esteban de Gormaz, Berlanga, and Valdorrey in the Sorian highlands which positions controlled access south into the lands of the *taifa* of Toledo and east into the *taifa* of Saragossa. A further outcome of these campaigns was the imposition of the payment of *parias* on the vanquished *taifas* of Badajoz, Toledo, and Saragossa.

Fernando alloted the rights to these tributes as well as his lands among his sons and heirs before his death in 1065. But when his son, Alfonso VI, had triumphed in the subsequent fraternal strife and reunited both, the new king was in a position to take up the policy of his father. In 1076 he seems to have begun a major drive to repopulate the lands south of the Duero and north of the Guadarrama, beginning with Sepúlveda and Olmedo and gradually penetrating south to Salamanca and Ávila. The appropriation of that 50,000 square kilometers would occupy him until his death. However, key to its success was the friendship or neutrality of the *taifa* of Toledo immediately to the south. Alfonso had been allied to its king al-Mamūn until the latter's assassination in 1075. He would support the heir, al-Qādir, against both his own subjects and the attacks of the *taifa* kings of Seville and Badajoz until the Leonese monarch became convinced that al-Qādir was not capable of maintaining the independence of Toledo.

Finally, Alfonso decided to depose the Muslim and annex his kingdom. This was effected with relatively little fighting on May 25, 1085. That city of some 28,000 thus became the largest of his realm and he was at pains to secure the loyalty of its Muslim inhabitants by guaranteeing their lives, freedom, possessions, and the continued practice of their religion. At a stroke another some 50,000 square kilometers were added to his kingdom which now embraced the basins of both the Duero and the Tajo in addition to the borderlands of Asturias, Galicia, and central and northern Portugal. Alfonso also despatched his lieutenant, Alvar Fáñez, to install his late ally in the *taifa* of Valencia, which realm had sometimes been a possession of Toledo. Al-Qādir was master in Valencia by the end of the year. At the same time, the Leonese king had enforced the payment of *parias* by the *taifas* of Granada and Seville in addition to those already paid him by Badajoz and Saragossa.

Suddenly, León–Castile had established itself as the largest and most puissant kingdom of the peninsula, Muslim or Christian. In response, led by al-Mutamid of Seville, the *taifa* kings of Andalusia appealed for assistance to the new Berber, fundamentalist empire of the Murābit in North Africa and Yūsuf ibn Tāshufin, the Berber emir and master of Morocco and a good part of modern Algeria, landed an army at Algeciras in the summer of 1086 and then marched north to the vicinity of Badajoz. There he and his allies fought and defeated an army hastily led south by Alfonso VI at Zalaca on October 23, 1086. Following the battle Yusuf retired to North Africa and Alfonso to Toledo but it was a harbinger of things to come. For the next twenty years, until the death of Yūsuf in 1106, the two would contest for the mastery of al-Andalus.

Twice more, in 1088 and 1090, the Murābit emir would lead African armies into Iberia only to meet with indifferent success in campaigns against Leonese positions in Murcia and La Mancha. Then, dissatisfied with the cooperation of his Andalusian allies, he would begin the outright annexation of the *taifas* into his North African empire. In the fall of 1090 Granada and Málaga became the first of his acquisitions. At his departure for Morocco, Yūsuf left a permanent military force under his cousin, Sīr ibn Abū Bakr, in Andalusia both to defend the south and to extend his control there. In 1091 first Cordova and then Seville were conquered outright when they attempted resistance. The smaller kingdoms of Jaén, Almeria, Denia, and Murcia submitted in the fall of that year.

Alfonso VI attempted without success to stem this growing threat. He had supplied military aid to the unfortunate al-Mutamid of Seville. He had taken as mistress the latter's daughter-in-law, Princess Zāida famed in later story, and had required the cession of Lisbon, Santarem, and Sintra, from al-Mutawakkil of Badajoz as the price of his protection. Nevertheless, the Murābit advance continued. Badajoz fell to them in 1094 and its king and his sons were murdered. In the fall Alfonso's forces in the west were defeated and Muslim control was restored at Lisbon. The basin of the Tajo in Portugal again became the most northerly bastion of Islam in the west.

But the Muslim was also on the advance in the east of Iberia. Alfonso, fearing the loss of his ally, al-Qādir of Valencia, made a strong demonstration before the city in the spring of 1092 but without effect. Instead, the former vassal of the Leonese, the Castilian minor noble and military genius subsequently to become the epic hero, Rodrigo Díaz de Vivar, *el Cid*, was to reap the immediate benefit. The Castilian had been militarily active in the east since his exile from León–Castile in 1081 and by 1092 had so far advanced his own fortunes there as to force not only the smaller *taifas* but Valencia itself to pay their *parias* to him as the price of his protection.

If that situation was intolerable for Alfonso of León, so too was it for Yūsuf ibn Tāshufin. The advance of the former in 1092 had caused *el Cid* to retire momentarily from the field and when Alfonso himself had to give up his attempt on the city, a revolt broke out there and the unfortunate al-Qādir was beheaded in October of the year. The rebels secured a small Murābit garrison to strengthen the city but sought to maintain their independence of all the rivals. The major initiative was taken by Rodrigo Díaz who began a siege in 1093 and forced the city to surrender to him in June of 1094. The Murābit response was a major expedition involving both Andalusian and North African forces. Nonetheless, that army was routed by *el Cid* at Cuart de Poblet outside Valencia in October of 1094. From then until Rodrigo's death in July of 1099 the Castilian noble was to be one of the great princes of the peninsula.

Yet those five years were to prove to be but an episode. Rodrigo's widow, Jimena Múñoz, would try to maintain herself in the city but with increasing difficulty. In the spring of 1102 Alfonso VI briefly occupied it but, deciding that it could not be held for long, evacuated it, taking its Christian populace with him to repopulate more defensible lands and firing the city behind him. By the beginning of May Valencia too had passed under Murābit domination.

In the east that left only the major *taifa* of Saragossa as an independent Muslim power. But the king there, al-Mustaīn, was protected by both distance, the strength of his realm, and a ductile diplomacy which kept his relations with Yūsuf ibn Tāshufin generally good. Though lands as far north as Barcelona itself might feel the wrath of the Murābit in 1102, Saragossa would endure up until the defeat and death of al-Mustaīn at the hands of Alfonso I of Aragon at Valtierra in January of 1110. Then a revolt broke out within the city against the former's son and presumptive heir and a Murābit governor took control instead. In the east as well as the west of the peninsula, Muslim Iberia had become coterminous with the Murābit Empire of Morocco, a series of provinces ruled from Marrakesh.

This contest between the empire of León and that of the Murābits had been waged in the center, on the plains of Castilla La Nueva as well. Yūsuf had sent an army north against the key redoubt of Toledo in 1090 without success. Another despatched in 1097 and yet one more in 1099 forced the Leonese back from Belmonte and Consuegra in La Mancha. An unsuccessful siege of Toledo itself ensued in 1100. The struggle swayed back and forth as Alfonso rushed forward the repopulation of Segovia, Ávila and Salamanca across the Guadarrama to the north in case Toledo and its lands should finally be lost. In 1104 he also took the key fortress of Medinaceli to protect the route towards Toledo from newly Muslim Valencia in the east. In 1104 and 1105 the Leonese raided deep into Andalusia about Seville and even Málaga as his aging foe was preoccupied with his own death and succession.

It was left to his heir, Emir Alī ibn Yūsuf, to score the great victory of Uclés in May of 1108 which would cost the life of young Sancho Alfónsez, Alfonso's only son and heir by the Moor Zāida, and roll the Leonese territories up to the very gates of Toledo itself. Alfonso VI died near that city on July 1, 1109, while seeing to its defenses against an inevitable attack. Indeed, for the next century Toledo was to be the advance bastion of the Leonese kingdom, by turns a fortress besieged by the Murābit and a staging area for Leonese–Castilian invasions of Muslim Andalusia.

The sudden and catastrophic collapse of an independent Muslim Iberia between 1090 and 1110 was due to a multitude of factors, some quite old and others quite new. Among the latter was the rise of a new northern society which was able to support a strong force of heavy, mailed, shock cavalry out of very limited resources. Operating in raiding parties of between 50 and 300, with absolutely essential supplies traveling by muleback, they were very mobile, covering distances of thirty to forty kilometers per day. From Palencia the lands of Toledo could be reached by such raiding parties in less than two weeks and later, from a reconquered Toledo, Cordova, Jaén, and even Seville were to find themselves vulnerable in much the same time. Such war bands could not take cities, of course, but they could wreak havoc on highway caravans and on small villages and livestock. They could hold cities to ransom, indeed the entire society, by threatening simply to girdle olive orchards whose trees required twenty-five years to reach full production. Since the grapevine was even more vulnerable and took almost half that time to mature well and *norias* were expensive to make but simple to destroy, the wealthy south found it simpler to pay the *parias*.

Even when the decision was made to fight them, such mobile bands were extremely difficult to bring to bay except as they decided that the advantage was theirs. Since the Muslim world continued to rely on essentially light cavalry, mounted archers in many cases, backed by infantry masses they had to depend on surprise, ambush, and on the invader hampering his own withdrawal by his unwillingness to abandon flocks and human chattels once seized. Those were difficult terms on which to fight an invader. Of course, when outright conquest became the object, then the northerner must stand and fight on defined ground. As Zalaca and Uclés attest, the superior numbers of the Muslims could then be brought to bear and victory often achieved. But even then, the heavy cavalry of the Christian world, when properly employed, remained without an adequate military answer from Islam in the west and the battle would often go to the smaller force as at Cuart de Poblet.

Notwithstanding, the remarkable advance of León–Castile in the half-century between 1057 and 1109 was due rather more to the particular weaknesses of al-Andalus than to the new strength of its enemy. With the collapse of the caliphate in 1009 Muslim Iberia had fragmented into a collection of seven major *taifas* and a usually uncountable number of lesser ones whose numbers waxed and waned with the ambitions of their neighbors. The ordinary determinants of political al-Andalus were geography and personal talent. That is, Badajoz had the Guadiana basin, Granada the bastion of the Sierra Nevada, Saragossa enjoyed the rich Ebro basin, Toledo the spare lands of the Tajo, Valencia sheltered behind the sierras of the east, and Seville and Cordova disputed the lush lowlands of the Guadalquivir. Within these limits a series of ambitious adventurers had made themselves masters by intrigue and war after 1009. Unconvincing as religious successors to a caliphal dignity and without family connections to the vanquished Umayyad dynasty, they one and all lacked any strength that legitimacy might offer.

For that reason alone, they found it dangerous to arm their own subjects. But, in addition, something like half of those latter were the

Christian Mozarabs who were at least passive in the face of attack from the north and sometimes even furnished the invaders with intelligence and supply. The *muwallad* masses were yet more untrustworthy, as they had frequently demonstrated against a far stronger caliphate, and the Muslim aristocratic families often conceived themselves as better entitled to rule than their current king. The caliphs themselves had increasingly tended to solve the same problems by the recruitment of mercenary forces, Christian European slave youths who could be raised as *mamelukes* or Berber tribesmen, both of whom lacked domestic roots in al-Andalus and who could be expected loyally to support their paymaster against all enemies. But that was the system which had broken down in 1009 and many of the *taifa* rulers had emerged, in fact, from the more ambitious members of just those two groups.

In any event, it had been an expensive solution for the caliphate and the new kings lacked comparable resources. Then too, the slave trade with northern Europe was becoming more complicated and the Berbers of North Africa were beginning to find a political sphere of their own more interesting. In short, to pay *parias* and to hope for better luck the next year was the simplest course. Perhaps the barbarians would attack one's neighbor then. Or, better yet, perhaps the nominal Christian ally and patron could be enticed to support one's own aggrandizement within the world of the *taifas*. Seville had early absorbed the lesser kingdoms of the Lower Guadalquivir and southern Portugal. In this latter area its ambitions clashed with those of Badajoz. Along the Upper Guadalquivir, Seville's interests ran counter to those of Jaén in the south and Toledo in the north. Cordova was an earlier contender which it had uneasily absorbed. To the east, the smaller Murcia viewed Seville's advance with fear. In fact, Alfonso VI had secured his first major opportunities by supporting Granada and Toledo against Seville.

But al-Andalus was far more resistant to the attacks of León–Castile than it was to be to the outright annexation of the Murābit. The greatest single weakness of the *taifa* kings was the insecure hold that they had upon the religious loyalty of their Muslim subjects. They could be tolerated by the latter as a matter of practical defense against the Christians to the north but they were essentially irrelevant to the religious and social ideal of Islam. However, in the eleventh century that ideal was being again asserted forcefully and that in an area with traditionally close ties. The Ummayad caliphs had long interfered with and manipulated the affairs of the Berber tribes of North Africa, Morocco in particular. They had hired its tribesmen as mercenaries, bought its gold, slaves, and ivory derived from the trans-Saharan caravan routes, and sometimes returned its exiles from Cordova to become its new chiefs. The rulers, warriors, merchants, *qāḍīs* of North Africa had long familiarity with al-Andalus.

Now these latter were themselves undergoing a religious conversion, beginning about the middle of the eleventh century. The semi-nomadic Sanhāja Berber tribe was its essential vehicle. One of their chiefs had made the traditional pilgrimage to Mecca and his zeal, inflamed by that pious practice, was further stimulated by contact with a famous Mālikite scholar in Kairouan, Abū Imrān al-Fāsi, on his return journey. When asked, the holy man agreed to dispatch one of his disciples for the edification of the Sanhāja for he himself had been a native of Morocco. That disciple, Abd Allah ibn Yāsin, was a former Moroccan as well from the region of Agadir.

The doctrine which he would preach was Mālikite in the technical sense. That is, it held to the notion of the Koran as uncreated and eternal. As such its language was literally inspired and must be understood literally. The devices of literary analysis or philosophical theology were heretical if applied to it. This view had given rise to a school of law of the same name which had become dominant in Iberia and in western North Africa. The doctrine of Abd Allah was not therefore new, strictly speaking. From contemporary description what seems to have been especially prominent in his message to the Sanhāja was a fundamentalism in the moral sense based upon that scriptural literalism. It rejected alcohol, music, womanizing, lying, and compromise of any type with the infidel, the latter most broadly defined. It emphasized once again the old message of Islam as a single community, united in brotherhood under the sole rule of the Koran.

This revival, for so we may call it, struck a responsive note among the Sanhāja who quickly would understand the true community of Islam as the tribe itself and those who accepted its leadership. The mission would transform the tribe into people of the *jihād* or holy war, the *mirabitum*, and its young men would practice both the ascetic life and military drill in the monastic fortress of the *ribāt*. By 1054 the new Murābit were both wresting territory from the Negro kingdom of Ghana in the south and the key oasis and caravan city of Sijilmāsa from the rival Zanata Berber tribe in the north. The movement had by now clearly become identified with the fortunes of the Sanhāja and all but religious leadership had been assumed by their chief, Abū Bakr ibn Umar. When Abd Allah ibn Yāsin was killed in the battle for control of the great central plain of Morocco that identification became even less circumstantial. Abū Bakr would associate his cousin, Yūsuf ibn Tāshufin, in the leadership with himself from 1070 and Yūsuf gradually overshadowed his patron and assumed supreme control himself on Abū Bakr's death in 1087.

Yūsuf was already a seasoned warrior and the victor of Zalaca by that time. After 1070, when the Murābit began the construction of their new cult center and capital at Marrakesh, we are told that he worked at its construction himself in the loincloth of the common laborer. His tastes were ascetic and he subsisted on a diet of barley, camel's meat, and camel's milk. Yūsuf seems to have combined the rude personal virtues of the Berber nomad, an instinct for military and religious leadership, and a rare sense of political possibility and timing. Obviously these were to be the imperial virtues of eleventh-century Islam in the western Mediterranean.

Assuming the traditional title of *amīr al-muminūn*, i.e., commander of the faithful, whose ambiguities suited his situation as well as it had the *taifa* kings of Iberia, Yūsuf captured Fez by 1075 and then the other lesser towns of Morocco. Proceeding northeast from Fez by 1082 the Murābit had taken Tlemcen and Oran but further progress in that direction was made problematic by the dominance in central Algeria of the Banū Hilāl Arab nomads. Yūsuf was to turn towards Iberia instead.

The small *taifa* of Ceuta had been a possession of the Umayyad caliphs in North Africa and its conquest by the emir did not necessarily commit him to the Iberian adventure. It did, however, bring him even more forcefully to the attention of the Andalusians. When the appeal came in 1085 from al-Mutamid of Seville Yūsuf's response was hardly that of a religious zealot. He apparently had been approached before and had refused to be involved. Now he agreed but stipulated that his expenses must be borne by the *taifa* rulers. As we have seen, for the initial four years, until 1090, the Moroccan would only attempt to succour his co-religionists rather than subdue them.

The movement towards annexation seems to have had at least as much support in al-Andalus as it did in Marrakesh. The very *taifa* rulers themselves deferred to him as suzerain from the beginning and appealed to him for the resolution of their quarrels. He seems to have had the support of the *qādīs*, or religious authorities, who declared favorably on virtually every action he took. Reassured by their common adherence to Mālikite orthodoxy, the *qādīs* urged the emir to act to free al-Andalus from the government of winebibbers, poets, fornicators, who paid tribute to the infidel instead of fighting them and who levied taxes not sanctioned by the Koran on the faithful in order to finance that tribute. Yet, despite his popularity there, Yūsuf avoided the simple assumption of power until the disarray and lack of cooperation among his allies had made only that course or complete withdrawal inevitable by 1090. A half-century later al-Andalus might seem to regret its Murābit masters but initially the Africans were received with considerable enthusiasm and idealism among wide sectors of its population.

THE PROLIFERATION OF CHRISTIAN KINGDOMS IN THE NORTH

The assumption of the imperial title by Alfonso VI of León–Castile in 1077 was, perhaps, required not merely as an assertion of Iberian independence vis-à-vis papal or Muslim pretensions but to establish its hegemony over Christian Iberia as well. In the first instance that meant Navarre, for that tiny kingdom had, under Sancho *el Mayor* (1000–1035), briefly overshadowed all of Christian Iberia. It had wrested the northern Rioja down to Calahorra from a Saragossa only then in the process of formation and had transferred its chief royal seat from Pamplona in the north to Nájera in that most fertile of valleys. Navarre even supplied León–Castile with its ruling dynasty. Beginning as the count of a subservient Castile, Fernando had gone on in 1037 to defeat and kill Vermudo III of León, to marry Vermudo's sister, Sancha, and to assume the royal dignity himself. In 1054 he had defeated and killed his brother, García Sánchez III (1035–1054) of Navarre, who had shared with him in the division of their father's patrimony twenty years earlier. Under García's son, Sancho García IV (1054–1076), Navarre was to be a tributary of León–Castile until his assassination in 1076 allowed the annexation of the better part of his kingdom by his cousin, Alfonso VI of León–Castile.

The other portion of Navarre fell to yet another cousin, Sancho Ramírez I of Aragon (1063–1094), and the former kingdom vanished from the political scene for the following sixty years. Aragon too had been a part of the holdings of Sancho *el Mayor*, and had been assigned to his son, Ramiro I (1035–1063) at the former's death. Ramiro I had added the counties of Sobrarbe and Ribagorza to Aragon after the mysterious death of yet another brother, Gonzalo, in 1045. In 1076, therefore, the new kingdom of Aragon was composed of four distinct parts. In language and culture, old Navarre, Aragon, and Sobrarbe, were largely Basque in origin but Christian from the Visigothic period and with significant Mozarab admixture so that, by this time, the vernacular was developing towards Castilian. In Ribagorza the language was Latin evolving towards the Catalan. On the other hand, Aragonese Navarre consisted largely of the lands about Pamplona, oriented towards the south and west by the flow of the Arga River. Aragon itself was merely a landlocked high valley running west along the Aragon River from Jaca. Both Sobrarbe and Ribagorza were constituted along north–south river valleys looking down towards the plains of the Ebro. The whole of this curious mixture did not then consist of more than 10,000 kilometers square. Nevertheless the family of Ramiro I would not only bind it together but would turn it into the second Christian realm of Iberia in the half-century between 1076 and 1134.

This tiny realm was sub-Pyrenean in climate and thus well-watered by Iberian standards. In the late tenth and eleventh centuries it was also undergoing the sort of agricultural evolution already described in the case of León–Castile and so was quite visibly experiencing the same pressure of population on available land. But there was no semideserted *meseta* anywhere to its south. Instead there was the 65,000-square-kilometer expanse of the *taifa* of Saragossa about its great cities of Saragossa, Huesca, Lérida, and Tortosa. That realm was one of the greatest of the *taifa* kingdoms of Iberia in extent, population and wealth, far overmatching any resources Aragon could hope to muster against it. Moreover, Saragossa was a client kingdom of León–Castile from the middle of the eleventh century and, as such, entitled to the protection of the latter's king, even against another Christian monarch.

Ramiro I of Aragon lost his life in 1063 in an unsuccessful attempt to take Muslim Graus, which town blocked the way south in Ribagorza. His son, Sancho Ramírez I (1063–1094), for two decades attempted futilely to breakout of the Saragossan chain of border fortresses to his south. He would lose his life in an unsuccessful siege of Huesca in 1094. Nevertheless, his reign pointed the road to eventual success by drawing French mounted chivalry into the peninsula to provide the necessary margin against the stronger Muslim. Geography facilitated that quest for the pass of Roncesvalles that opened the way north into Gascony, and Aquitaine lay just north of Pamplona, and the Somport pass leading into Bearn and Bigorre was situated just north of Jaca. Sancho Ramírez brought his little kingdom into close relationship with the papacy, turning Aragon into a papal fief in 1068. He also arranged the marriage of his son and heir, Pedro I (1094–1104), to the daughter of the duke of Aquitaine in 1086. However, it was only during the last ten years of his reign that changed conditions allowed Sancho some success against his major enemy.

That is, from 1083 Alfonso VI and León–Castile were increasingly preoccupied with the Toledan and then the Murābit problems. In that year too, al-Muqtadir of Saragossa died and the *taifa* was divided into Saragossa in the west, ruled by his son al-Mutamin, and Lérida and Tortosa in the east, subject to his son al-Mundir. The two were usually hostile to one another. The major problem that Sancho Ramírez had to face was the presence now in the east of Iberia of the Castilian adventurer Rodrigo Díaz de Vivar. *El Cid* entered into the service of al-Mutamin initially and helped defeat Sancho in 1083 and 1084. But after 1090 the growing weakness of Valencia under al-Qādir and the death of al-Mundir at Lérida would draw the Castilian away and a series of small successes were scored on the northern border of al-Mutamin before Sancho paid for his ambitions with his life at the siege of Huesca in 1094.

Pedro I of Aragon would achieve what his father could not by taking Huesca in 1096. To do that he had to defeat the army of al-Mutamin in the open field when it advanced to break his siege. Moreover, that army was strongly reinforced by Castilian elements. But Pedro had prepared for this eventuality by drawing large French contingents into his own service. On his victory he rewarded French prelates and abbots out of the spoils and made Huesca, at a population of about 3,000 by far the largest town of his kingdom, his chief city. The same combination of forces gave him Muslim Barbastro in 1100. He even attempted a descent on Saragossa itself in 1101 though without success. But the death of *el Cid* in 1099 and the fall of Valencia to the Murābit in 1102 created a new situation in the east of the peninsula which would block further major gains during Pedro's lifetime.

Just to the east of this developing kingdom of Aragon was another collection of tiny realms united almost solely by a language ancestor to modern Catalan. The geography of the eastern Pyrenees makes of the area a sort of gigantic fan of river valleys whose western rib is the Segre River of Urgel flowing down past Muslim Lérida; a central rib is the Llobregat which brushes past Barcelona and into the Mediterranean. The River Ter runs almost due east past Gerona and into the same sea. The River Tet works northeasterly to meet the sea by Perpignan. In their valleys, under the distant patronage of the Carolingians and then the Capetians, a series of tiny counties, usually ten in number, had taken shape, with an equally curious heritage combining Visigothic, Frankish, and Mozarabic elements.

In the third quarter of the ninth century a local dynasty would rise to prominence under one Wilfred "the Hairy," at once count of Barcelona, Gerona, and Osona, from 878. With the exception of the county of Pallars, farthest to the west, from that time forward all of these Catalan realms were to be ruled by some member of that dynasty. The combination, however, in the hands of the count of Barcelona not only of three contiguous counties but also of their three bishoprics of Barcelona, Gerona, and Vich, ordinarily gave to the Barcelonan count an easy pre-eminence in the family. Still today the archeological evidence is clear for the early and intensive agricultural exploitation of these valleys. In the eleventh century they were heir to the same pressure of population on resources experienced farther west but their peculiar geography dispersed and weakened its effect.

In addition, they faced, in Iberia proper, a formidable enemy immediately to the south and west in what was sometimes the *taifa* of Lérida when it was not the more formidable *taifa* of Saragossa. As early as 1026 a Barcelonan offensive seized Cervera on the eastern edge of the plain of Lérida but that was to be the highwatermark for the next century. Under Count Ramón Berenguer I (1035–1076) the 8,000-square-kilometer principality had spent its energies mostly in the more promising north. A loose Barcelonan hegemony emerged gradually over Narbonne, Béziers, Carcassone, Agde, and Montpellier in which that county seemed in a fair way to recreate the old Visigothic Septimania in the Midi. But the concentration of much of the dynasty's interests in the north, and severe dissension within that family itself, made it difficult for Barcelona to make headway in Iberia even against a Lérida and Saragossa divided against one another after the death of al-Muqtadir in 1083.

The rule of Berenguer Ramón II (1076–1097) saw a continuation of dynastic strife and the count was eventually forced to abdicate and go into exile, reputedly as penance for the murder of his twin and earlier co-ruler, Ramón Berenguer II (1076–1082). But the former had earlier allied with Aragon and Lérida only to be defeated with them at Almenar in 1083 by Saragossa and *el Cid*. Lérida, under al-Mundir, paid what was probably a subsidy to Barcelona during this period. It is assimilated to the tribute, or *parias*, by most historians but was more likely the price of such military assistance when needed. Berenguer Ramón had designs on Valencia but was consistently frustrated there by the activities of Rodrigo Díaz de Vivar. In 1090, on the death of al-Mundir of Lérida, *el Cid* was able to establish himself as guardian of the political fortunes of al-Mundir's minor sons in that *taifa* despite the combined efforts of the Barcelonan and al-Mutamin of Saragossa, both of whom the Castilian defeated at Tevar in that year.

Finally, the count's political rivals in Barcelona were able to force him into exile and to replace him by the fifteen-year-old son of his twin. Ramón Berenguer III (1097–1131) came to power just as the Murābit threat was becoming acute in the east. After their occupation of Valencia in 1102 the Murābit would raid extensively through his lands. An attempted counterattack in concert with his cousin, Count Armengol V of Urgel, was roundly defeated at Mollerusa in 1102 and the latter lost his life there. Fortunately, the regency for the young Armengol VI was assumed by his maternal grandfather, the great Leonese magnate, Pedro Ansúrez. In 1104 Barcelona cooperated with Pedro Ansúrez in the conquest of the Muslim fortress of Balaguer on the lower Segre River on the northern edge of the plain of Lérida. Yet a portion of that town had to be ceded to the Aragonese for its capture had suddenly put Barcelona into effective communication with that realm for the first time. The capture, by this date, of most of the strongpoints on the northern edge of the plain of Lérida had made regular traffic between Barcelona and now Aragonese Huesca feasible for the first time since the Muslim conquest of the eighth century. At the same time, it effectively posed the question of the future relationship between the two principalities.

The long and successful reign of Alfonso I *el Batallador* of Aragon (1104–1134) was to make that question even more pressing. The Aragonese monarch's first great opportunity for aggrandizement came with the death of Alfonso VI of León–Castile in 1109. The latter had died without a male heir and had designated his daughter, Urraca, as his heir but also had directed that she be married to Alfonso of Aragon. With the Murābit hammering at the very gates of Toledo the old king wanted a proven warrior to guard his newly swollen kingdom. The marriage, though dutifully performed at Monzón near Palencia in October of 1109, proved however to have too many enemies.

Urraca had been married previously to Count Raymond of Burgundy. The count had been made royal vicar for Galicia and promised the right of succession but he had died in September of 1107. Nevertheless Count Raymond had sired a son, Alfonso Raimúndez, who was four years old in 1109 and had a claim on the throne himself. The marriage agreement between Urraca and Alfonso of Aragon carefully protected his rights against every eventuality except such a child as the two might subsequently conceive. In addition, Alfonso VI had also married his natural daughter, Teresa, to Count Henry of Burgundy and had entrusted the two with the county of Portugal in 1096. Teresa too had a claim on the throne and was by this time probably pregnant with the future Alfonso Enríquez who would have a claim as well. The prospects for political intrigue were thus almost infinite, especially given the additional burdens of the marriage.

Urraca and Alfonso of Aragon shared a common great-grandfather in Sancho *el Mayor* of Navarre and were thus related within the degree of kindred prohibited by the church. Archbishop Bernard of Toledo had objected to the marriage, presumably on those grounds, and Pope Paschal would condemn it in 1110. The standard of revolt was raised early in Galicia in the far west by the guardians of Alfonso Raimúndez, Count Pedro Froílaz of Galicia and Bishop Diego Gelmírez of Santiago de Compostela. At Coimbra Henry and Teresa held aloof from all parties for the moment. In January of 1110 Alfonso of Aragon defeated and killed al-Mustaīn of Saragossa at Valtierra but the victory would redound to the benefit of the Murābit when their partisans in that *taifa* delivered it up to the Africans rather than to the fallen king's heir, Abd al-Mālik. Furthermore, an invasion of Galicia in 1110 by Alfonso had most disappointing results. But the most crucial failure of the year was that Urraca did not become pregnant. An heir to the embattled couple would have provided a possible solution to the dynastic crisis but none was to appear. It seems most likely that Alfonso of Aragon was sexually impotent or at least sterile. Late in the year Urraca seems to have separated from her spouse.

In the meanwhile, the Murābit under Emir Alī ibn Yūsuf, had taken Talavera de la Reina on the Tajo, threatened Toledo itself, ravaged the lands about Guadalajara and Madrid, and in 1111 would proceed to the reconquest of Santarém on the Portuguese Tajo. Alfonso of Aragon took possession of Toledo in response to that threat and Count Henry of Portugal would recruit troops in France while Urraca allied herself with the Castilian nobility by taking Count Gómez González of Lara as her lover. In Galicia the supporters of the boy, Alfonso Raimúndez, had him anointed king in the cathedral of Santiago de Compostela. At Candespina in October of 1111 Count Gómez was defeated and killed by the allied troops of Alfonso I and Count Henry. Urraca, however, then managed to separate the two by a short reconciliation with the Aragonese. Late in the fall Alfonso of Aragon also defeated the Galician supporters of Alfonso Raimúndez who had marched on León to install the boy in power.

The following year saw the death of Count Henry in Astorga in May and, with that threat removed, Urraca made the definitive break with her husband and began to associate her young son by Count Raymond with herself in royal documents. For the next five years war would be endemic between her and Alfonso of Aragon. The tide of battle swayed back and forth over the *meseta* but the Rioja and Old Castile together with Burgos, Castrojeriz, and Carrion de los Condes, were ordinarily in the hands of the Aragonese, while Sahagún itself sometimes acknowledged him. He also held the trans-Duero *meseta* along with what was left of the lands of Toledo.

Finally, to attend to what they conceived as other, more pressing necessities, the two initiated a series of three-year truces at Burgos in February of 1117 that were to be renewed up until Urraca's death in 1126. Urraca accepted the status quo in order to be free to put down the chronic state of rebellion in Galicia and deal with her insubordinate sister, Teresa, in Portugal. She would manage to do the first and also to install her son, Alfonso Raimúndez, in the Toledan lands, effectively displacing the Aragonese there despite the truce. In 1124 Urraca also managed the reconquest of Muslim Sigüenza and Atienza, closing the gap leading down toward Toledo between the Sierra de Albarracín and the Sierra de Guadarrama to Aragonese penetration. But Teresa, who had begun to style herself queen, succeeded in maintaining her independence in the old county of Portugal.

Alfonso of Aragon was to utilize the truce to effect the conquest of Saragossa from the Murābit. For that he had to draw on the already carefully cultivated French connections. Present at the siege of Saragossa, begun in the spring of 1118, were the Normans, Rotrou of Perche and Robert Burdet, the Bearnese Count Gaston and his brother, Viscount Centulle of Bigorre, Count Bernard of Comminges, Viscount Bernard Atto of Carcassonne, and scores of others. Pope Gelasius II raised the effort to the dignity of a crusade from a council held in Toulouse. Murābit attempts to relieve the great city proved vain and on December 18, 1118, it surrendered. The Aragonese monarch hastened to consolidate his victory. Tudela submitted in February of 1119 and Tarazona in May. By the following spring he was campaigning in the south where he occupied Daroca and laid siege to Calatayud. The ultimate Murābit effort to reverse what had occurred came near Daroca at Cutanda where, on June 17, 1120, Alfonso I destroyed a relief army despatched from Seville.

The conquest of the former *taifa* of Saragossa can only be compared to the conquest of Toledo thirty odd years before. By it one of the great, traditionally Muslim seats of power in Iberia passed irrevocably into Christian hands and altered, in major fashion, the balance of the two in the peninsula. The kingdom of Aragon itself was at least doubled in size, reaching about 40,000 square kilometers. Its population leaped from about 125,000 to about 500,000. For the remaining years of his life Alfonso I would be occupied in consolidating his control of a vastly swollen kingdom containing, initially, more Muslim than Christian subjects.

Muslims were guaranteed the exercise of their religion, their rule by Muslim officials, their lives, property, and freedom of movement within the realm or emigration from it if they wished. Still, within a year of their capitulation, they were to move from the city to the countryside for the cities of this new kingdom had to become Christian fortresses if the land was to be held. In 1125 *el Batallador* mounted a spectacular raid in force into Andalusia which lasted for some nine months. Its function was to deter attack on his new possessions from that quarter. On his return his army escorted large numbers of Andalusian Mozarabs, perhaps even 10,000, to new places of settlement in Aragon.

But powerful Muslim neighbors and a newly conquered, internal Muslim majority in his realm were not the sole problems of the Aragonese. After March of 1126 he faced a León–Castile ruled by an ambitious former stepson, Alfonso VII (1126–1157), who reversed the policy of his mother, made peace with Teresa of Portugal, and set out to recover those lands which *el Batallador* had held since 1113. In 1127 the young Leonese monarch retook Burgos and Carrión de los Condes. To prevent the collapse of his position Alfonso of Aragon first invaded Castile and then agreed to recognize his losses in hope of preventing further ones and of keeping his hands free in Aragon. That hope proved vain. In 1127 Alfonso VII secured a marriage with Berengaria, daughter of Count

Ramón Berenguer III of Barcelona, and an alliance with that count. Aragon was soon involved in a struggle with Barcelona which also had repercussions north of the Pyrenees. It drew him to a siege of Bayonne against the Count of Aquitaine, ally of Barcelona, in 1130 in support of his own allies at Toulouse, Bearn and Bigorre. While he was so occupied, his Leonese rival took Castrojeriz and overran the last Aragonese positions west of the Sierra de la Demanda.

At the same time, the struggle for predominance in the east of the peninsula raged back and forth. Alfonso I defeated a major Murābit army at Cullera south of Valencia in May of 1129. But in 1130 the Murābit governor of Valencia defeated an Aragonese force, killing both Bishop Stephen of Huesca and Viscount Gaston of Bearn. Back from the Aquitaine after 1131, Alfonso decided on the conquest of the lower basin of the Ebro. The key points were Fraga and Lérida and the siege of the first was undertaken. However, after several attempts to relieve the city had miscarried, the forces of Valencia, Lérida, and Fraga combined to defeat the Aragonese near the latter on July 17, 1134. Less than two months later Alfonso I died of wounds received there.

A wild melée now began in eastern Iberia that would endure for three years. *El Batallador* had died without children. Sterile or impotent, he had not married before or after his unfortunate marriage to Urraca of León–Castile. No liaisons were reported. Instead, by will, Alfonso I had provided for his kingdom to be divided among the three religious orders of the Templars, the Hospitallers, and the Holy Sepulcher. None of the three, born out of the context of the First Crusade in the Levant, had yet existed for as much as even three decades. While they had already begun to develop a support structure in western Europe, it was minuscule and generosity on this scale was unprecedented. The will was destined to be set aside, although some satisfaction would later be made to its designated beneficiaries.

Already in September of 1134, in the old royal city of Jaca, a good portion of the Aragonese nobility had recognized as new king Sancho II (1134–1137), brother of *el Batallador*, monk, former abbot, and former bishop-elect. To be sure, papal approbation would be necessary for the return of the new king to the laic life, for his subsequent marriage, and above all for his inheritance of lands already the property of the church in virtue of a will. Worse, by the end of the year another great-great-grandson of Sancho *el Mayor*, by an illegitimate lineage, had been recognized in Pamplona as García Ramírez IV *el Restaurador* of Navarre (1134–1150). Of course, the struggle of the two for possession of the kingdom of Aragon had to contend with Alfonso VII of León–Castile as well.

The latter invaded Aragon in the fall of 1134, quickly and finally recovering eastern Old Castile and the Rioja west of the Ebro. But the new lands of Saragossa were another great prize and Alfonso VII allied by turns with each of the other two in order to secure them. The confused warfare that resulted only began to move toward solution when Sancho II of Aragon (1134–1137) married Agnes, daughter of Duke William IX of Aquitaine in 1135. Thus an heir if yet a girl, Petronilla, was born to the pair in 1136. Finally, in 1137 the infant heir was betrothed to Count Ramón IV of Barcelona (1131–1162). The latter was made the protector of the realm initially and its sovereign when, in 1150, he should marry Petronilla. Sancho II abdicated in their favor and returned to monastic life, surviving until 1158. García Ramírez IV continued the fight for another seven years but ended by settling for a restored kingdom of Navarre, of perhaps 10,000 square kilometers and a population of about 75,000, limited to Pamplona and the Rioja down to Tudela. Alfonso VII accepted the situation, which apparently he could not or would not alter, in 1137 when Ramón Berenguer agreed to pay homage to him for the territories of Saragossa. The two then waged joint war against García Ramírez, with Alfonso detaching the Basque lands of Alava, Vizcaya, and Guipúzcoa from the Navarrese in the process.

But if Alfonso VII had profited from the death of his former father-in-law, Alfonso I of Aragon, to reclaim Old Castile and the Rioja and to establish the hegemony of León–Castile over the Basque territories, he had also to accept the emergence of a rival Christian realm of unprecedented proportions. Under Ramón Berenguer III (1097–1131) the county of Barcelona had begun to assume something more like the shape of Catalonia. Already count of Barcelona, Gerona, and Osona, by a mixture of marriage and diplomacy he had added to them the hereditary control of the county of Besalu and the territory of Vallespir in 1111 and of the county of Cerdanya with the territories of Conflent, Capcir, and Berga in 1117. The Catalan counties of Pallars, Urgel, Empúries, and Roselló would long continue to escape direct control but clearly Catalonia was to take shape about Barcelona. Ramón Berenguer had also himself married the Countess Dolce of Provence in 1112. As a result, the control of the house of Barcelona along the entire southern coast of Languedoc was long ensured.

But even if we disregard the lands north of the Pyrenees, Ramón Berenguer IV from 1137 ruled the second most powerful Christian kingdom in Iberia. Now "Prince of Aragon" as well as "Count of Barcelona," his territories there comprised some 50,000 square kilometers with a population of about 700,000. That was, perhaps, but half of the population of León–Castile and scarce a third of its land mass.

Nevertheless, the hybrid Aragon–Barcelona that took shape first in 1137 would grow, become yet more diverse, and would dispute the leadership of the Christian peninsula with León–Castile down to the unification of the fifteenth century.

While the Christian northeast saw the slow emergence of a unified Aragon–Barcelona, the west of Iberia was witness to the contemporary formation of a Portuguese kingdom. Though the pressures of a growing agricultural society were similar there, other contributory factors were markedly different. For one thing, the western coast of the peninsula is constituted by a single low plain, seldom more than thirty kilometers wide, that stretches from Galicia in the north to Lisbon in the south. A variety of rivers, the Miño, the Limia, the Duero, the Mondego, and finally the Tajo, run down from the central *meseta* in the east to flow into the Atlantic. The eastern mountains of Portugal, through which they flow, are broad and rugged and effectively isolate the Portuguese coast from the interior of the peninsula even today.

In the early medieval period, that had meant that the area was something of a border district even though it had never been deserted to the extent of the Duero basin area of the *meseta*. It was approachable, although distant, from the south and Muslim Lisbon and Santarém were in constant touch by sea with the dār-al-Islam. Therefore, politically, the plain had been loosely controlled by the caliphate of Cordova and afterwards by the *taifa* of Badajoz. But this Portugal was also approachable from Galicia in the north and, during the ninth century, had been overrun as far south as Coimbra on the Mondego by Alfonso III of Asturias. That proved a tour de force but Christian control did perdure in the north between the Miño and Duero Rivers, which territory was long a mere district of Galicia whose inhabitants spoke a Latin derivative sometimes called Gallego-Portuguese and indistinguishable from that of the remainder of Galicia. Beyond the Duero, Muslim occupation must have been scant north of the Lisbon–Santarém–Coimbra triangle. Certainly there was a quite large Mozarab population.

Fernando I of León–Castile had moved into these lands, taking Lamego on the Duero in 1057, Viseu on the Mondego in 1058, and Coimbra farther down on the same river in 1064. Leonese rule there seems early to have been based on the hegemony of the Mozarab count, Sisnando Davídez of Coimbra, but from 1096 the territory was entrusted to Count Henry of Burgundy, married to Alfonso VI's natural daughter, Teresa. Just before the death of Alfonso in 1109, the pair objected to his plan to marry Urraca to Alfonso I of Aragon and withdrew from his court to Coimbra. Effectively, they never returned and the independence of Portugal may be said to date from that time.

However, the plans of Henry and Teresa were to accede themselves to the throne of León–Castile rather than to create a new, previously unknown kingdom. To that end they intervened regularly in the affairs of the latter until the death of Count Henry himself in Leonese Astorga in 1112. Teresa was weakened for a time thereby but in 1117 reacted to Urraca's truce with Aragon and recognition of Alfonso Raimúndez as heir to León–Castile by herself taking the title of queen. Teresa did not specify the realm to which her title pertained but she did begin actively to extend her control northward over the towns and bishoprics of Túy and Orense in the valley of the Miño. She also allied herself, about 1119, with the powerful Galician house of the Trastamara and took Fernando Pérez of that lineage as her lover.

Queen Urraca of León–Castile reacted forcefully against this threat and the two struggled for control of the valley of the Miño until Urraca's death in 1126. Then Alfonso VII of León–Castile, who preferred to undertake the recovery of his eastern territories from Aragon, made peace with his Aunt Teresa. However, a reaction in Portugal itself against the influence of the house of Trastamara was headed by Teresa's son and heir, Alfonso Enríquez. In June of 1128 Teresa and Fernando Pérez were defeated at San Mamed, near Guimarães, by her son and forced into exile.

Under Alfonso Enríquez (1128–1185) a frankly independent kingdom of Portugal emerged although he too long hesitated over the best course to pursue. From 1128 to 1135 Alfonso merely styled himself *infans* and stressed his own relationship to his grandfather, Alfonso VI of León–Castile. Then, in the latter year when his cousin, Alfonso VII was to have himself crowned *imperator* in León, the Portuguese dynast began to use the title of *Portugalensis Princeps*.

In 1137 the two cousins fought an inconclusive border war for the lands of the Miño. But Alfonso Enríquez was also active in the south where he strengthened the border of Coimbra by erecting a strong castle at Leiria. When the Murābit responded to the challenge by mustering a major army of invasion he marched boldly into the Algarve itself and scored a great victory over them at Ourique in July of 1139. Turning to the north again, the Portuguese prince launched an invasion of the Miño valley that invited a counter by Alfonso VII in 1141. The result now was a clear defeat for León–Castile and a truce of indefinite time was arranged. Sometime during this latter period, certainly by July of 1140, Alfonso Enríquez had begun to call himself *Portugalensium Rex* in his charters. In this fashion a fourth Christian kingdom, albeit of not much more than 30,000 square kilometers and a population of 200,000, had begun to emerge in the peninsula.

THE ASSAULT ON MURĀBIT IBERIA

Despite his obvious and necessary concerns with Christian Iberia during the first fifteen years of his reign, Alfonso VII had gradually begun some further steps towards a continuation of the *reconquista* against Islam in the south. Clear opportunity was presented by the weakening there of the Sanhāja Murābit empire. In Morocco the Murābit were increasingly threatened by the rise of the Muwāhhid sect enshrined in a rival Masmūda Berber confederation. Every preoccupation or reverse there found echo in intrigue and disaffection within their Iberian provinces. In 1133 and again in 1137 Alfonso had led great sweeps deep into Andalusia. In 1139 he had reclaimed the fortress of Colmenar de Oreja northeast of Toledo from the Murābit. In June of 1142 he had retaken the Extremaduran town of Coria, in the gateway between the mountains of Portugal and the Guadarrama, which led from the plains of the lower Tajo to those of the western Duero. It had fallen to the Murābit in the dark days of 1111.

But preparations were in train which would lead to a much more general attack on Murābit Iberia. Ramón Berenguer IV had finally signed a peace with Navarre in 1142. September of 1143 saw a great council of León–Castile at Valladolid. Cardinal Guido, the papal legate was present along with representatives of the kings of Portugal and Navarre. Recognition of the regal status of Alfonso Enríquez, along with a variety of other disputes, was negotiated. June of 1144 saw the nuptials of Urraca, natural daughter of Alfonso VII, and García Ramírez IV of Navarre. The result of all this activity would be a series of extraordinary advances of Christian Iberia which coincided, roughly, with the launching of the Second Crusade in western Europe to reclaim the fallen county of Edessa in the Levant.

By the beginning of 1145 revolt against the Murābit had become general in the upper basin of the Guadalquivir. During the spring of 1146, while the Second Crusade was being launched at the court of Louis VII of France at Vezelay, Alfonso VII had reduced Cordova itself to vassal status. In September he signed a treaty with Barcelona and Genoa that provided for a joint attack upon the Muslim port of Almeria. In November he arranged the adhesion to it of García Ramírez of Navarre. Alfonso then reduced the Murābit fortress of Calatrava in La Mancha in January of 1147, which success safeguarded the road into Andalusia. Pope Eugenius III, meanwhile, issued a new crusading bull that listed Iberia along with the Levant and the German frontier with Slavdom as official spheres of crusading endeavor. Although the means and the extent of coordination between the crusade and the Iberian *reconquista* remain less than entirely clear, that the former would powerfully reinforce the latter is obvious.

Alfonso Enríquez of Portugal scored the first success with a surprise attack by night on Muslim Santarém which fell to him in mid-March. Having thus isolated Lisbon from reinforcement except by sea, he immediately undertook the siege of that town. Then, in June, a combined English, Flemish, and German fleet bound for the Holy Land arrived off the coast of Portugal. Negotiations quickly persuaded the crusaders to cooperate in the siege of Lisbon, which fell to the combined forces on October 24, 1147. During the same summer Alfonso VII and García Ramírez of Navarre had marched south through upper Andalusia, subduing that territory and then joining the combined forces of Genoa, Aragon–Barcelona, and Montpellier before Almeria. That town fell to them on October 17, 1147. The following year, as had already been agreed, the Genoese, Ramón Berenguer, the forces of Montpellier, and Toulouse, joined even by some elements of the crusading fleet that had helped to reduce Lisbon, united before Muslim Tortosa on the lower Ebro. That town surrendered in December. Less than a year later, in October of 1149, Ramón Berenguer, aided by contingents from Bearn, Urgel, and the Templars of his kingdom, captured both mighty Lérida and Fraga.

For a variety of reasons this momentum could not be maintained in the years that followed. However, in the space of less than three years the remainder of the basin of the Ebro from Saragossa to the Mediterranean had passed under the permanent control of Aragon–Barcelona. In the west, the new kingdom of Portugal now stretched from the valley of the Miño in the north to that of the Tajo in the south. The gains of León–Castile would prove ephemeral for neither Almeria nor upper Andalusia could be permanently held but some of the advances in La Mancha allowed for further repopulation there on the southern *meseta* in what was becoming *Castilla la Nueva*. Of the five great river valleys of Iberia, three had passed now under Christian control and only those of the Guadiana and the Guadalquivir remained to Islam.

THE STRUCTURE OF ELEVENTH- AND TWELFTH-CENTURY SOCIETIES

From the beginning of the eleventh century to the middle of the twelfth the political relationships of the two worlds of al-Andalus and of Christian Iberia interacted increasingly and yet the two underwent their own, autonomous developments in other respects. Although always with the massive reservations that must be understood of any society before the age of the Industrial Revolution, al-Andalus may be described as becoming yet more urban. That is, the total area devoted to agriculture was contracting somewhat as the full impact of the new agriculture came to be felt and lands earlier utilized for that purpose now became unnecessary and hence uneconomic. Total agricultural production nonetheless probably increased and more than sufficed to feed a population that seems to have at least stabilized and may even have begun to decline.

The increasing emphasis on irrigation farming at some expense to dry farming made the riverine character of the civilization of al-Andalus even more pronounced. But while hundreds of villages thus clustered more closely about its great cities, the latter seem not to have grown in any great degree. There were readjustments as Seville grew perhaps to 40,000 in the age of the *taifas* while Cordova shrank from the 90,000 it had attained during the age of the caliphate to something like 75,000. Other *taifa* capitals gained, sometimes greatly, as with Granada swollen to 20,000 and Badajoz to 21,000. Just as significant, because it points to the increasing volume and importance of overseas trade, was the growth of Almeria to 18,000, and of Valencia to about 20,000.

Indeed, in economic terms, the rise of the Murābit empire in North Africa was beneficial to al-Andalus. The pacification of Morocco and western Algeria and their political union with Muslim Iberia converted the former into a convenient and major market for the textiles, leathers, metalgoods, glasswares, timber, and a host of other products of al-Andalus. Andalusian merchants often maintained branches in cities such as Fez, Marrakesh, Tlemcen, and Algiers. Andalusian artisans, artists, and poets, found employment in those cities that increasingly were graced with mosques of Iberian design and houses and salons which aped its manners and interests. At the same time, the expansion of North African agriculture made it often able to provide cereal grains by sea to coastal Iberian cities such as Almeria and Málaga with insufficient hinterlands to produce it for themselves. In times of poor harvests in the peninsula, the ease of water transportation from Africa made that area supplier for any Iberian city so reachable.

But the greatest single contribution of North Africa was its gold, derived from beyond the Sahara. Not only have six Murābit mints in North Africa been identified but no less than fourteen more in Iberia can be counted. From them flowed the premier coinage of the entire peninsula, the gold *morabetino* as it was called in the Christian north. It reinforced the power of government and enlivened and stabilized the economy. From Africa as well came *exotica* such as the black household slave and ivory to be worked by the artisans of Seville and Cordova.

Except on its frontiers, al-Andalus seems to have experienced increasing prosperity even while its political fortunes were clearly on the wane.

At the same time, one must note the absence of any marked political or institutional development in contrast with its agricultural and techno-logical innovation. Aside from a perhaps increased use of written communication, while the Murābits brought political unity they did not bring political innovation. The government of the emirs was simply household government. They ruled as the commander of the faithful and their sons, brothers, cousins, and nephews, furnished the provincial governors. These were appointed and removed at will in the traditional fashion and governed, most often, the lands of the former *taifa* kingdoms from the old *taifa* capitals.

As before, it was a distinctly urban government. The city elites, religious, social, and economic, were consulted informally by the wiser governors. But these privileged subjects had no right to be consulted embodied in a permanent institution. The governor was an autocrat appointed by an autocrat. Hopefully he was benign. No one dreamed of consulting the countryside. As always, the governor ruled the city itself for even his capital had no individual personality. Politically it too was merely the expression of his *imperium*, exercised through his appointment of *qādī* and *muhtasib*. No more than its elites was the city a corporate *res*.

In almost every respect the Christian north was a different world. Its so-called towns about AD 1000 were essentially cult centers, their stable population a function of the cathedrals and monasteries that furnished their essential *raison d'être*. At that date the royal city of León itself could not have boasted more than 1,000 inhabitants and the same was true of Astorga, Barcelona, Burgos, Jaca, Lugo, Oviedo, Palencia, Pamplona, and Santiago de Compostela. They were tiny indeed but what is significant is that they were, with the possible exception of Jaca, growing and had at least doubled and likely tripled their size by 1157. At the same time a host of new towns of much the same size were springing up in the trans-Duero as Segovia, Salamanca, and Ávila, were awakened from their ancient sleep.

But while this phenomenon was important it was dwarfed by the instant urbanization achieved by the success of the *reconquista*. The fall of Toledo, with its population of 28,000, in 1085 tripled the urban population of León–Castile in a day. The conquest of Huesca, population 3,000, doubled that of Aragon and the subsequent conquest of Saragossa, population 16,000 within the walls, almost tripled it again. One and the same process continued to operate down until the end of the period as Lisbon and Santarém became the major cities of Portugal and Lérida and Tortosa were added to the realm of Aragon–Barcelona.

Nevertheless, the Christian north remained much more fundamentally a world of agriculture. With few exceptions its growing towns remained simply the occasional focus of the surrounding countryside. In return for the latter's produce, they now supplied it with shoes, pottery, and metalgoods, as well as with religion. To the extent that some towns were beginning to be a bit more diverse yet, that change was the result of one of two factors. For every town from Jaca west, a major stimulus was the growth of traffic along the pilgrim road to Santiago de Compostela from the eleventh century. From all over western Europe they came over the Somport Pass and down into Jaca or over Roncesvalles and down into Pamplona, from there to make their way west to the Atlantic. At every point along the "way of Saint James" there developed the business of ministering to this constant and predictable stream with rooms, food, drink, clothing, draught animals, and carts, all of the necessities of travel over great distance in a strange land. Such humble opportunity on a growing scale redoubled the existing market characteristics of the towns along the route.

But a more general trade is difficult to detect still. Some traffic in salt, to be sure, and some in iron. Some Flemish woolens were already reaching the peninsula but in what number is impossible to say. The Atlantic was still more often a source of danger than a highway of trade and, for all its seacoast, León–Castile was effectively landlocked. Such manufactured goods as came to it came largely from the Muslim south: fine textiles, fine leathers, fine metalgoods, fine jewelry, and even wine and olive oil. When the costs of such were not met in the gold of the *parias* they were probably paid in livestock: cattle, sheep, but above all horses.

What was to become the kingdom of Aragon–Barcelona was another world in which another factor operated. That is, its parts touched intimately on a world of trade, the old exchange between the land of the French and that of Islam. Established trade routes ran through both the Somport and Roncesvalles from the south of France down to the rich Muslim emporia of Tudela, Huesca, Lérida, and above all Saragossa already in the tenth century. Pamplona and Jaca participated in its largesse. Commercial life was reinforced by this current of trade as well as by that of pilgrimage and Sancho *el Mayor* of Navarre (1000–1035) seems to have struck a silver coinage in Pamplona and his grandson, Sancho Ramírez of Aragon (1063–1094), certainly did in Jaca. In León–Castile it appears that Alfonso VI (1065–1109) began to issue a silver currency only somewhat later but by the end of his reign his kingdom boasted no less than six operating mints.

But yet farther east a still richer current of trade had begun to develop in the triangle formed by the eastern coast of Iberia, the southern coast of France, and the northwest coast of Italy. There was a land route that reached from Valencia and beyond in al-Andalus north past Barcelona and on into the Midi. But from the beginning of the eleventh century the sea lanes were clearly open, carrying an increasing traffic, and joining Muslim Almeria, Valencia, and Balearics with Christian Barcelona, Montpellier, Genoa, and Pisa. Barcelona's early part in this was largely limited to the supply of agricultural goods, iron, and salt to others' shipping although doubtless it possessed a local fishing fleet of its own. The city's central position in both land and sea trade already made Count Ramón Berenguer I (1035–1076) the only Christian prince of his time able to issue a stable gold coinage. While we are largely uninformed of its particulars, that the trade of Barcelona would develop rapidly in the twelfth century is evidenced by the central position of its count in the abortive attempt by the Christians of Genoa, Pisa, and Montpellier, to conquer the Muslim Balearics in 1114. Already Barcelona was marked by its singular geography for the very singular political and economic destinies which it alone among the Christian Iberian powers would realize during the medieval period.

On the whole then, the towns and the commerce of Christian Iberia were diminutive by comparison with those of al-Andalus at mid-twelfth century, except where the former were indeed recently conquered Muslim towns. Nonetheless, all of them were undergoing an institutional development without parallel in the world of Iberian Islam. In the largest sense, there was the rise of a specific municipal law embodied in the *fueros*. This law by turns complemented and superseded what may be called the ordinary law of the realm. It would be a long time before there was any codification of *fueros* and each towns had its own particular law but all such local codes provided for civil status and criminal procedures unique to the individual town, its own law. Curiously enough, this recognition of a particular urban status was wellnigh universal being granted in one place by the crown, in another by a bishop or abbot, and in still others by a local noble.

Moreover, this individual legal existence was granted to that corporate body which was made up of the citizens of the town. That collection of "good men," the *concejo*, had a right to participate in the administration of their own municipal code. The earliest form of participation was doubtless simply that of corporate witness to the provisions of the law, to an individual's identity as a subject of that law, or to some specific application of that law. When this passive participation gave way to a fuller self-administration of the law by elected urban officials it is confused by the fact that most *fueros* continued to be living documents into which later amendments were simply incorporated without indication as to date. Clearly the first half of the twelfth century was transitional here. In 1118

Queen Urraca granted to the town of Burgos only the right to have its royal judge, or *juez*, named by her from among its citizens, and Burgos was a most important town. Still, the long revolt against abbatial authority in the town of Sahagún between 1111 and 1116 and the briefer revolt against episcopal authority in Santiago de Compostela between 1116 and 1117 were struggles whose results were embodied in *fueros* that specified not just rights but the selection of officials to administer those rights. Even though both struggles ended in setbacks for the popular forces, the very direction of their initiatives indicated the shape of the urban future.

HIGH CULTURE IN ELEVENTH- AND TWELFTH-CENTURY IBERIA

The same sort of prosperity in adversity which marked the economic life of al-Andalus during the *taifa* and Murābit period was reflected as well in its intellectual life. If anything, the courts of the *taifa* kings were agents of variety and diffusion in the traditional learning for they continued the patronage of arts and letters of the caliphate while multiplying the possibilities open to the scholar or artist. The *taifa* king was, himself, most often literate and able to participate personally in the intellectual contest. In Seville al-Mutamid (1068–1092) was a poet of some ability and in Granada Abd Allah (1073–1090) was able to compose a history of his own decline and fall. Both rulers passed the closing years of their lives in exile in Murābit Morocco of course and the Berber emirs are often made responsible for the blighting of the high culture of al-Andalus. That judgment must be considerably qualified.

Insofar as that brilliance is seen as the product of an interaction between the distinct Muslim, Jewish, and Mozarab traditions of al-Andalus, the charge is sustainable. Under the Murābit, and later the Muwāhhid emirs, life became much more difficult for the latter two communities and increasingly its more able and talented members found refuge in the Christian north or, in the case of Iberian Jewry, even in Egypt or the Levant. Yet, as we have seen, there were considerable elements in traditional al-Andalus which welcomed the restoration of the ideal of Muslim unity, the suppression of the influence of non-Muslim communities within it, and an attempted return to a more fundamentalist stance in its own life. Moreover, both Berber regimes were themselves, in turn, seduced by the intellectual refinements of Iberian Islam and often functioned as patrons of its practitioners to the extent that their circumstances permitted. It is well to recognize that the fundamental ideals of all three of the communities concerned were mutually exclusive and that they could have finally maintained the circumstances that gave rise to the high culture of the period only by yielding up their own several identities.

The three cultures of Iberia could well understand, if not empathize with, one another because all were fundamentally religious. More, they were all religions of a Revelation, that is, a book whose interpretation was central to their faith. In addition, at least some of the traditions, practices, and even persons, of their several faiths were the same. All three were, then, in some degree literate cultures by definition. They also shared the same essential literary genre, scriptural commentary. One needs to remember that the central intellectual and literary endeavors of all of them were centered upon scriptural exegesis, the reexamination of the work of previous exegetes, and on the construction of catechetical and ethical works. To some extent, therefore, their scholarly labors could be mutually appropriated, as with the influence of the construction of Arabic grammar and linguistics upon such Hebrew studies in the period of the caliphate. Nevertheless, it must be recalled that the basic vehicle of the learning of each was centered upon an institution, mosque, synagogue, or church, in each case of necessity closed and even hostile to the other.

Of course the separation of learning and life can only be a mental device and the former found a secondary focus in court circles and, to a lesser degree, familial and social ones that were not quite so impenetrable. This had always been true under the caliphate and will remain so for some time in this period. However, Mozarabs had always been more to the periphery of these circles than Muslim or Jew and will be increasingly so.

The court produced its own genres, of course, and these could be a matter of common participation and collaboration in some measure. The most basic of these was that poetry which is always the main vehicle of a wider and fundamentally pre-literate society. The main strand here was that traditional Arabic lyric poetry that celebrated nature, love, the hunt, and war. A famed theologian, ibn Hazm (994–1064), composed perhaps the most famous piece of this sort, *The Ring of the Dove*. Though the exemplars were Islamic in origin, such themes could be utilized indifferently by Jew or Christian. The noted Jewish theologian, Solomon ben Judah ibn Gabirol of Saragossa (d. 1070), composed love poetry in both Hebrew and Arabic and used the lyric Arabic forms to compose hymns for the synagogue as well. On the other hand, the growing departure from the traditional metres in Muslim poetry could result in the borrowing from Christian popular circles of the *muwashshah* and *zajal* forms for a new lyric which became all the rage in Murābit times.

But prose writing becomes gradually more prominent, probably reflecting the increasing ability to read in wider and wider polite circles.

Ibn Tufayl of Almeria (1105–1185) chose it to construct his romance, *Alive, son of Awake*, that detailed the adventures of two young religious reformers, one raised in nature and the other in civilization, as they attempted to cope with society. Prose was also the medium of the *adab*, that is, the genre combining biography and history so dear to Arabic literature. Most strictly historical literature of the period has perished but what remains of the *Djahira* of ibn Bassām of Lisbon (d. 1147) is still useful. The Cordovan who worked in Granada, al-Muwāīnī (d. 1168), also employed prose for his *The Comfort of Hearts and the Protection of Youth*, a seven-part scheme of the classification of knowledge. By and large, the matter of prose tended to be less adaptable to the several traditions except, spectacularly, in the realm of philosophy and of the sciences.

Precisely in these disciplines all three cultures possessed an overlapping secondary tradition, that of the Graeco-Roman world, that could and did furnish the area for their most fecund collaboration. Most of the still existing corpus of Greek science and philosophy, as distinct from its general literature, had been translated into Arabic at Damascus in the eighth century and at Baghdad in the ninth. From that time it had become the subject of commentary and elaboration within the dār-al-Islam and furnished the basic scheme of the Muslim approach to science, as illustrated by the work of al-Mawāīnī. For example, the polymaths of Islam were thoroughly familiar with the medical works of Hippocrates and Galen to which they made significant additions in the realm of botany, pharmacology, and medical diagnosis. A geographer such as al-Idrīsī (1100–1166), who was born in Ceuta and educated in Cordova, constructed his geography of the world by modifying the work of Strabo and Ptolemy and adding to it his own formidable knowledge of the twelfth-century Mediterranean.

But the scholars of Islam had appropriated not simply Greek science; to the astronomy of a Ptolemy or the geometry of a Euclid they had added the ancient Persian astronomical knowledge and the mathematics and astronomy of the Hindu Indian world. This process had largely taken place in the great days of the Abbāsid caliphate at Baghdad and had seen a marvelous enrichment of the classical lore in the Near East by figures such as al-Battānī and al-Khwārizmī. The intellectual dependence of Muslim Iberia on the Levant made inevitable the reception of such advances in the west and the peculiar social configuration of al-Andalus facilitated their transmission to the Jewish and Christian worlds.

The profound intellectual ferment that resulted was reflected in the efforts of the Muslim theologian and philosopher ibn Sīna (980–1037), Avicenna to the Christian world, to express the religious outlook of Islam in the terminology and conceptual apparatus of Greek, Aristotelian philosophy. In the west ibn Hazm of Cordova (994–1064) would take up this venture although somewhat more tentatively. The fullness of this effort in al-Andalus was only realized by the Cordovan ibn Rushd (1126–1198), Averroes to the medieval Christian west.

All of this theoretical adventuring was transmitted to the Jewish culture of al-Andalus of course. Abraham bar Hayya (1065–1136) based his astronomical and mathematical works on Islamic science and mediated the latter to the Hebrew world of Catalonia. This procedure was widely diffused but the greatest Jewish thinker of al-Andalus was Moses Maimonides of Cordova (1135–1204). Like his Muslim contemporaries he was a polymath writing on religion, medicine, and philosophy in terms of that antique tradition conveyed by Islamic scholars. He also took up a task analogous to that of his older contemporary, ibn Rushd, essaying in his *Guide for the Perplexed* to reconcile Aristotelian philosophy with the religious inheritance of Judaism so as to make of the former an intellectual vehicle for the latter.

This diverse and singular brilliance of the society of al-Andalus should not be minimized either for what it constituted in itself or for the contribution it was to make to later advances in the same fields. Nevertheless one cannot help but think that its full promise was never realized, either in eleventh- and twelfth-century Muslim Iberia or in the dār-al-Islam or Jewish world subsequently. There was a drawing back from the contemporary logic of the intellect and a turn, rather, towards fundamentalist thought which left the former incomplete, at least in terms of its original aspirations.

The final fate of ibn Rushd himself is instructive. Of good family, introduced to court through the famous scholar ibn Tufayl (1105–1185), promoted to *qāḍī* in Seville and then in Cordova, and finally court physician to the emir himself in the times of the Muwāḥḥid sovereigns Abū Yaqūb (1163–1184) and Abū Yūsuf (1184–1199), ibn Rushd nonetheless was forced into exile in Morocco in 1195 where he died four years later. The Mālakite *faqīh* of al-Andalus profoundly distrusted his advocacy of philosophy as a road to metaphysical truth independent of religion. His statements on the possibility of the duality of truth as seen from the religious and philosophical perspectives, the possible eternity of matter, and the unity of the active intellect in all rational beings were viewed as evidence of the dangers of philosophical speculation. Ultimately, even the Muwāḥḥid emir was not only unable to protect him but forced to direct the burning of his books. Muslim scholars of similar bent, such as ibn Bājjah of Saragossa (1070–1138) in his *The Rule of the Solitary* and ibn Tufayl of Almeria (1105–1185) in his *Alive, son of Awake,* emphasized the usual inability of society to appreciate correctly either religion or philosophy and counseled the solitary life of study and prayer. However, even one such as ibn Arif of Almeria, Saragossa, and Valencia (1088–1141), who preferred the way of mysticism and contemplation to that of philosophical disquisition, could find himself too the object of the suspicion of the guardians of orthodoxy and exiled finally to Morocco.

A similar experience awaited Maimonides. He had early become an exile from his native Cordova at the time of the Muwāhhid conquest of the same. When the first fervor of that sect against the Jews relaxed some-what he spent some time in Morocco at Fez but finally departed for the near East in 1165 where he spent the last years of his life as physician at the court of Saladin in Cairo. During all this time he suffered more at the hands of orthodox rabbis than at those of the Muwāhhid. The Jewish community as a whole was unprepared to accept his affirmation of the possibility of a natural religion independent of Revelation, his clear distinction between faith and reason, and his defense of the latter despite its inability to affirm or deny some of the crucial truths of holy scripture. That community found more congenial the admonitions of the poet Moses ben Ezra (d. 1135) who had also fled al-Andalus for the shelter of León–Castile but who preached there a radical cultural separatism for Iberian Jewry. It also preferred the denunciation of natural theology by the poet Judah Halevi (d. 1150) of Toledo who opposed the accommo-dation of the Jewish community to either the Muslim or the Christian one. Judah's most famous work was the *Kusari*, an imaginary dialogue in which the tenth-century Khazars are wooed successively by Christian, Muslim, and Jew, which demonstrated the superiority of the Revelation and the Covenant of Israel. Eventually Halevi journeyed to the Near East and never returned.

The participation of the Christian community in this intellectual ferment was to take an unprecedented form. That is, its locus was to be the new Christian kingdoms of the north rather than the Mozarab community of al-Andalus as such. Now the much ruder northern kingdoms were not simply newly come to the learning of Muslim Iberia. Long since they had received from it the texts of their own church law in the *Hispania* and the theory, at least, of their own secular law in the *Liber Judiciorum* from Mozarabs who found their way north. The great Catalan monastery of Ripoll and the Navarrese one of San Millán de La Cogolla also had had access to some of the mathematical learning of the Muslim world. But, by and large, the north had been a world where formal learning consisted of Biblical and liturgical study and the epic stories of popular culture found their way into the Latin chronicles of the clergy most irregularly and late. This traditional mental culture would continue, blossom, and find new vehicles but it would also be massively enriched by the brilliant contemporary achievements of the world of al-Andalus.

These new vehicles were, practically to exclusion, the reformed monasteries but, above all, the newly formed cathedral chapters. The royal court as center of high culture was not yet and, in stark contrast with the Muslim world, no Christian prince could even read, so far as we can ascertain. But the monasteries and the cathedral chapters became those centers where the new Roman liturgy must be absorbed. In that process, and often under the aegis of new French bishops or abbots, the Latin language itself began to be more rigorously defined and to be separated consciously from the vernacular of ordinary life. Often this process was reinforced by the recruiting of French monks and priests and by the despatching of Iberian ones to France for study.

A fitting symbol of this "new learning" is the contemporary spread of Romanesque architecture across the ecclesiastical map of northern Iberia. From Jaca at the foothills of the Pyrenees to Santiago de Compostela on the Atlantic a new esthetic proclaimed the new consciousness. Nevertheless, the traditional Latin learning and literature continued to be pursued and refined. Learning remained, in the first instance, Biblical study and commentary and training in liturgical competence. But one finds as well the blossoming of the episcopal *vita* as a literary form. One was done of the French Archbishop Bernard of Toledo (1086–1125), and of the French Archbishop Gerald of Braga (1097–1109), and a most famous one, the *Historia Compostelana*, of Archbishop Diego Gelmírez of Santiago de Compostela (1100–1140). At different poles the former court bishop, Pelayo of Oviedo, and an anonymous monk of Sahagún both chose to rework the eleventh-century chronicle of Sampiro and to bring it down to the times of Alfonso VI. In quite a different fashion another anonymous monk of Sahagún chose rather to record the troubles of his monastery with its own neighbors and subjects during the civil wars between Urraca of León–Castile and Alfonso I of Aragon. In the traditional fashion, some learned notice continued to be taken of popular literature. Some epic materials found their way into the *Historia Silense*, for instance, and a Latin poem concerning the exploits of *el Cid*, Rodrigo Díaz de Vivar, the *Carmen Campi Doctoris*, was composed.

Yet, in the largest sense, all of this very creditable activity pales before the wholesale appropriation of current Muslim and Jewish learning which took place in the same circles during the first half of the twelfth century. Although this endeavor was widespread the cathedral chapter of Toledo under the French Archbishop Raymond (1126–1151) appears to have been the most important center. The Italian scholar Gerard of Cremona worked there, until he disappeared about 1187, and made something in the order of eighty-seven translations. These included such works as Aristotle's *Physics*, Euclid's *Elements*, and Ptolemy's *Almagest*, all previously unknown in the Latin west. Gerard was also responsible for the translation of al-Kindi's *De Intellectu* and his *De quinque Essentiis*.

What drew someone such as Gerard to Iberia at precisely this time is unknown in its particulars but it is clear that many of the scholars of the European west had become aware of the richness of knowledge available there. Yet the phenomenon was by no means purely foreign. While Gerard worked at Toledo he was contemporary of a Jewish convert to Christianity, one John of Seville, and with John's collaborator, Dominic Gonzálvez of Segovia. These two produced translations of the tenth-century Muslim philosopher al-Fārābī and of the eleventh-century philosophers ibn Sīna, ibn Gabirol, and al-Ghazzālī. They were responsible as well for a variety of scientific translations including al-Battānī's *Liber de Consuetudinibus*, Sīr al-Asrār's *Secretum Secretorum*, and the *Liber Alghoarismi*.

For some period of time the German scholar Herman of Carinthia also worked at Toledo. Eventually he was to translate the *Planisphere* of Ptolemy, publish the astronomical tables of al-Khwārizmī and a variety of other works on astronomy by Jewish and Muslim authors. Herman translated as well two Muslim catechetical works on the doctrine and the genealogy of the prophet Muhammad. These two were to accompany a contemporary translation of the Koran into Latin carried out by a number of Herman's associates and friends.

This extraordinary undertaking was the fruit of the resolve of Abbot Peter the Venerable of Cluny (1122–1156) who traveled to Iberia in 1142–1143 to solicit financial support for the Burgundian abbey from Alfonso VII of León–Castile. He appears to have formulated the idea after meeting some of the future collaborators at Nájera in the course of his journey. His secretary, Peter of Poitiers organized the project and one Peter of Toledo acted as editor of the manuscript. Herman of Carinthia was drawn into this circle by his English friend Robert of Ketton who worked on it along with a Muslim scholar known only as Muhammad.

Obviously this intellectual revolution extended well beyond Toledo. Working rather in Barcelona during the reign of Ramón Berenguer IV (1131–1162) the Italian Plato of Tivoli collaborated with the Jewish scholar Abraham bar Hiyya to produce translations of Ptolemy's *Quadripartitum*, al-Battānī's *De Motu Stellarum*, and ibn al-Saffar's work on the astrolabe. Plato translated as well Abraham's *Liber Embadorum* which furnished the first known solution of a quadratic equation to the medieval west.

At roughly the same time, Hugh of Santalla, an Iberian, was busy at the cathedral of Tarazona in Aragon on a translation of Arabic astronomical tables. Robert of Ketton was for long associated with the cathedral of Pamplona and, in addition to his work on the Koran, collaborated with Plato of Tivoli in Barcelona, translated a variety of astronomical and mathematical works, and himself composed a set of astronomical tables for the longitude of London.

In this wise, the process set in motion in the *taifa* states of al-Andalus and enriched there by the cooperation of their diverse constituencies would be prolonged and mediated in the emerging Christian north so that its fruits became available to the scholars of all of medieval western Europe. Just as Arabic numerals, as we call them, were assimilated there, so was much of that corpus of additions to classical knowledge made by the scholars of Islam working in part with materials derived from the far worlds of Persia and India. On this base were to rise the scientific endeavor and teaching of the universities of the medieval and early modern west. Even more critical was the inheritance of the most profound philosophical and theological thought of Islam and Judaism. Under the influence of their findings and methods, the west would develop that intellectual stance to be known as scholasticism by which Albertus Magnus, Thomas Aquinas, and Bonaventure, would press the competence of the rational mind to its then outer limits.

In Iberia itself, however, the process of "spoiling the Egyptians" was to be continued into the latter twelfth and thirteenth centuries. Yet, at the same time, the Christian north was establishing its independence of al-Andalus and its solidarity with Europe to the north of the Pyrenees in matters of the mind as well as in matters of war, politics, and economics. Though only the most foolhardy of the time in Iberia would have dared to assert it, the balance of worlds in the peninsula was slowly inclining towards the preeminence of the north.

5

THE DEFINITION OF IBERIAN
AUTONOMY, 1157–1295

The death of Alfonso VII, *el Emperador*, of León–Castile in 1157 marked the end of four decades of triumphant progress on the part of the Christian principalities of the north of Iberia and the beginning of another six decades of the painstaking consolidation of prior gains in the face of considerable adversity. All things considered, the pause in that expansion was beneficial. The resources then to hand long proved barely adequate to maintain stability in the northern principalities, already swollen beyond all recognition from their shape and size even at the beginning of the twelfth century. That is not to suggest that fellows of our species were any more inclined than we to recognize the merits of moderation or the foolishness of the gambler's throw. Rather, this fortunate restraint was forced upon them by the new strength of their enemies and the crippling contradictions inherent in their own constructions.

The newfound vigor of the most obvious enemy, Islam, came from a familiar source. For the prior seventy years the military and political potency of al-Andalus had resided in the Moroccan empire of the Murābit of which it had become a part. For most of that time, the reigns of Yūsuf ibn Tāshufīn (1070–1106) and of his son Alī ibn Yūsuf (1106–1143), the Murābit emirs had ruled strongly but had been unable either to define the religious mission of their movement once it had become victorious or, alternatively, to construct a frankly political structure that could capture the consent of those beyond the family and tribal complex that was the government. Consequently, they now fell victim to that most ubiquitous of phenomena in Muslim society, another fundamentalist religious reform embodied in another tribal confederation.

The challengers were the Muwāḥḥid. Their founder and initial leader had been ibn Tūmart (d. 1130), a member of the Masmūda Berber confederation who had undertaken the traditional pilgrimage to Mecca, and returned to Morocco sometime about 1120 with the selfproclaimed mission to reform the Islamic community there. He appeared at the court of Alī ibn Yūsuf in Marrakesh but his preaching was rejected and he retired to Tīnmal in the Atlas Mountains where he was shortly accepted by the Masmūda as their religious leader, or *imām*. Emboldened by his recognition, ibn Tūmart in 1121 proclaimed himself the *mahdī*, that is, the inspired teacher sent by Allah to restore Islam.

The central tenet of his teaching was the oneness of God and his followers were therefore the *al-muwahhidūn*, or those who accept that doctrine and its corollaries. The chief of these, practically speaking, was that one must depart occasionally from the literal text of the Koran if one is to avoid objectifying the attributes of Allah and thus multiplying gods. Inasmuch as the reigning Mālikite jurists of the Muslim west and their Murābit supporters were firmly identified with the literal interpretation of Revelation they were polytheists and infidels by selfdefinition and ibn Tūmart declared the holy war, or *jihād*, against them.

The new *mahdī* was hardly original or profound in the doctrinal sense. With few exceptions he resembled very closely the early Murābit reformers. That is, the popular perception of his message was that it promised moral reform. A right order would be restored to the dār al-Islam in which the community and equality of male believers would be restored. The seclusion and virtue of women would be reaffirmed. Dancing, music, winebibbing, and the like would be suppressed. Only taxes sanctioned by the Koran would be imposed on the faithful. The infidel within that world would be reduced to a proper and abject obedience. The infidel without would taste the wrath of an aroused and victorious Islam. The novelty of all this lay chiefly in the new zeal with which it was asserted, the absolute mercilessness with which it was imposed, and the use of the Berber tongue for religious instruction.

But if ibn Tūmart was not particularly original he was, obviously, most apt at politics and the leadership of men. He welded together the tribes of the Masmūda confederation and led them into a guerilla war against the Murābit from the fastnesses of the High Atlas. When he himself was killed in battle in 1130 the leadership in that crusade was taken by one of his early followers, Abd al-Mūmim (1130–1163). Gradually the Muwāḥḥid began to make headway and after the accidental death of Alī's son, Tāshufīn ibn Alī (1143–1145) the collapse of the Murābit empire was almost immediate. The regime by which it was replaced featured the frank replacement of the Sanhāja by the Masmūda Berbers as at once the faithful of Allah and the rulers of Islam in the west. Abd al-Mūmim would take the step of declaring himself caliph and would gradually replace the uneasy balance of the personal followers of ibn Tūmart and the council of tribal chieftains with a family despotism in the traditional fashion.

As all of this transpired in North Africa the Murābit provinces of Iberia were being shaken by revolt from 1143 onward. That disorder was to allow the conquest of Lisbon by Portugal in 1147, the conquest of Tortosa in 1148 and Lérida in 1149 by Aragon–Barcelona, and the occupation of most of upper Andalusia and Almeria by León–Castile in 1147. Almost from the beginning Abd al-Mūmim had been approached by one or the other parties in Andalusia asking his intervention but his major interests long lay elsewhere. In 1151 his armies overran Algiers and Bougie in modern Algeria but the remainder of his life was required to secure the expulsion of the Norman kings of Sicily from their captured strongholds in present-day Tunisia. He had achieved that aim by 1162 but his death the following year prevented a major descent on Iberia. That task was left to his son and successor, Abū Yaqūb Yūsuf (1163–1184).

However a Muwāhhid army had landed in Iberia as early as 1146 and by the following year had subdued the Algarve in Portugal as well as the lower basins of the Guadiana and the Guadalquivir up to Badajoz and Seville. In 1148 the Murābit prince, ibn Gāniya surrendered Cordova itself to them rather than continue to submit to the claims of Alfonso VII. Nevertheless, the Muwāhhid were to remain simply one of the players in the tangled politics of al-Andalus for nearly a quarter of a century to come. Not until 1154 did they manage to displace the Murābit rulers of Málaga and Granada withstood them until 1156. Only then were they able to coordinate the advance on Almeria that would free that city from the control of Alfonso VII of León–Castile in October of 1157.

But several portions of al-Andalus continued to defy the new North African imperial power. In Valencia and Murcia the adventurer ibn Mardanish (1147–1172), whom the Christians called "el rey Lobo," seized power. He would maintain himself there until his death, collaborating with León–Castile against the Muwāhhid and surrendering to his allies the key fortress of Uclés just south of the Tajo. The new Muslim *taifa* king also signed commercial treaties with Genoa and Pisa in 1149 which granted them factories in the ports of Valencia and Denia and he signed a treaty of alliance with Ramón Berenguer IV, agreeing to pay *parias* to the Barcelonan in return for military aid. In 1162 he penetrated and subdued most of upper Andalusia before being defeated near Granada. In 1165 he even laid siege for a time to Cordova. For another ten years he waged a stubborn defense in Murcia but at his death he advised his sons to submit to the Muwāhhid. His career is testimony to the aversion many in al-Andalus felt to its becoming once again a province of a Moroccan empire.

In the islands of the Balearics too the descendants of the Murābits long maintained themselves. They waged active war at sea against the Muwāhhid and sometimes launched descents on the coast of Andalusia. But more often they combined with the opposition to the Muwāhhid in the latter's rebellious province of Tunisia, rebellion which occasionally penetrated as far west at Bougie. Not until 1203 did the Moroccans finally solve the problem by the conquest of the Balearics. The capture of those islands was to prove the highwater mark of the Muwāhhid counter-offensive in Iberia but it still fell well short of the reconstitution of the Murābit dominions there. Lisbon, Santarém, Lérida, Tortosa: all these had been lost to the northern enemy forever as it eventuated.

During this period of internecine warfare in Muslim Iberia the Christian north as well was experiencing its practical equivalent. Typical of the slight contemporary differentiation between dynasty and kingdom, Alfonso VII had provided for the division of his realm between his two surviving sons at his death. The elder, Sancho III (1157–1158), became king of a Castile which included Asturias de Santillana, the Basque provinces, the Rioja, a greater "Old Castile" which included *meseta* lands as far west as Carrión de los Condes, and Avila, and "New Castile," or the lands of the old *taifa* of Toledo stretching south into La Mancha. The younger, Fernando II (1157–1188), became king of a León which included Asturias de Oviedo, Galicia, and a somewhat abbreviated Leonese territory which reached south into Extremadura about Salamanca and Coria. With Castile was associated the traditional hegemony over Navarre and the newer one over Aragon–Barcelona for the Saragossan lands. With León was associated the hegemony over the new kingdom of Portugal.

This fragile arrangement began to dissolve almost immediately when Sancho III died scarcely a year later leaving a son, Alfonso VIII (1158–1214), of but two years. In the regency that followed the great Castilian families of the Lara and the Castro vied for control of the boy king and the latter, who lost, looked to Fernando of León to recoup their fortunes. Fernando attempted to control Castile without success and eventually Alfonso VIII came of age in 1169 and married Eleanor, daughter of Henry II of England and Eleanor of Aquitaine. The match gave Castile a claim on Gascony, Eleanor's dowry, and also well illustrates the increasing interpenetration of west European and Iberian politics.

The relations of Fernando II with Portugal were generally hostile until he made peace with Afonso Enríquez at Pontevedra in 1165 and married the latter's daughter, Urraca. Unfortunately the couple had a common greatgrandfather in Alfonso VI of León–Castile and Pope Alexander III would finally declare the match null in 1175. Subsequently Fernando II would enter a liaison with, and then marry, the noblewoman Urraca López of the house of Haro and a son, the *infans* Alfonso, was born to them. When Fernando died in 1188 the accession of his son by the Portuguese marriage, the future Alfonso IX (1188–1230), was then disputed on behalf of her son by Urraca López on grounds that Alfonso was illegitimate. As a result, Alfonso VIII of Castile now had ample opportunity to intervene in Leonese affairs.

Generally he was no more successful in controlling the affairs of León than had been his late uncle in directing those of Castile during his own minority and border raids and intermittent hostilities ensued. Finally, an attempt was made at a general peace in which Alfonso IX married Berenguela, daughter of Alfonso VIII and Eleanor of England at Valladolid in 1197. This time, of course, the problem was that Alfonso VII of León–Castile was the grandfather of the Leonese king and the great-grandfather of the Castilian princess. Pope Innocent III would pronounce the marriage invalid in 1198 but the royal couple continued in wedlock until 1204 at which time they finally separated. However, in the interim that Fernando III had been born who would reunite the two kingdoms in his own person after 1230, who would carry out the *reconquista* of Cordova and Seville, and who would finally be canonized by Pope Clement X over four hundred years later in 1671.

In northeastern Iberia during the years after the reconquest of Tortosa and Lérida the activities of Ramón Berenguer IV were largely directed towards the Midi. There he allied with Henry II of England in the hope of protecting Provence against Count Raymond V of Toulouse and strengthened his own overlordship in Bearn, Bigorre, Béziers, Montpellier, Narbonne, and Carcassonne. In the peninsula he did sign a treaty with Alfonso VII at Tudején in 1151 which provided for their joint partition of both Navarre and the Muslim *taifa* of Valencia–Murcia but that ambitious program was never realized. When he died in 1162 his heir was his son, Alfons II (1162–1196), just five years old. Not until the latter's knighting in 1174 did he assume real direction of the realm. At that time he was married to Sancha of Castile, the aunt of Alfonso VIII.

THE CONTEST WITH THE MUWĀHHID

Within the space of five years, the coming of age of Alfonso VIII of Castile (1169), the death of ibn Mardanish of Valencia–Murcia (1172), and the majority of Alfons II of Aragon–Barcelona (1174), set the stage for a climactic struggle of more than three decades between the forces of Islam and of Christianity in Iberia. Indeed the one northern principality that had experienced no dynastic crisis already had made some surprising headway. Afonso Enríquez of Portugal (1128–1185) profited from the exploits of Gerald the Fearless, the knight-adventurer Giraldo Sempavor, who took Trujillo and Cáceres in 1165 and Badajoz itself in 1169. But Fernando II of León was thoroughly alarmed by the Portuguese advances and intervened to defeat both Gerald and Afonso Enríquez. The Leonese monarch then took control of Trujillo and Cáceres but left Badajoz independent under its local leaders.

In 1171 however the caliph, Abū Yaqūb Yūsuf, came personally to the peninsula to deal with his assorted enemies. He received the surrender of ibn Mardanish's sons in 1172 and the same year led a great army against Huerte northeast of Toledo and but twenty-five kilometers from the Tajo. He narrowly failed to take it but in 1174 he had more success against León, reclaiming Cáceres and then Alcántara before failing in the siege of Ciudad Rodrigo on the southern fringe of the Duero basin itself. Yet when the affairs of Africa again demanded his personal attention, Alfonso VIII of Castile and his vassal, Alfons II of Aragon–Barcelona, captured Cuenca in 1177 and so secured the eastern border of La Mancha. Two years later at Cazorla the allies signed a treaty by which they agreed to partition all of Iberia, Christian and Muslim between them. In return for his assistance, Alfonso VIII recognized the king of Aragon–Barcelona as an equal and released him from the obligation of doing homage for the old lands of Saragossa. Over the next seven years the major Christian powers raided deep into al-Andalus and when Yūsuf returned to the peninsula in 1184 he had again to clear them from positions in Extremadura and the Portuguese Algarve. However, when the African attempted a siege of Santarém Afonso Enríquez of Portugal was joined by his old opponent, Fernando II of León, and Yūsuf lost his life in the retreat.

The latter's son, Abū Yūsuf Yaqūb (1184–1199), was again long detained in Africa by revolts there. Castile and Portugal utilized his distractions to advance once more in the south while simultaneously launching destructive raids deep into the basin of the Guadalquivir. In 1191 Yaqūb returned and in a single campaign obliterated the Portuguese gains in the Algarve but then was forced to attend to conspiracies and rebellions in Africa for the next four years. He came again to Iberia in 1195 and this time his objective was Castile which power had been raiding into Andalusia, bolstering its position on the middle Tajo at Trujillo and Plasencia, and even fortifying Alarcos at the northern edge of the Despeñaperros pass, which gave entry to Andalusia from the north. Although pledged assistance from León and Navarre, Alfonso VIII of

Castile advanced to meet the Muwāhhid alone and was resoundingly defeated at Alarcos in 1195. The Castilian positions in southern la Mancha and the middle Tajo were rolled up and in 1196 the Muwāhhid were joined in attacks on Castile by León and Navarre. In 1197 Yaqūb ravaged the lands of Toledo even laying siege, without success, to Madrid. Only the invasion of Tunisia by the Murābit of the Balearics forced him to grant the Castilians a five-year truce, which was once renewed by his son and successor, Muhammad al-Nāsir (1199–1213).

This interim offered little of novelty as León and Navarre continued to quarrel with Castile and the new Portuguese king, Sancho I (1185–1211), busied himself with repopulating his eastern border with León. Alfons II (1162–1196) of Aragon–Barcelona was concerned about his northern lands and the perennial struggle there with the counts of Toulouse. His position was consolidated when in 1172 Barcelona moved yet a step closer to identity with Catalonia as the count of Roussillon died without heir and that realm to the north was absorbed. In 1192 the last member of another such lineage ceded the county of Lower Pallars to Barcelona. Alfons' son, Pere II (1196–1213), was to be largely preoccupied by problems in the Midi where circumstances were to lead to the Albigensian Crusade and, eventually, his own death in battle there at Muret. In Iberia his reign was remarkable for the peaceful absorption of the Catalan county of Urgel in 1209 and his participation in the great victory over the Muwāhhid at Las Navas de Tolosa in 1212.

The Roman popes had been attempting since Alarcos to inspire a united Christian counterattack in Iberia without success but in 1210 Innocent III took up that quest anew. The expiring truce with the Muwāhhid was not renewed and Alfonso VIII opened offensive action in Upper Andalusia in 1211. Stung by assaults against Baeza, Jaén, and Andújar, the caliph struck into La Mancha and captured the Christian base at Salvatierra in late summer. Alfonso VIII now decided upon a direct trial of strength for the following year. His appeals for assistance would be answered by Pere II of Aragon–Barcelona and by Sancho VII of Navarre (1194–1234) but Alfonso IX of León (1188–1230) and the new King Afonso II of Portugal (1211–1223) held aloof for the time. Considerable contingents from beyond the Pyrenees under the bishops of Nantes, Bordeaux, and Narbonne also made their appearance in response to papal encouragement. Alfonso VIII assumed the expenses, requiring his clergy to contribute half their annual income for the year, and the host was launched against the Muwāhhid in June of 1212.

Muhammad II also took the field, moving east to the vicinity of Jaén. The Christian army spent a month clearing the Muslim positions in La Mancha. After the surrender of Calatrava, the majority of the French decided that they had done enough and marched north for home. In Andalusia Muhammad now advanced to Las Navas de Tolosa just south of the Sierra Morena. Alfonso in turn advanced through the pass of Despeñaperros, which was inadequately held, and the battle was joined on the next day, July 16, 1212. What followed was typical of the tactics of the battles of the *reconquista*. Despite an apparent inferiority in numbers, the Christian knights launched an attack against the Muslim center, composed largely of infantry. While their center held, the Muwāhhid reserves attempted to use their numerical superiority to envelop their opponents but the committing of the Christian reserve allowed a breakthrough and the battle became a rout. The Muwāhhid camp was taken, Muhammad fled on horseback to Jaén that day, and to Morocco immediately afterwards, but the Muslim foot were ridden down by the Christian horse and perished by the thousand. Not even the victors could have realized immediately the full significance of the event.

Indeed, the principals among the victors were soon to vanish from the scene. Before the end of 1214 Alfonso VIII of Castile was dead, having done little more than secure his hold on La Mancha. To his place succeeded an eleven-year-old son, Enrique I (1214–1217), who would not live to govern himself and meanwhile the kingdom was rent by the efforts of the house of Lara to control the regency. Pere II of Aragon had in 1213 already met his death at Muret in the Midi campaigning against the north-French baron, Simon de Montfort; Pere's son, Jaume I, was but five years old and a long regency would ensue there as well. Alfonso IX of León had taken Alcántara on the Tajo in the west in 1213 but thereafter became himself entangled in the question of the control of the Castilian throne. In Portugal, Sancho I had died just before the climactic battle and been succeeded by his young son, Afonso II (1211–1223), whose internal political troubles were joined to the disease of leprosy of which he finally died without having effected any notable conquests.

Fortunately for the Christian princes the empire of the Muwāhhid was falling into even greater disarray. Muhammad II fled from Las Navas de Tolosa to Marrakesh to die there in the following year. He was succeeded by his son, Yūsuf II (1213–1224), who proved quite unwilling to assume the responsibilities of leading that sprawling empire. He left it instead to a council of Masmūda sheiks whose primary interests were in Africa. For a decade then, the fortunes of the contestants in the peninsula were left largely to local forces and the fighting swirled back and forth furiously. Gradually the tide turned in favor of the Christians however. In 1217 a northern fleet on its way to the Fifth Crusade in the Levant was persuaded by Bishop Sueiro II of Lisbon to join in an attack on Alcácer do Sal at the mouth of the Sado River, which stronghold was then taken opening a road into the Algarve. The crusading fleet itself continued on its way, sacking Faro and Cádiz in the south en route. Nothing quite so spectacular was achieved in the center of the peninsula where the brunt of the fighting was borne by the military orders of Calatrava and of Santiago and by forces rallied by the doughty archbishop of Toledo, Rodrigo Jiménez de Rada (1208–1247). Still, the mopping up in La Mancha was completed and by the beginning of 1222 the king of León, Alfonso IX, had returned to the fray with determined if not yet successful sieges of Cáceres.

Then in 1224 the simmering crisis of the Muwāhhid regime boiled over at the death of Yūsuf II. The Masmūda sheiks in Marrakesh chose his genial great-uncle, Abū Muhammad Abd al-Wahid (1224). But the Muwāhhid governors of al-Andalus, with the exception of Abū Sāid of Valencia, refused to recognize him and rose in rebellion. At first, Yūsuf II's brother and governor of Murcia, al-Adil (1224–1227), seemed about to consolidate his power for, after he declared himself caliph, the sheiks of Marrakesh strangled al-Wahid and recognized him. But his cousin, Abū Muhammad al-Bayyasi, declared himself independent in Cordova, Jaén, and Baeza in Upper Andalusia and allied with his brother Abū Sāid of Valencia and with Fernando III of Castile who invaded Andalusia in 1225. Both rebel brothers became Fernando's vassals and al-Adil fled to Morocco where he was first accepted and then murdered by the Masmūda sheiks. The latter then named caliph Yahya (1127–1236), the sixteen-year-old brother of Yūsuf II but in Seville al-Adil's brother and governor, Abū Ula al-Mamūn (1227–1232) also had himself proclaimed caliph. The year before al-Bayyasi had been betrayed and killed by the Cordovans so in late 1228, master of most of the basin of Guadalquivir for the moment, al-Mamūn crossed into Morocco to reclaim the throne of the Muwāhhid. He would die there in 1232 in the midst of a civil war and neither of his sons, al-Rashid (1232–1242) and al-Sāid (1242–1248), nor his nephew, al-Murtada (1248–66), proved capable of reuniting the empire.

What then remained of al-Andalus in 1228 was a series of *taifas* most of which proved to be very shortlived. These were the Balearics and Valencia, independent under nominally Muwāhhid governors, and the remainder of Andalusia and Murcia which had recognized Muhammad ibn Hūd, a soldier and adventurer of Saragossan background who had risen in the civil war and now recognized the Abbāsid caliph at Baghdad to underscore his piety along with his independence.

Unfortunately for ibn Hūd, when Enrique of Castile had died in 1217 his older sister and the former wife of Alfonso IX of León, Berenguela, had quickly summoned her son by Alfonso to her and had him proclaimed king at Valladolid before even her former husband understood what she was about. So installed, it took the young Fernando III some time to placate his father and close to seven years to complete his control of the unruly nobles. But by 1225 he was ready to invade Andalusia in support of al-Bayyasi and at the death of the latter in 1226 Baeza passed finally into Castilian hands. Farther west Alfonso IX of León, who had been besieging Cáceres for some time, captured it in 1229 and then went on to take both Mérida and Badajoz in 1230. The middle basin of the Guadiana thus passed finally into Christian control.

But the succession crisis had now come to an end in the kingdom of Aragon–Barcelona as well and Jaume I (1213–1276) at nineteen years of age had taken the reins firmly in hand by 1227. His first objective was Majorca and that island kingdom was conquered in 1229–1230. The Muslims of Minorca recognized Jaume as their sovereign in 1232 and the occupation of Ibiza was left to the archbishop of Tarragona in 1235. The Balearics conquered, Jaume now turned to the *taifa* of Valencia. The Muwāḥḥid Abū Sāid had been overthrown there in 1229, fled the revolt into Jaume's lands, and had accepted Christianity as well. Pope Gregory IX declared a crusade and the invasion began in 1232. The resistance was spirited, however, and not until 1238 did the capital itself surrender.

Meanwhile, Fernando III, having secured the kingdom of León on his father's death and settled the details of the reunion of León and Castile, returned to Andalusia to capture Ubeda in 1233. But his hold on Upper Andalusia only became secure with the surrender of Cordova in 1236. Ibn Hūd, having proved unable to prevent the Castilian's advance, was murdered by his followers in 1238. Immediately another adventurer, Muhammad ibn Yūsuf al-Ahmar who had been vying with ibn Hūd since 1132, declared himself king and was recognized in Almeria, Jaén, Málaga, and Granada. Nominally recognizing the Muwāḥḥid al-Rashid in Marrakesh, al-Ahmar will in fact become the founder of the Nasrid dynasty of Granada as Muhammad I (1238–1273) and the initiator of the famous Alhambra, symbol of that last of the *taifas* there as well.

In Murcia, on the other hand, the local Muslims preferred to recognize Fernando III as sovereign. Preoccupied with these and other matters, the Castilian monarch did not return to Andalusia until 1244 and then immediately attacked al-Ahmar. In 1246 he succeeded in reducing the almost impregnable Jaén by siege and al-Ahmar agreed to yield the city to him and to become his vassal. The way to Seville was now open and siege lines were established around that city in 1247. The great city resisted until November, 1248, but with its surrender Muslim resistance in the valley of the Guadalquivir collapsed. Since the Portuguese had simultaneously been carrying out the conquest of the Algarve and Faro in the extreme south would fall in 1249, Muslim political power in Iberia was reduced to the southern littoral in the hands of al-Ahmar of Granada, himself a vassal of Fernando III and the various lands of Murcia also subject to the latter monarch. By the death of Fernando III in 1252 the long struggle was all but over and now it was Islam that would survive in Iberia only on the sufferance of its old rival, Christianity.

THE SINEWS OF TRIUMPH

The first explanation of this changed state of affairs is that combination of military and political events detailed above. However, those factors were, in large measure, the products of more fundamental changes in the societies of the Christian north. First among these was the demographic increase that was general in all regions of those principalities. The new kingdom of Castile had roughly tripled in size to some 355,000 square kilometers by 1300 but, at the same time, its population had increased by the same factor, from one to three millions, so that the average density remained steady at about 8.5 persons per square kilometer. By that date it was also a fairly homogeneous kingdom for in the new, former Muslim lands a continuing exodus south of the Muslim population, finally to Granada and North Africa, and a rapid assimilation of the Mozarabs had occurred. Except for Murcia, where it was probably still a majority, the Muslim population did not amount to more than 8 to 10 percent. The most visible minority was, in fact, the Jews but their numbers did not surpass 2 percent in all likelihood.

In the new Crown of Aragon of 120,000 square kilometers the population density would have been about the same for its numbers reached about 1,000,000 at the same period. Aragon's population was far less homogeneous, for although the Muslims only amounted to about 2 percent in Catalonia, in Aragon proper that rose to almost 25 percent and in the new realm of Valencia they still reached 75 percent. There too Jews were a very visible minority and they seem to have numbered about 5 percent. Portugal swollen to 90,000 square kilometers and perhaps 800,000 inhabitants resembled Castile more than Aragon in its demographic composition but at 12 persons per square kilometer its population density would have exceeded that of either by some 50 percent. Little Navarre with its area of only 10,000 square kilometers and some 100,000 people still had a Muslim minority of about 10,000.

Everywhere the business of life was agriculture and the latter's rhythms dominated war, politics, religion, and culture. In the northern half of the peninsula by 1300 the agricultural revolution based upon the plow, the watermill, iron or iron-edged tools, and garden-style irrigation, had been carried through and generalized. At the same time the size of the average farm had probably doubled, realizing the potential of the new technology, for the perennial availability of new lands to the south had more than counterbalanced the pressure of rising population everywhere except in tiny Navarre. Climate continued to control the traditional crops of the north although sorghum and hard wheat had come up from the south and the olive had been coaxed into the lands of the Tajo and the grape into those of the Duero. Mozarab and Muslim skill had been instrumental in that respect. Clearly the agricultural land was sufficiently prosperous to allow the increasing dedication of marginal lands to stockraising even in the north though, as in the terrible years of 1213–1214, spectacularly bad weather could still produce very real famine.

In the southern, formerly Muslim half of Iberia agriculture continued the evolution already begun in the last years of the caliphate. That is, it was marked by the twin phenomena of a declining population and an ever-greater concentration on large-scale irrigation in the river valleys and the contraction of the area devoted to cereals. Some land went out of cultivation everywhere and in La Mancha and the Upper Guadiana valley dryfarming had virtually ceased only to be revived again with the Christian occupation of the thirteenth century. That repopulation was only partial, of course, and in Andalusia proper the decline of the Muslim population was only very slowly replaced. As a result, cereal lands continued to contract, the less intensive cultivation of the olive and the grape expanded yet more sharply, and the lands devoted to stockraising soared exponentially. The same was largely true of the Portuguese Algarve. On the other hand, in Valencia and Murcia, where the Muslim inhabitants remained in very large numbers, the structure and practice of agriculture changed very little though it was increasingly directed by the conquerors.

Perhaps the best indication of the good health of the countryside is to be found in the experience of the towns of the period. With the exception of some formerly Muslim cities, it is one of uniform and sometimes spectacular growth That is, the countryside could feed such urban agglomerations at the same time that it swelled them with its excess sons and daughters. Certainly such great centers as Seville, Cordova, and Cádiz were smaller in 1300 than they had been in 1200 by reason of the exodus which followed on their conquest. Farther north, once Muslim Saragossa, bereft of its status as capital, had shrunk from perhaps 18,000 to a still respectable 12,000 by 1300. On the other hand Muslim Lisbon of 5,000 people in 1147 was now of the order of 15,000, and once Muslim Toledo of 28,000, which had certainly contracted after the conquest in 1085, recovered and may have reached 45,000 by 1300.

Nor was this new Christian Iberia of 1300, like that of 1150, wholly dependent on the conquest of Muslim cities to flaunt an urban character. In the Duero region older towns such as León and Burgos had apparently doubled in size since then to reach something like 8,000–10,000 apiece. Zamora had 7,000 or so and the scarcely settled Salamanca and Valladolid of 1100 had reached 15,000 and 25,000 respectively. Once tiny Barcelona now had become the metropolis of the north at 48,000 inhabitants.

Such urban complexes depended for their life on trade that went beyond the mere servicing of the surrounding countryside although that component remained the essential precondition of all other activities. The great bulk of this trade consisted of the exchange of natural products between regions differently favored by climate and soil. Thus the wheat and wine of the Duero basin went north and west into Asturias and Galicia and in return came salt and dried or salted fish. In the late twelfth century the Leonese kings had patronized the development of ports such as La Coruña in Galicia and of Avilés and Gijón in Asturias and the commercialization of the resources of the sea had developed very quickly. The rise of Lisbon also, particularly in the thirteenth century, had increased the exploitation of the Atlantic fisheries and the distribution of processed seafood had become peninsular in extent. Closely allied to it was the distribution of salt derived from coastal districts.

In Aragon proper the same phenomenon was yet more dramatic once the lower course of the Ebro had been opened up by the conquests of 1148 and 1149. That great river offered a highway down which Aragonese wheat, wood, fruits, and vegetables, flowed to the chronically hungry Barcelona and beyond to Majorca and Valencia. The products of the sea came back, to be sure, but also such things as the oranges and the rice of Valencia. The conquest of the valley of Guadalquivir in the thirteenth century meant the yet more unrestricted passage of the olive and olive oil, the wines, and the fruits of that region towards the valleys of the Tajo and the Duero. That conquest permitted, as well, the extension of a local into a great peninsular transhumance which would bring the flocks of the Duero, Lower Aragon, and the Tajo basin into Andalusia. The semi-annual passage of the sheep brought concern but also rentals and tolls into the coffers of those along its route.

By comparison with the trade in natural products, that in manufactures was relatively small. Nevertheless, it too had expanded greatly. The textiles of Cordova, Seville, of Cuenca, and Valencia, now began to experience competition from those of Segovia and those of Barcelona above all. The leather goods of Cordova and the steels of Toledo still found buyers but the weapons and armor of Aragon and Barcelona prospered as well. Toledan ceramics began to contest the peninsular market with those of Malaga and the glass and carpets of Murcia found acceptance everywhere as heretofore. This trade, transported mainly by pack animal but sometimes by cart for the rivers of Iberia seldom offered a dependable alternative, had its regular routes, local fairs, and toll stages and by the end of the thirteenth century had found something like a peninsular institution in the great fairs held semi-annually at Medina del Campo. Already too the business of such fairs was tied into a financial network which covered all of western and central Europe. Archbishop Sancho of Toledo borrowed 4,000 *solidi* of Tours from a French merchant in 1256, the agreement stipulating that it was to be repaid at the fair of Alcalá de Henares after Easter or the fair at Pamplona after the feast of the Ascension. Some thirty years later Archbishop Gonzalo of Toledo was able to borrow 20,000 *maravedi* against his projected income from the three annual fairs at Alcalá de Henares.

Trade with the world beyond the peninsula was composed of three main complexes. One was that of Catalonia, and after mid-century Valencia, which had emerged in the twelfth century from the leading strings of the Muslim south or Italian Genoa and Pisa. Bolstered by the control of Provence and much of the Midi by the dynasty of Barcelona, and successively reinforced by the conquest of the Balearics and Valencia in the 1230s and the annexation of Sicily in 1282, the seagoing merchants of Catalonia bid fair to dominate the trade of the western Mediterranean. In this case though, the flag followed the trade. For a century before the acquisition of Sicily the Catalans had become very active players in a maritime trade which, as in antiquity, was based essentially upon the traffic in wheat, slaves, and piracy. Vessels coasted from Montpellier to Genoa to Palermo to Tunisia and Almeria in search of occasional cargo, such as the silk of Valencia and the paper of Játiva, which might be saleable in other climes, but the great staples were those three.

At home both Barcelona and Valencia now possessed an organized and fertile hinterland in Aragon from which and to which they could tranship. The seagoing merchants of the first had already begun to put together their *Costums* which later would be formalized as the famous *Libre del Consolat del Mar*. Jaume I provided institutional framework for these several advantages when he organized the maritime sector of Barcelona in 1257 as the *universitat de la ribera*, virtually a city within the city, and his son, Pere III, did the same for Valencia in 1283. These sovereigns also negotiated favorable conditions for their merchants with the various portions of the decayed North African empire of the Muwāhhid and even in Alexandria with the caliphs of Egypt. To accommodate the results Pere III began the issuance of a heavier silver coinage, after the precedent of the Italian towns, better adapted to use in the European market.

In Seville in the second half of the thirteenth century, the merchants of Castile attempted to continue and dominate the established trade with North Africa. Vessels of the average size of three hundred tons could still navigate the Guadalquivir up to that city. However, most of that trade was to fall into other hands. Since the conquest itself there existed in Seville a large and aggressive colony of Genoese merchants who increasingly monopolized the distribution of the manufactures and natural products of the Guadalquivir basin to the Moroccan and Algerian coasts opposite. The Genoese also participated in the newly activated Mediterranean seaborne trade with the North Sea market of England and Flanders, utilizing Seville but also Cádiz and Sanlúcar de Barrameda as points for transhipment and local redistribution of goods derived from either. In this latter the Genoese found competitors not so much in Seville and its merchants but in the Basque seacaptains and merchants who had participated in the siege of the city and subsequently retained both interests and privileges there.

To the north in Portugal, Lisbon repeated this phenomenon although on a smaller scale. That city possessed the finest harbor on the Atlantic coast and owed its liberation from Muslim hands in 1147 to its place on the sea routes from the north to the Mediterranean. The city continued to enjoy the benefits of its placement as an essential point en route in a growing trade in the Atlantic, as did Oporto and La Coruña farther north to a lesser degree. By the end of the thirteenth century merchants of Genoa and Venice had established residence in Lisbon and Portuguese merchants trading with England, France and Flanders had begun to organize for purposes of insurance and protection. Portugal's contribution to this cosmopolitan trade came above all in wine, olive oil, and salt but also in cork, hides, wool, and dyestuffs.

Now the trade complexes of Barcelona and Seville had precedent and predecessors in antiquity and Muslim times. That of Lisbon, and yet more so that of the Cantabrian coast to the north, however, was something new under the sun. From the late twelfth century Alfonso VIII had promoted the growth of ports and trade on the coast of Cantabria. Castro Urdiales, Santander, Laredo and San Vicente de la Barquera were called into being and began to carry Asturian timber, livestock, meat, hides, fish, and salt, north along the coast of the Bay of Biscay to France and to England and Flanders as well. To these products were soon added the iron ingots worked from the mines of Alava and the wool collected at Burgos from all over the peninsula. The artery of trade so opened would create the most important landroute in the peninsula, bearing the Flemish cloths landed at Santander south through Burgos, Medina del Campo, Salamanca, Seville, and so far as Cádiz. Among other goods, dyestuffs, ivory, and gold, collected from North Africa made the return trip back through Cantabria to the North Sea markets. When Fernando III decided to launch his final siege of Seville at mid-century he had secured the service of a Basque fleet arranged by a merchant of Burgos.

POLITICAL SOCIETY UNDER THE MONARCHY

The constantly increasing ability of the new agriculture to produce an excess of wealth between AD 1000 and 1300 supported the burgeoning of both towns and trade in the north of the peninsula. But, of course, the very appearance of both indicated that ever more sophisticated diversification and specialization in northern society by which the surplus wealth created on the land was increasingly appropriated by the non-agricultural classes. One of these was that of the townsmen whose rise was spectacular in the period 1157–1300.

By the first of these dates the inhabitants of towns of any size virtually everywhere had achieved recognition as juridical persons subject to a particular body of law unique to their own locale. By the second date most of them will have secured as well a considerable degree of local self-government under their own elected officials. Though the variation is endless, nonetheless certain common essentials may be remarked everywhere. The municipal council, *concejo*, at once executive, legislative, and judicial in nature, was the mainspring of its government and a variety of officials were usually chosen by it such as a mayor, *alcaide* though that term is flexible, judges (*alcaldes*), notaries, and market supervisors (*zabazoques*). The influence of Muslim precedent is evident but the *concejo* itself had no such counterpart. By the first half of the thirteenth century most such administrations will possess their own corporate property and, as a necessary corollary, their own seal. They will have secured a local taxing power as well, especially in connection with the maintenance of the town walls, the latter as much a symbol of the town's status as its seal.

Nevertheless, even within the walls the jurisdiction of the *concejo* was one shared with other powers, whether with regard to civil, criminal, religious or political and military matters. The great figure was the king, to be sure, and his castellan, if there were a palace or royal fortress within the town, and his *merino* or *veguer*, if only royal property and judicial rights required exercise, possessed an independent jurisdiction to be exercised in concert with that of the *concejo* or to override the latter if need be. Almost as omnipresent as the independent authority of the king was that of the bishop, the urban figure *par excellence* in the age. The bishop administered the property and the persons of the clerical estate within the town for these were, in theory and ordinarily, beyond any secular jurisdiction, town or crown. But, especially in the north of the peninsula, the bishop might also wield a secular authority derived from hallowed royal concession that made him the chief royal official of the town as well. Finally, often in the smaller towns a local noble house, perhaps the original founder of the town, still retained property and a restricted jurisdiction within the walls.

The town was, then, a genuine political world of competing rights, each of them defined in law or custom. However, it was as well a world of competing interests. The citizen class was usually composed of those burghers who possessed a house or a business within the walls and this class monopolized the town's elections, the *concejos*, and the related offices. But the more numerous artisans and casual laborers thus excluded from ordinary political life could still affect it in times of stress when their physical support was sought by one or the other rival jurisdictions of crown, town, or church, or indeed of factions within the citizen class itself. Such factions were a regular part of civic life for that class divided often into proprietors who were wholesale merchants, those simply engaged in the retail supply of the town and its countryside, and that peculiar group of minor nobles who possessed sufficient property to be able to maintain themselves as mounted warriors of the day, in Castile the so-called *caballeros villanos*.

Then too one must remember that divisions within the royal dynasty often found echo within the town as might, at a lesser level of intensity, dynastic divisions within or between the great noble houses. Nor was the church monolithic under its bishop. The rise of the cathedral chapter provided a competitor for property and jurisdiction for him within his own house. That competition was often embittered by the fact that the bishop was usually a royal appointee lacking local support and the canonries of the chapter were ordinarily filled by the scions of local powers among the town bourgeois or nobility. Moreover, the growth of Roman papal jurisdiction in the church of the twelfth and thirteenth century meant that a disappointed party could always appeal to Rome. Finally, the bonds of family and patronage crossed and complicated all of these lines of jurisdiction and interest. In a small urban society, ordinarily of less than 10,000 people in all, these circumstances provided for an active civic life to say the least.

Nevertheless, this pluralism and devolution of political authority proved workable, successful, and an element of strength rather than sterile discord in those times. The towns seemed to have achieved local self-government during a period such as that of the division of León and Castile into competing kingdoms after 1157 that made their loyalty worth purchasing. Fernando II of León mediated the ambitions of the men of

Lugo and of Túy vis-à-vis their bishops then. Busy cobbling together an unlikely union, Alfons II of Aragon–Barcelona allowed elections to the men of Cervera on their border. But the external factor of the *reconquista* had much to do with the development as well. Especially prominent in León–Castile were the urban militias of Segovia, Ávila, and Salamanca, which led attacks of their own on Muslim Andalusia in the twelfth and thirteenth centuries as well as supplying an essential stiffening to royal expeditions; town forces were important everywhere to royal purposes and were rewarded accordingly. Portuguese *fueros* routinely mandated the maintenance of a military forces by the towns and the men of Barcelona were in the forefront of the conquest of Majorca and subsequently of Valencia. This military potential of the town made it difficult not to accord it a place either in deliberations or in determining its own proper life.

Similar general circumstances determined the increasing rule of the surrounding countryside from the towns. As the Christian princes advanced south they encountered, in the trans-Duero region of La Mancha and the Beira Baixa or the Beira Trasmontana later, semi-deserted regions in need of an immediate governing structure. The simplest way to do this proved to be the extension of town jurisdiction over the lands and hamlets surrounding it, the *alfoz* and the *aldeas* respectively in León–Castile. In lands formerly effectively occupied by the Muslims a new government had to be installed in a foreign and still latently hostile countryside which could not itself be repopulated in any substantial measure. Very largely this need too had been met by expelling the Muslims from the cities, concentrating the Christian population therein, and again making them the legal centers for the administration of the countryside.

Of course this growth of urban local autonomy and its extension into the countryside was analogous to what was happening elsewhere in western Europe in the period and differed largely in degree and extent. The same may be said of the rise of an Iberian nobility. Everywhere in that Europe an older, clan and tribal aristocracy was transforming itself into a more explicitly political, economic, and military class. This was being done under the pressure of a rising dynastic monarchy, a changing agriculture, and an emerging complex of military weapons and techniques which favored the mounted warrior. In Iberia a number of special circumstances had magnified this common development though perhaps not so much as popular mythology would have it.

These, of course, were the *reconquista* against a powerful, rich, and culturally alien society in al-Andalus which gave an even stronger social premium to military prowess. Associated with it was the possibility for continuing reward of that prowess through *parias* or simply booty extracted from the enemy and the replication of noble holdings almost indefinitely as the northern societies expanded at the latter's expense. Moreover, climate, soil, and demography conspired to make trans-humance stockraising an economically more feasible activity than it was in northern Europe and that way of life and business provided its own emphasis on the superiority of the mounted warrior. In Iberia, as else-where, this nobility was never a closed corporation for the fortunes of war, the favor of the crown, the biological failure of established houses, and marriage alliance and economic success to a lesser extent, made entry into it from below far from uncommon.

By AD 1300, the Iberian nobility had taken a varied shape. At its apex were the great lineages, in Castile styled the *ricos hombres*. There they consisted of about thirty-four great houses, such as the Haro of Vizcaya, the Trastamara of Galicia, or the Castro and the Lara of Castile. In Aragon there were some fifty, in Navarre only five or six, in Portugal a rough dozen. The characteristics of such houses were a carefully exaggerated family history, great wealth in land, and personal acquaintance with the crown. Below them was a much more numerous and lesser nobility, the *hijos de algo* or *hidalgos*, propertied in land as well, that strove to associate itself in some degree with one of the great lineages. Finally, the lowest reaches of the nobility were made up of the *caballeros villanos*, urban originally as the name implies; but whose financial means ordinarily rested upon agricultural receipts and of such means economically as to be able to afford the accoutrements of the mounted warrior.

Three centuries of progress in agriculture and in warfare had been kind to this class as a whole. It had enlarged its estates in the countryside, multiplied its leaseholders, and was fortified both by the acquisition of ordinary civil and criminal jurisdiction over those who worked the lands. The *caballeros villanos* more often than not dominated the *concejos* of the towns. According to its various means the nobility competed with the crown for the right to exploit the bishoprics, the abbacies, and the canonries of the church for its own benefit and that of its retainers. The greatest houses even sought to control the monarchy itself during periods of royal minority and to profit from crown offices or patronage at all times.

The third great power in Iberia was that of the Christian church. From a handful of bishoprics in AD 1000 the secular church in 1300 had become a world in itself of forty-four episcopal sees divided into five archepiscopal provinces reconstituted as the *reconquista* progressed, Toledo (1086), Tarragona (1089), Braga (1100), Santiago de Compostela (1120), and Seville (1248). In Portugal and Aragon, the archepiscopal provinces of Braga and of Tarragona had consciously been fashioned as coterminous with the lands of the kingdom. The sole see of Navarre, Pamplona, had been absorbed into the province of Tarragona, however, and the kings of Castile had been unable to prevent the proliferation of ecclesiastical provinces within their sprawling realm although Toledo was ordinarily their preferred instrument.

While the Iberian churches were dispensers of spiritual comfort, religious instruction, and physical charity, they were also great institutions wielding a spiritual jurisdiction embodied in their own separate courts and entitled by law to the greatest regular tax of the age, the clerical tenth (tithe) levied annually on the income of every Christian household. They also possessed that power and wealth which came from a great landed endowment and the rents that derived from it. Finally, the bishop, as agent of the crown, frequently wielded outright political power as well, especially in the great towns of the north, more often in the council chamber but sometimes even on the battlefield.

No monarch could afford, then, to allow a bishopric to pass into other than friendly hands. Invariably the king had a candidate for any vacant see, usually a trusted member of his curial clergy, not infrequently a member of his family. The great houses of the realm competed too on behalf of members of their families or supporters and the more ambitious prelates of the kingdoms had theirs. In theory the right of election belonged to the cathedral chapter but that essentially local institution had ever greater difficulty making its wishes prevail in an increasingly cosmopolitan world. Already in the twelfth century it had been those who could make their voice heard at Rome, for the pope must confirm any election as legitimate, who prevailed in a contest and that usually meant the king.

But a bishop chosen, as they usually were, at court found himself forced to deal with a variety of more homely forces within his diocese. The first of these was his own cathedral chapter which had its own officers and seal and very often the largest claim on the landed income of the cathedral church. Most of the canons with whom he had to deal were scions of local burgher families, of local noble families, but sometimes even the king's sons or officials of the papal curia. Although these latter were not ordinarily in residence but merely the recipients of income attached to the canonry, they could give the chapter access to circles uncomfortable for a too ambitious bishop. Bishops had to cope as well with established monasteries in the diocese, which enjoyed a large degree of independence in canon law, and their sometimes conflicting claims to clerical properties and even to the clerical tithe. Then again, of late there had appeared the orders of friars who would contest the monopoly of the secular clergy of the diocese to preach, shrive, marry, and bury and so compete for their income. Lucky was the bishop who did not have a building program to boot.

Scarcely less active and influential were the regular clergy. These were, in the first place, the Benedictine monasteries affiliated with French Burgundian Cluny which had spread through Iberia in the late eleventh and early twelfth century. In the middle of the twelfth century they were joined and not infrequently replaced by the sons of the French monastery of Citeaux about which a new international monastic order was taking shape; Portugal had its Cistercian Alcobaça and Aragon its Poblet and Santes Creus, and Castile its great convent of Cistercian nuns at Las Huelgas in Burgos. Such international organizations had their own links to Rome and home, their own independence of episcopal and sometimes royal control, and their own ambitions for a proper share of the instruction, and of the generosity, of the Christian Iberians. These traditional monastic orders had been joined at the turn of the twelfth century by the more modern friars who modified their liturgical life to allow for a largely urban apostolate of preaching and teaching. San Domingo de Guzmán (d. 1221) was himself a Castilian who had studied at Palencia and had been a canon of Osma so that the Dominican Order of Preachers that he founded struck natural roots in the peninsula. Saint Francis of Assisi (d. 1226) had made his own pilgrimage to Santiago de Compostela in 1213 and Franciscan houses followed the saint himself to the peninsula at small remove. Both orders of friars were marked by the rise of notable convents of women and the life of the regular religious found an almost bewildering variety of expressions over and above those mentioned.

Most spectacular, perhaps, among these were the military orders. The first half of the twelfth century saw the introduction of both Templars and Hospitallers into Iberia and the second half of the period was their greatest time of growth. The thirteenth century, by way of contrast, saw the rise of strictly Iberian military orders. The defensive needs of the La Mancha territories led Sancho III of Castile to entrust Calatrava to religious so inclined in 1158 and their successors were recognized as the Order of Calatrava by Pope Alexander III in 1164. In 1176 Alexander also formally recognized the Order of Alcántara which the necessities of the border in Extremadura had called into being. The Order of Santiago emerged from the same cauldron at Cáceres in 1170 to be encouraged by Fernando II of León and subsequently also by Alfonso VIII of Castile. At Evora in the south of Portugal the same circumstances gave birth to the Order of Avis about 1176. After the conquest of Muslim Andalusia in the thirteenth century, these orders would become the masters and owners of massive tracts of lands there.

Presiding over all of these burgeoning activities and forces were the new monarchical governments of the thirteenth century. Common to all of them was the attempt to establish a territorial government in itself, distinct from the mere operation of the royal fisc, which intention became visible in the creation of *merindades* which were geographical units rather than simply fiscal ones. This entailed, among other things, the coordination and standardization of the activities of local *merinos* or *veguers* by the creation of supervisory officers, one such was the *Merino mayor* instituted for Castile by Alfonso VIII. After the reunion with León in 1230 and the conquest of Andalusia at mid-century, such administrators are appointed for the major areas of Galicia, León, Castile, Murcia, and Andalusia, though they come to be called *Adelantado mayor*. In the crown of Aragon, the analogous office, *Procurador*, was established for each of the historic units, Catalonia, Aragon proper, and Valencia after the conquest. The *Procurador general* was usually the royal heir. In Portugal the lesser size and relatively greater homogeneity of the realm seems to have accommodated a single *mordomo-mor*.

Increasingly the activities of such officials were largely confined to judicial matters as the finances of the realm were entrusted to a separate set of administrators. Although no kingdom essayed a budget during this period, the need for some greater control over royal finances was embodied in such offices as the *Maestre racional* which emerged under Pere II in Aragon and the royal *Almojarife*, or chief tax collector of Alfonso X of Castile. In all realms the actual collection of taxes was farmed to Jewish officials in the thirteenth century and well beyond that time in Castile and Portugal.

Attempts to regularize and rationalize contemporary government were more typical in law than in finance. In Catalonia the *Usatges* were drawn up about 1150 and a century later were translated into Catalan and made the official law code there. Aragon received its *Fuero de Aragon* in 1247 and Valencia its *Furs* in bits and pieces before 1271. In Castile Alfonso X had issued the *Fuero Real* about 1255, intending that it should gradually supersede other law in effect. In Portugal the analogous attempt was made by Alfonso X's grandson, King Dinis (1279–1325).

In general, however, these activities were perceived by their subjects, along with the increased utilization as judges of men trained in the law in the universities, as manipulation of the customary rules of the game and bitterly resisted. Only most gradually did anything like a single royal law strike roots anywhere in the peninsula.

But if the traditional functions of the king were the tending of his own dynastic garden, the maintenance of peace and the administration of justice within the realm, to these were conjoined the leadership of the same realm against its enemies. Changes made in this latter activity were quite uneven over the various realms. In all, of course, armies remained little more than the royal bodyguard in peacetime. Nevertheless, Castile had developed a system of regular, annual payments to those nobles who were thereby required to produce the requisite squadrons quickly when need arose. Partially due to this arrangement, Castile was apparently able to field armies of about 4,000 heavy cavalry regularly in time of war while Aragon struggled to assemble as many as 1,500. Conversely, while both powers paid some attention to naval necessities, the Castilian war fleet ordinarily available seems seldom to have exceeded fifteen galleys of their own and had to be supplemented by hiring from abroad when possible. Aragon must have maintained about thirty or more galleys in some state of readiness and could swell them in wartime from a carefully cultivated merchant marine which its peninsular rival almost entirely lacked. The means of a Portuguese monarchy relegated it to that of a minor power in both categories and gave its kings little reason to innovate in either sphere.

At the center of this growing web of responsibilities was the royal court. As everywhere in Europe it remained peripatetic. The king remained its one indispensable member but the *majordomo*, the *alférez*, and the chancellor of earlier days have been joined by a vice-chancellor and by an assortment of jurists learned in the Roman and canon laws. Various families and clergy had already developed standing claims to one or the other office and the crown had responded by depending often on trusted *familiares* vested with occasional authority to deal with critical matters. Within the *curia regis* itself a special royal council had emerged to expedite the more important executive business and to act as a high court. Indeed Pere II (1196–1213) of Aragon found it necessary to issue the first general Ordinance defining the duties of the various members of the court.

To an unprecedented degree, all business of the court was conducted in writing and the chancery was the essential and one true department that had already emerged. With Alfonso X of Castile the official language of the government became Castilian and Latin was reserved for international correspondence. Portugal adopted the vernacular for its chancery under King Dinis. Because of the greater pluralism of languages in the Aragonese kingdom, Catalan would wait on Latin into the fourteenth century. However, the conquest of the Valencian lands delivered the paper mills of Játiva into the hands of the Aragonese and the chancery of that kingdom quickly began the use of paper rather than parchment for government documents. The greater convenience and economy of the former allowed the practice of keeping registers of copies of official documents there and we begin to have such records about the middle of the thirteenth century for the crown of Aragon.

Both the increased size and the increased activity of the Iberian governments demanded an increase of royal revenue that was to be obtained only with the gravest difficulty in the thirteenth century. Public opinion was conservative in the extreme, demanding that the ruling dynasty live "of its own" just as any other family. The dynasties never had, of course, but their shortfalls were larger and more frequent because the success of the *reconquista* had brought an end to the *parias* which could be exacted from the south, except for those Granada sometimes paid to Castile. The familiar resources of the annual taxes owed by Jewish and Muslim subjects could be and were exploited and the traditional monopolies and tariffs on trade squeezed but the greater activity of the crown and the new world within which it functioned made the old revenues increasingly inadequate. Even the virtually permanent possession of the royal third (*tercias*) of the tithe in the realm of Castile, originally granted to it by the papacy as a crusading concession, and the occasional grant of special permissions to all of the kingdoms to tax church incomes when a war could be presented as a crusade of some sort did not remedy their financial straits.

In that sense, it is no exaggeration to assert that the rise of the representative assembly of the Middle Ages, in Iberia as elsewhere, was a response to a financial crisis. Already in the twelfth century one can detect, in a rough way, the increasing tendency of the crown to secure more widespread support for the most important policies or initiatives by summoning more and more magnates and prelates to court. The resulting larger meetings were sometimes called a "general curia" or a "general council" by the chroniclers. The practice will continue but when townsmen as well are summoned to attend them we are wont to call them *cortes* or *corts*. It appears that the first such assembly in Iberia took place in León in 1188 on the troubled accession of Alfonso IX. While the record is not entirely clear, by the first quarter of the thirteenth century such meetings are being held in all of the Iberian kingdoms. They treat of questions of war and peace, of the royal succession and of dynastic marriage but above all they meet to consider the crown's request for a special grant-in-aid. Most frequently, to obtain his funds the king had to promise that he would not debase the currency for a stipulated period, often seven years.

This new institution can claim to represent the realm in a particular way. It will come to have its own organization; usually the three houses of clergy, nobles, and burghers, each with their own speaker. They will develop their own procedures; meeting jointly to hear the requests of the crown from the royal chancellor and to deliver their own petitions for redress of grievance, deliberating separately on the crown's agenda, and reassembling with the other houses to respond to the latter. These assemblies will come to validate the credentials of their own members and to keep records of their own proceedings. They will, at various times, attempt to control the selection of royal ministers, the disbursement of royal revenues, the implementation of royal policies, and even the business of their own regular convocation, without obtaining final success in any one of these. Nevertheless, by 1300 the *cortes* have become not only a central institution but also a symbol of the realm in a degree second only to that of the king himself.

THOUGHT, ITS VEHICLES, AND ITS ENVELOPES

One cannot reflect too often on the fact that knowledge, in the society which concerns us here, was still above all what one's father, mother, grandparents, priest, rabbi, or *imām* had told one. It was practical in content; how to make the land yield its fruit, how to make a barrel or a pair of shoes, how to deliver a child or roast a hare, or how to placate the "God of Hosts" and so win through to a better life beyond. The mode of communication of all of these things was oral. Letters were another and mysterious world, for most somewhat frivolous and somewhat suspect. Most people came into contact with it only through the notary, the judge, the cleric, and sometimes more pleasantly through the wandering minstrel both in and out of the court of the local noble, bishop, or even king when he passed through with his entourage.

The overwhelming majority of people, then, lived in three mental worlds. The first was constituted by the nature to which they lived so close. It was the vegetative round of life, death, and life again that provided their sustenance, conditioned their everyday life, and dominated their mental images. In it everything was in motion but nothing ever changed permanently. Within the peasant world life was a mysterious gift, but a hard one, from mysterious powers that must constantly be placated. The second world was that of religion. The three monotheisms of the peninsula all asserted that the world of nature was a creation of God, that human beings were His special concern, and that as they served Him so would He reward them ultimately. But all three faiths were closely attuned, in their liturgical rhythms and ritual practices, to the round of the natural year. Their Scriptures drew their analogies, their ethical examples, from that background, which illustrations they then presented to the faithful in the oral form of the sermon. Except for their common assertion of a historical beginning and of a final apocalypse, none of them did much directly to modify the conception of human existence as an eternal round.

The third mental world of the ordinary Iberian was, however, the kaleidoscopic and fabulous one of the occasional passing traveler, the itinerant minstrel, the court of the local abbot, bishop, noble, and above all of the king or prince. Indeed, so changeable was this world that preachers of all the faiths inveighed against it as a deception and an illusion for the ordinary faithful from which they should resolutely turn their gaze to meditate on the eternal verity of the faith.

Nonetheless the Christian church had itself become a part of that process of change in a fashion that was observable even by the humblest of its adherents. Iberian Islam or Judaism might experience change as decay or disaster but the Christian saw it as triumph or even progress. Moreover, aside from the successes of the *reconquista* itself, the age saw the great pilgrimage to Santiago de Compostela reach its apogee. Counts, bishops, royalty, from beyond the Pyrenees made their way along the *camino de Santiago* in numbers substantial enough to bring a glimpse of a wider world to all along their path. An Englishman became bishop of Lisbon, French quarters became familiar in most large Castilian and Aragonese towns, and whole towns passed under the control of French nobles in Aragon and Catalonia while Genoese and Pisan sailors and merchants pressed into the seaports of the latter. In the most striking and durable reminder of all, everywhere in the peninsula old churches were torn down and rebuilt in new styles no less than twice as the French Romanesque succeeded the Mozarabic in the twelfth century and then the French Gothic succeeded the Romanesque in the thirteenth. Most spectacularly this occurred in Castile where great Gothic piles rose majestically at Toledo, Burgos, and León in the thirteenth century.

Still, the impact of even such dramatic change was limited by the fact that neither the popular nor the formal learning of the time offered much of an intellectual context to accommodate it. The popular poets and minstrels whose works were accessible to the common folk, be they Muslim, Jewish, or Christian, sang of the eternal themes of love and nature whether they sang in Arabic, Gallegan, or Catalan. The one form that they all utilized, the *zajal* derived from Muslim literature, would not have impressed them for they were ignorant of its derivation. Another popular form was the poetic glorification of war and noble prowess and manners. As early as Alfons II in Aragon and Fernando II in Castile the royal court itself patronized the bards and both of those monarchs are supposed to have tried their own hand at composition. But the genres of *gesta* and Romance, which also would have reached the populace in some measure, supplied only a fabulous background of King Arthur, Charlemagne, and Alexander the Great.

In the world of formal learning the twelfth and thirteenth centuries were ever more marked by a Christian predominance which mirrored, in its own way, the arena of politics. That is, Jewish and Muslim literature and thought continued to be dominated by the traditional themes and interests and their institutional basis functioned unchanged, if in a contracting sphere. On the other hand, the formal learning of the Christian kingdoms continued to be marked by institutional development and a reaching beyond its own traditional form and content to assimilate the products of both Europe beyond the Pyrenees and of Islam and Judaism within the peninsula.

Elsewhere in western Europe in the twelfth century some of the cathedral schools were developing more or less spontaneously into the medieval universities. That transfiguration was reflected in Iberia too but in a tardier and more artificial fashion. There may have been some natural growth of that sort at Palencia before it was recognized by Alfonso VIII of Castile in 1214 and again at Salamanca before Alfonso XI of León began to patronize it in 1218 but it is hard to specify in either case. In any event, Palencia hardly survived the century while Salamanca was to have a brilliant future. In Portugal King Dinis established a university at Lisbon which had a most chequered history, moving back and forth between that metropolis and Coimbra. In 1300 Jaume II of Aragon erected the first university in that realm at Lérida. All of these foundations owed their beginnings largely to the contemporary royal interest in the promotion of the study of Roman and canon law which long monopolized graduate studies at them. Even then, bishops and cathedral chapters preferred to send their most promising students abroad to study theology at Paris or law at Bologna.

In the peninsula the pursuit of theology flourished rather within the schools, or colleges, established by the mendicant orders of Dominicans and Franciscans at their most important convents. To these two new orders, as well, the age owed its most remarkable educational experiment, the study of the Arabic language. Arabic had been, of course, one of the working languages of the peninsula and some Christians had always known it. Castilian, like all of the peninsular languages absorbed a great deal of the vocabulary of Arabic and most of those 4,000 or more borrowed terms seem to have entered the former in and after the thirteenth century. But even the formal study of Arabic was given new impetus in the latter thirteenth with the inclusion of large numbers of Muslims in the kingdoms swollen by the reconquest of Valencia, Murcia, and Andalusia. Both friars and kings were much interested in Arabic as a tool of conversion. The Dominicans opened schools of Arabic studies in Murcia in Castile, at Valencia and Játiva in Aragon, and even briefly in Tunisia. Ramon Lull persuaded Jaume II of Majorca to sponsor a Franciscan school of Arabic there in 1276. By and large, these schools would disappear in the fourteenth century as the resistance of the Muslim community to even the best-versed missionaries became clear.

At the same time, the knowledge as well as the language and form of Islam was the object of great interest, especially at the court of Alfonso X *el Sabio* (1252–1284) of Castile. In part this movement simply continued the great age of translations begun in the twelfth century at Toledo. There in the thirteenth, and under the patronage of Archbishop Rodrigo Jiménez de Rada (1208–1247), the science of antiquity and Islam continued to be rendered into Latin by scholars such as Michael the Scot and Herman of Germany. But for the first time, under the patronage of the king himself, works on subjects as various as astronomy, government, ethics, literature, and chess were being rendered from the Arabic into Castilian, leading to the rapid development of that language as a formal intellectual tool.

Contemporaneously, the court had an enormous effect on literary development as well. Alfonso X himself was directly involved in the production of the *Cantigas de Santa Maria* which combined hundreds of lively tales of the Virgin and her devotees with musical scores and unselfconscious miniatures by way of illustration in a volume written in Gallegan, the Iberian language of poetry at the time. The work had a large impact in the literary circles of the day. In the realm of historical writing, the court made notable contributions as well. The reign of Fernando III of Castile had seen the appearance of the *Chronicon Mundi* by Bishop Lucas of Túy closely followed by Rodrigo Jiménez de Rada's *De Rebus Hispaniae*. The good archbishop also found time to do a *Historia Arabum*. These came to be complemented at the court of Alfonso X by a history of Spain, the *Primera crónica general*, and by a universal chronicle, the *General Estoria*, both done in Castilian. It is notable that from Lucas of Túy's *Chronicon* onward these histories of Iberia were written as the history of the separate Christian realms rather than as the history of a single political society.

The exigencies of contemporary government also had their part to play in the scholarly activity of the court. The newly swollen realm of Castile already in the time of Fernando III led him to arrange a translation of the Visigothic law code, the *Liber Judiciorum*, into Castilian as the *Fuero Juzgo*. Under the same stimulus, Alfonso X saw to the preparation of a variety of law codes in Castilian, from the *Fuero Real*, to the *Especulo de las leyes*, and finally to the famous collection of legal philosophy and essays known as the *Siete partidas*. Most of this latter work would not come to be embodied in the actual usages of the courts for more than another half-century but the achievement would not be lost.

Alfonso X seems to have envisaged himself as a sort of "royal troubador" and in this he conformed to what was transpiring in the contemporary crown of Aragon as well. The developments there were somewhat less extensive but were solid nonetheless. From the time of Alfons II (1162–1196) the kings of Aragon had been patrons of the Provençal troubadors and he and his successors at least played at poetic composition personally. As we have already seen, they presided as well over the elaboration of a series of general law codes for Aragon, Valencia, and Catalonia. Jaume I, the Conqueror (1213–1276), not only followed closely what was occurring at the court of his son-in-law, Alfonso X, but was the only medieval king up to this point to leave us an autobiography, the *Libre dels feyts*, written in Catalan. His patronage also lay behind the foundation of the friars' schools of Arabic in his realm.

Turning from the learning of the courts of the time to that diffused throughout society, it is difficult to distinguish the two areas very sharply. In general one may assert that formal learning remained distinctive only of the clergy. Still, the higher clergy often were former court figures, indeed, had secured their episcopal appointments as a result of their position at court, and continued a close relationship with it. So, for example, we have Bishop Vidal de Canyelles of Huesca who compiled the *Fueros de Aragon*, promulgated in 1247, and the great Dominican, Ramón de Penyafort (1175–1257), whose *Decretals* and *Summa de casibus* in canon law can hardly be separated from his active life so closely supported by the court of Aragon. Similar figures in Castile are the historians Lucas of Túy who became bishop of that tiny frontier town and the lordly Rodrigo Jiménez de Rada who wrote while primate of Iberia and close collaborator of the crown in the work of the *reconquista*. Occasionally the process might be reversed as with Vincentius Hispanus who was a master at Bologna and ended as archbishop of Braga.

At the same time there is more than enough evidence that illiteracy in Latin still marked at least a fair proportion of the cathedral canons who were, supposedly, the most educated portion of the secular clergy even when the former could read the vernacular, as illustrated by the translation of summaries of theology into the latter for their benefit. There were also translations of the Bible into Castilian from both the Hebrew and the Latin and into Catalan from the Latin. Probably this was a side effect of the rise of systematic theology in the schools, a change that made the Latin at once more professional and less relevant for ordinary pastoral work. Still, one suspects that the ordinary parish clergy would rarely have known more Latin than was essential for liturgical purposes and that largely simply memorized. By and large, the outstanding learned clerical figures of the age were friars such as Ramón de Penyafort or his fellow Dominican Ramón Martí (d. 1286) who was fluent in both Hebrew and

Arabic, was active in court-sponsored attempts to convert the Jews, and authored not only a *Pugio fidei contra Judaeos* but also an Arabic–Latin vocabulary.

Yet it would be incorrect to imagine that formal learning was simply confined to the clergy. One of the greatest figures of the age was Ramón Lull (d. 1315) who began as a minor noble at the court of Jaume I and never did become a cleric although his life changed abruptly after he experienced a religious conversion. Lull largely taught himself although he was familiar with the universities. He became a master of Arabic and wrote in both it and Catalan while his Latin remained simple and it was his devotees who translated his works into the latter. The great purpose of his later writings and life was the conversion of the Muslim, to which end he traveled from Paris and Rome to Tunis and Cyprus. He became conversant with the religious and philosophical thought of Islam and his writings aimed to convert them by rational discussion; he brought about the foundation of a school of Arabic studies on Majorca, and, in his *Liber de Fine*, advocated a crusade to recover the Holy Land.

Still, contemporary Islam largely ignored Lull while he became famous in Iberia and western Europe. He could and did write love poetry in the Provençal style. His *Libre del Orde de la Cavalleria* dealt with the knightly ideal as it should be informed by the Christian faith. In his *Ars Magna Generalis Ultima* Lull attempted a highly original resolution of the tension between a philosophical faith and one based upon Revelation. In the *Art de Contemplacio* he wrote as a Christian mystic but with some Sufic influence obvious. Finally, he was famous for his novel, *Blanquerna*, that now furnishes the historian with an invaluable mirror of the late thirteenth century.

The very range of Lull's genius makes him unique, of course, but he was not alone as an educated layman in his age. Arnau de Vilanova (d. 1311) was a famous physician at the courts of Pere III and Jaume II of Aragon. He had studied medicine at Naples and Montpellier and taught at the latter university. Arnau was a controversial figure in his own age for his attacks on corruption within the church and even wrote a tract, *De Adventu Antichristi et Fine Mundi*, predicting that it would bring about the Apocalypse in the mid-fourteenth century. Nevertheless, he was an accomplished physician and scholar, able to read Arabic and Hebrew and fully conversant with classical and Islamic medicine. In addition to his roughly seventy translations he also wrote a variety of original medical works.

There was, of course, a host of poetic works which may have been popular in their origins but were being reduced to a written form at the time, doubtless often by laymen. Cases in point are the more scholarly but still popular histories of the day, strongly informed by local or regional feeling. The *Acts of the Counts of Barcelona* seem to have been written by a priest attached to the monastery of Ripoll in Catalonia, but the chronicler Bernat Desclot (d. 1288) who wrote of the glories of the crown of Aragon under Jaume I and Pere III was a layman and probably a minor noble. The first form, the *Costums*, of the *Libre del Consolat del Mar* were done about 1230 and were certainly due to lay initiative at least.

In Castile a mere secular priest attached to the monastery of San Millán de la Cogolla, Gonzalo de Berceo (d. 1250), became the foremost poet of his age writing *vitae* of San Millán and of Santo Domingo de Silos as well as his most famous *Milagros de Nuestra Señora*. The *Poema de Fernán González*, written about mid-century, has been attributed to a monk of San Pedro de Arlanza but breathed the popular air of Castile and Castilian chauvinism. There too popular poetry was being written down as well as composed but, outside of the court, we do not have lay figures of the type of a Lull or Arnau in the Christian community. On the shores of the Atlantic in Portugal, these developments were generally weaker still and often a good fifty years later in their appearance. All regions of the peninsula had their vernacular religious narratives, of course, although we are ignorant of their authorship and a religious drama in Latin. The nuns of Las Huelgas in Burgos even pioneered the use of French liturgical music in Castile.

But although we may see the novelty of portions of popular literature, for contemporaries such borrowings, once accomplished, blended rapidly with the traditional and became almost immediately indistinguishable from it. The sense of motion or change was negligible. As for the formal learning of the day, all in all, we may say that despite its brilliance and variety, it remained yet a closed world, minimal in its impact upon the society in formation around it. Dynamic as it was in its continuing absorption of Islamic and Jewish philosophy, science, and medicine, that inheritance would remain encapsulated in the scholarly and professional community to affect future society far more than its contemporary one.

6

THE EVOLUTION OF THE MEDIEVAL ORDER IN IBERIA

For the historian the treatment of the fourteenth and fifteenth centuries in Europe presents a series of particularly difficult problems. From the collapse of the Holy Roman Empire in Germany and Italy to the Hundred Years War in France, from the decline of the Plantagenet in England to the tragedies of the Avignonese papacy and the Great Western Schism of the Christian church the period often seems to be one of unrelieved decline that finds a successful issue only in the birth of the modern world about the beginning of the sixteenth century. One, or more even, of these crises and convulsions could be blinked but their concurrence and universality would seem to require a more general explanation which nonetheless continues to elude us. To simply conclude that "time is out of joint" is more satisfying emotionally than intellectually and mystical Spenglerian hypotheses of organic growth and decline in civilizations distance themselves rather too much from the data to be accommodated.

So much, at least, needs to be said by way of context for the Iberian experience of the period. Whatever the possibilities had been for peninsular society at the end of the Roman period, by 1300 it had been increasingly a part of the medieval west for at least four centuries. Its rhythms, from the steady growth of population, to the emergence of Christian dynastic monarchy, to the rebirth of towns, and to the rise of parliaments, had substantially mirrored those of the wider west. With its own particularity, its "time of troubles" would do so as well. Nevertheless the crises of the times were largely those of a by then traditional growth and unrealistic ambition which overreached the practical possibilities.

A case in point is the attempt of Alfonso X of Castile to secure the office of Holy Roman Emperor after 1256. The Hohenstaufen emperor Frederick II had died in 1250, Conrad his son and successor lived only until 1254, leaving the throne in turn to his infant son, Conradin (1254–1268), but papal fears had raised an anti-emperor against both and the bastard son of Frederick II, Manfred (1254–1266), actually ruled the old Norman kingdom of southern Italy and Sicily. Alfonso X had, in the circumstances, a perfectly proper claim to seek the imperial election. In 1219 his father, Fernando III, had married Beatrice of Swabia, grand-daughter of Frederick I Hohenstaufen, at Burgos. The logic of dynastic politics and the growing interrelationship of all of the western European kingdoms gave a lunatic plausibility at least to Alfonso's quest for the imperial dignity, pursued for twenty years and at great cost until the papal sponsorship of the first Hapsburg emperor in 1273 finally convinced even Alfonso of its futility.

Quite as traditional as dynastic aggrandizement was the hallowed pursuit of the *reconquista*. Here, one thinks, Alfonso X might well have been grateful for a respite. With the fall of Seville in 1248 the last of the great Iberian river basins had been effectively appropriated by the Christian kingdoms. What remained of Iberian Islam had been reduced to the vassal *taifa* of Granada, some modest and scattered cities along the Atlantic seaboard, and the semi-occupied territory of Murcia. From the eastern highlands about Baeza and Ubeda to the lush flats about Seville almost 300 kilometers to the west the major problem, as the Muslims fled or were expelled in good number to Muslim North Africa or Muslim Granada, was to find Christian peasants to till the land, Christian merchants and artisans to fill the cities, and nobles and churchmen to root the framework of settled life. However traditional, further advance would risk only the collapse of that achieved so recently.

Moreover, that North Africa from which so many threats had issued in the last two centuries was in the throes of political disintegration. On the heels of their expulsion from Iberia the Muwāhhid dynasty and sect was collapsing at home as well. Their last attempts to rule perished with the defeat and death of the Caliph al-Sāid when he attempted to reduce Tlemcen to obedience in 1248. Farther east the Hafsid governors of Tunisia had already asserted their practical independence in 1229. In 1236 the emir, Abū Zakariyya, arrogated the title of caliph and the mantle of leadership of the Muwāhhid religious movement to himself, asserting that the dynasty of Marrakesh had strayed from the one, true path. Under his son and successor, Abū Abd Allah Muhammad al-Mustansir (1249–1277), the Hafsid empire grew to include Tripolitania, and Algeria west beyond Constantine to Bougie and Algiers. With varying fortunes the regime so founded would endure past the reign of Uthman (1435–1488) into the period of the coming of Ottoman power to the west.

In western Algeria the former governor of Tlemcen, Yaghmurāsan ibn Zayyan (1235–1283), cast off the Muwāhhid yoke and seized Oran and Sijilmāsa as well as founding a new Zayyānid dynasty. Unlike the Hafsid in Tunisia, the Zayyānid at Tlemcen repudiated Muwāhhid teaching as well as the dynasty and based their Islam on a thoroughly Mālikite orthodoxy and the support of the Zanāta Berbers of which the family represented a minor branch. Though often severely squeezed by their neighbors to east and west, the Zayyānids also survived down till the coming of the Ottomans in the modern period although the kingdom was seldom of real importance after the fourteenth century.

The most proximate of the new Muslim regimes to Iberia was that established by the Banū Marin in Morocco. These were another Zanāta Berber people who had begun to infiltrate Morocco under the Muwāhhid who sometimes employed them as mercenaries. After the defeat of the Caliph al-Sāid near Tlemcen in 1236 they began a struggle of some thirty years which only ended with their conquest of Marrakesh itself in 1269. Under Abū Yūsuf Yakūb (1258–1286) the Marīnids established a new capital at a refounded Fez. The Marīnids now became the most energetic of the successors to the Muwāhhids and for the next century would threaten to absorb Zayyānid Tlemcen and sometimes even Hafsid Tunisia. Internal decline set in from the mid-fourteenth century, however, and neither the dynasty nor its internal rivals, the Wattāsids who replaced them in 1472, were able to maintain a strong government thereafter.

All through this period Muslim North Africa was experiencing more than simply a political decline. It appears that its population was shrinking in absolute terms and that the land under cultivation was also contracting as the flocks of the desert nomads encroached upon it. Indeed, this phenomenon gave rise to the brilliant speculations of the Muslim historian and philosopher, ibn Khaldún (1322–1406), about the relationships between settled agricultural peoples and wandering pastoral ones. Paradoxically, however, this period saw an ever more thorough Arabicization of the Berber peoples of North Africa and, in the end, their more thorough rooting in Islam as well through the medium of both a restored and fundamentalist Mālikite orthodoxy in the towns and villages and a strong Sufic missionary Islam that spread through the more remote and nomadic peoples. Under such conditions these Berber kingdoms experienced no institutional development, their fundamental structure remained tribal with an overlay of religious authority as cement, and their armies consisted largely of nomad or Christian mercenaries whose loyalty was at purchase to the dynasty.

Despite the fact that none of the developments across the straits boded anything but more respite to Castile, Alfonso X saw the African disorder as opportunity. Further conquest beckoned irresistibly as the main chance not to be missed. In 1259 he attacked and took Cádiz, in 1260 an expeditionary force descended on Salé in Morocco and sacked it, and Niebla in lower Andalusia was taken in 1262. Under these circumstances, Muhammad I of Granada entered into a conspiracy with the subject Muslim population of Andalusia and Murcia which rose in a great insurrection in 1264. Alfonso had to appeal to his father-in-law, Jaume I of Aragon, who subdued Murcia for him while he invaded Granada. Everywhere the rising was put down and new expulsions and emigrations of the Andalusian and Murcian Muslims took place further retarding the recovery of that region.

In 1275 while Alfonso was parleying with the pope in France over the question of the imperial title, Abū Yūsuf and the Marīnids entered into a pact with Muhammad II of Granada, who ceded Tarifa and Algeciras to them. The Marīnids then landed in Iberia and raided as far east as Cordova while the Granadans threatened Jaén. Alfonso's eldest son, Fernando de la Cerda, died on campaign against them, the Christian forces were routed and the *adelantado de la frontera*, Nuño González de Lara, killed. Although the Marīnids withdrew after six months they now possessed ports of entry to the peninsula and they would return in 1277 and 1282 as North African circumstances permitted.

The sole benefit that accrued to Castile from the episode was that Alfonso X was moved to a more pacific policy with his continental neighbors thereby. Prior to it he had already given up his claims to Gascony in negotiations with Henry III of England. Alfonso agreed that his rights should be vested in his daughter, Leonor, who would then marry Henry's son, Edward. In the peninsula proper, Alfonso by 1256 had dropped his demands against the new king of Navarre, Thibault II (1253–1270). During the revolt of Andalusia the Castilian monarch placated Afonso III of Portugal, when he solved the border question by ceding all claims to the Portuguese Algarve in 1264.

Nonetheless, the Marīnid invasion of 1275 had left a fatal legacy in the form of a succession dispute to the Castilian house. The centralizing policies of the king, his ambitious international plans, and the funds necessary to pay for these two, had already led to disaffection headed by the great nobles and even his own brothers, some of whom took refuge in Granada and then in Aragon. Now, in 1275 his eldest son and heir, Fernando de la Cerda, died on campaign in Andalusia. The sons of

Fernando and his wife Blanche, the daughter of Louis IX of France whom he had married in 1269, were the *infantes de la Cerda* and they were now the presumptive heirs of Alfonso X. But the latter's other son, Sancho, had undertaken the struggle against the Marīnids in Andalusia with some success and claimed the right of succession for himself. The *cortes* of 1278 supported Sancho's claim and Alfonso X finally admitted it himself.

However, Queen Violante, Blanche of France, and her sons the *infantes*, sought refuge in Aragon. For the remaining six years of his reign Alfonso turned one way and the other in attempts to solve the inheritance problem while satisfying France, Aragon, Sancho, and their respective partisans. In the *cortes* of 1282 Sancho usurped the reins of government while his father retired to Seville and called in the Marīnids to support him. The latter raided north even into the valley of the Tajo and Alfonso gave them the crown of Fernando III as surety for their expenses. When Alfonso X died on April 4, 1284, he disinherited Sancho, leaving his kingdom to Alfonso de la Cerda, eldest of Fernando's sons, and *appanages* or dependent realms in Seville and Murcia for his own younger sons, Juan and Jaime.

Sancho IV (1284–1295) yet managed to block his father's desires and to rule the kingdom until his own death. Still, his supporters against his father among the nobility claimed their rewards and the powerful houses of Haro and Lara might have controlled the realm completely but for their rivalry with one another. The king was hampered as well by the fact that his marriage with his cousin, Maria de Molina, was not recognized by the papacy as licit until 1301, well after his death, and so their sons were officially illegitimate. That strengthened the still active claims of the *infantes de la Cerda*. He did succeed, by allying with the Nasrid of Granada and with Aragon, in capturing Tarifa in 1294 and momentarily at least in excluding the Marīnid from the peninsula.

His son, Fernando IV (1295–1312), succeeded at nine years of age and only the strength of his mother, Maria de Molina, saved his throne. He secured his legitimization by the pope and took advantage of the divisions of his enemies, especially the houses of Lara and Haro. In 1304 Aragon was brought to abandon its support of the *infantes de la Cerda* by the cession of northern Murcia. But when Fernando himself died at twenty-six he left a one-year-old son to inherit.

During the long minority of Alfonso XI (1312–1350) Castile continued to be run by Maria de Molina, her younger son, and her brother-in-law. After the death of the two latter in 1319 and of the old queen herself in 1321 the lesser members of the royal family almost divided the realm in halves in their bids for support. That order survived at all was due to the basic strength of the dynastic monarchy as an ideal and that of the society of the kingdom as a whole. When he assumed personal rule in 1325 the new king considered that he had little alternative but to resort to the outright murder of former advisors in order to free himself from them and their fellow conspirators. In his domestic policy the new king now imposed the procedures of Roman law on the whole kingdom by the *Ordenamiento de Alcalá* of 1348. The *Siete Partidas* of his greatgrandfather, Alfonso X, were now added officially to royal and local law. Royal judges traveling on circuit through the realm were instituted and all castles were declared to be subject to royal control. To support his new and ambitious framework of royal action the king decreed the enactment of a general sales tax, *alcabala*, on all business transactions throughout the kingdom.

The king also returned to the business of the *reconquista*. During his minority success had rested largely with the Muslims of Granada and two of his regents and relatives perished at their hands in 1319 when a Castilian counteroffensive against the Nasrid had miscarried. As Alfonso XI gradually bolstered his authority at home and reinforced Andalusia after 1325, however, the Granadans decided once again to appeal to the Marīnid in Morocco for assistance. At that time the latter were led by Emir Abū al-Hasan (1331–1351) who was the last of their great rulers. Al-Hasan was to conquer the Zayyānid kingdom of Tlemcen in 1337 and that of the Hafsid in Tunisia in 1347. When his forces first intervened in Andalusia they were victorious there as well. In 1333 they retook Gibraltar which was one of the few places conquered by Castile during the reign of Fernando IV. A truce followed for six years but in 1339 the fighting resumed and the Emir's son was killed in battle. A Castilian fleet was defeated in the straits in 1340 and that cleared the way for al-Hasan himself to cross the peninsula with a great army.

In September of 1340 the Marīnid, joined by forces of Yūsuf I of Granada (1333–1354), laid siege to the fortress and port of Tarifa at the narrows of the Straits of Gibraltar with an army that has been said to number almost 70,000. Whatever the accuracy of that, Alfonso XI came to the relief of the port with an army numbered at 8,000 horse and 12,000 foot, which is large for the day but at least imaginable. He was accompanied by Afonso IV of Portugal (1325–1357) with another 1,000 horse, again a large but possible figure. The two forces came together on October 30, 1340 at Río Salado and both resorted to their ordinary tactics. The Christian host charged frontally, counting upon the weight of their horses and armor to shatter the Muslim center. It seems to have had some effect but a Marīnid counterattack threatened to envelop the Christian line when a sally of the garrison of Tarifa struck the former's rear and reduced their ranks to utter confusion. Abū al-Hasan escaped to Algeciras and then to Morocco and Yūsuf I to Granada but the Muslim infantry perished on the field and its cavalry fared not much better. The victory at Río Salado marked the end of the great North African interventions in Iberia.

Two years later Alfonso undertook the siege of Algeciras itself to bolster further the defenses of Iberia against the Africans. The struggle lasted until the port surrendered on March 26, 1344 to a force which had included at various times not just the army of Castile but volunteers from Navarre, Aragon, Gascony, and even England. A Catalan fleet had assisted with the necessary blockade. Alfonso XI then attempted to complete the sealing off of the Iberian side of the straits by the capture of Gibraltar, whose siege he began in 1349 with the aid of Catalan ships and troops. However, the arrival of the bubonic plague in the peninsula, in the army before Gibraltar, and the death of Alfonso XI himself in the camp on Good Friday of 1350 resulted in the breaking up of that effort.

The urge to continue the *reconquista* was much less in evidence in the territories of the crown of Aragon. Jaume I did respond to the plea of his son-in-law of Castile during the great rising of 1264 and intervened to pacify Murcia. Doubtless the alternative would have been to encourage the recently conquered Muslim majority of Valencia to join the rebels. To be sure, the great Marīnid invasion of Andalusia in 1275 did supply the incentive for a general Muslim revolt in the former that outlasted the life of Jaume himself. In 1287 Alfons III (1285–1291) rounded out his hold on the Balearics by the conquest of the formerly vassal kingdom of Minorca and enslaved its Muslim people. Jaume II (1291–1327) extorted the northern portion of Murcia from the regents of Fernando IV of Castile in 1304 and then went on to cooperate with that king in 1309 in a joint war with Granada in which the latter besieged Algeciras and the former Almeria. Both attacks failed, the Almerian one disastrously, and it marked the last Aragonese attempt on Granada. The assistance rendered by Pere IV (1336–1387) to Alfonso XI's assaults on Algeciras and Gibraltar were inspired by the desire to break the power of the Marīnids at sea and their hold on Tlemcen which kingdom was a major trading center for Aragon in North Africa.

Jaume I also had resisted the temptation to rebuild a Catalan empire in the Midi where Capetian influence had grown steadily after the defeat and death of his father, Pere II, at Muret in 1213. By the treaty of Corbeil with Louis IX of France in 1258 the Aragonese monarch renounced his claims to Toulouse, Narbonne, Carcassonne, Béziers, Foix, Nimes, and Albi. In return the French king, as successor to the Carolingians, renounced any claims of his to Barcelona, Gerona, Vich, Urgel, Empúries, Cerdanya, Conflent, and Roselló. Charles of Anjou, brother of Louis IX, had earlier married the heiress of Ramón Berenguer V of Provence, which province had marked the easternmost holdings of the house of Barcelona for almost a century and a half. Jaume of Aragon now renounced his claims on Provence in benefit of the Capetians and the daughter of Ramón Berenguer V, Margaret. Finally, the bargain was sealed by the betrothal of Jaume's daughter, Isabel, to Louis IX's son and heir, Philip.

As we have seen, Jaume I's efforts had gone into the conquest of the nearby Balearics and then contiguous Valencia. But despite his caution, he was to leave the crown of Aragon a fateful legacy in the western Mediterranean. In 1262 he arranged the marriage of his eldest son, Pere, to Constance, the daughter of Manfred, bastard son of Frederick II Hohenstaufen, ruler of southern Italy and Sicily. Protests from the papacy and Charles of Anjou, who were deep in intrigue over the fate of those lands, was immediate but Jaume assured them that he had no designs upon the latter territories. To be sure, Aragon made no moves when in 1265–1266, with the blessing of Pope Clement IV, Charles of Anjou invaded them, defeated and killed Manfred at Benevento, then Conradin at Tagliacozza in 1268, and subsequently became king of the old Norman realm of Sicily and a papal vassal.

All of this appeared to be of little import for Aragon had already realized the prestige accruing to the crown from a foreign marriage. Especially so when Jaume I so early as 1262 divided his realms, leaving Aragon, Valencia, and most of Catalonia to his eldest son, Pere III (1276–1285), but Cerdanya, Roselló, Montpellier, and the Balearics to his second son, Jaume II (1276–1311), who took the title of "King of Majorca." The latter was later forced by Pere to do homage as his vassal. With the division the temptation of a Mediterranean policy would seem to have evaporated for the crown of Aragon itself. Nothing was further from the fact.

Pere III, married to Constance of Sicily, had every intention of asserting his dynastic claim to that territory from the outset of his reign. However, the concerns of his first few years were to put down the revolt of the Valencian Muslims that he had inherited from his father. He had also to deal with a revolt of the barons of Catalonia. Both had been resolved by 1280. He then turned to an alliance with Castile, effected by 1281.

By this time Charles of Anjou and his French retainers had made themselves thoroughly hated in the new Italian territories. In addition, a new level of taxation had been imposed there to support the other ambitions of Charles, which aims included nothing less than an attempt to conquer the Byzantine Empire itself. The Byzantine emperor, Michael VIII, sought allies against the coalition Charles was assembling, which cabal included Pope Martin IV (1281–1285) and the French nobility in control in the Pelopponese since the Fourth Crusade. Naturally the emperor encouraged Pere III to strike at Charles' rear and promised him financial aid if the Aragonese did so. In 1281 Pere prepared an expedition officially destined for a crusade against the Hafsid emir of Tunisia. Still, when the conspirators on the island rose in the "Sicilian Vespers" on Easter Monday in March of 1282 and slaughtered French officials and garrisons all over the island, the Aragonese monarch seems to have been as surprised as was Charles of Anjou himself. Pere's fleet and army sailed for Africa in June but it was not until the end of August that he landed in Sicily at the invitation of the rebels. By that time the Angevin had failed in his summer campaign to retake the island but he had convinced the rebels that their only viable course was to throw themselves into the arms of Aragon.

Thus began the Aragonese empire at sea in the Mediterranean. Since Charles of Anjou was his ally and Sicily was formally a papal fief, Pope Martin excommunicated and deposed Pere and awarded his kingdom to Charles of Valois, son of Philip III of France. The latter was encouraged to invade Aragon to carry out the papal sentence. That French invasion took place in 1285 and failed despite the sympathies of much of the baronage of Aragon proper and of Pere's brother, Jaume II of Majorca. But in November of the same year Pere died when about to launch an invasion of Majorca to punish his brother.

The king had left the crown of Aragon to his eldest son, Alfons II (1285–1291), who carried out his father's planned invasion and overran the Balearics, reuniting them to his own kingdom. The new kingdom of Sicily had been passed to a second son, Jaume. The outrage of the papacy and of the house of Anjou continued, of course, and the lands of Aragon lay under papal interdict for ten years. Alfons had violent troubles with his nobility at home but both he and his brother maintained themselves, although shortly before his death Alfons had to agree to desert his brother's cause, make a pilgrimage of penitence to Rome, and then a crusade to the Near East. Instead of any of this happening the king died in 1291 and his brother suddenly was the ruler of all of the Aragonese territories, Sicily included.

Jaume II of Aragon (1291–1327) used every resource of diplomacy to maintain his position but finally yielded, it appeared, to his enemies at the Treaty of Anagni in 1295. There he surrendered his claim to the Balearics and they were returned to his uncle, Jaume II of Majorca. He made his peace with the French and a marriage to Blanche, daughter of Charles II of Naples, ensued. He also agreed to help to return Sicily to the house of Anjou but his brother, Frederick, who had been his viceroy there refused to accept that decision and had himself crowned king at Palermo in 1296.

But as part of the settlement Pope Boniface VIII (1294–1313) already had recognized Jaume as king of Sardinia and Corsica.

Jaume II did honor his promise to the papacy to the extent of campaigning against his brother, Frederick of Sicily (1296–1337), in 1298 and 1299 but without decisive effect and Sicily remained an adjunct of the house of Aragon. The king also took seriously his new papal titles and intrigued long and hard to make them a reality. Yet it was not until 1323 that he was able to despatch a fleet and army which carried out the subjugation of Sardinia.

The keystone to this structure was restored by Pere IV (1336–1387) of Aragon when he decided that the opposition of the cadet branch of the dynasty on Majorca was no longer tolerable. In 1342 he summoned Jaume III (1324–1343) of Majorca to his court and when the latter did not appear he was condemned as a rebel vassal and his fiefs declared confiscate. Pere IV then sailed to Majorca and overran it quickly and subsequently Jaume's mainland possessions in Cerdanya and Roselló were conquered as well. In the following year Pere solemnly proclaimed the indissoluble union of the Balearics and Roussillon with the crown of Aragon.

The adventures of a half century had now established Aragon as a major power in the western Mediterranean and provided a legal, logistic, political, and economic framework for Catalan trade therein. This had been carried through successfully against the resistance of the papacy itself, the house of Anjou, and sometimes that of France. The achievement was impressive but the cost remained to be discovered. The occupation of Sardinia had been effected at the expense of the Pisans who were expelled from that island. However, the real opposition to the Catalan initiative was to come not from that declining power but from a rising Genoa. After their destruction of Pisan naval power at Meloria in 1284 the Genoese were not inclined to brook another serious rival in the western Mediterranean and certainly not one established in Sardinia at their very doorstep. The net effect of these Catalan successes was to be an almost perpetual state of hostilities with Genoa at sea over the next century. It meant, as well, the more or less regular cooperation of Genoa with Castile and against Aragon in the affairs of Iberia.

We are inclined to observe the rising trade of Barcelona in the Mediterranean and to regard, therefore, this aggrandizement of the crown of Aragon as necessary if it was not to be permanently crippled economically. Moreover, Genoa was not necessarily an invincible enemy. But one must be careful of motives and one's ability to perceive them correctly over the centuries. That the Angevin house in Sicily would have been an insuperable obstacle to the flourishing of Aragonese trade with that isle is easier to assert than to prove. Quite as much to the point, was trade or dynasty the real motive? As for Sardinia, the benefits of its acquisition may very well have been outweighed by cost of its continuing occupation. Finally, while Barcelona suffered from both the commercial prowess and the political independence of the independent Baleàrics after 1276, to what degree did dynastic claims outweigh those more mundane, in the mind of the age, considerations?

Actually, while dynastic turmoil is easily perceived as a major problem for Castile from 1275, the problems of the royal family were almost as responsible for the direction of events in the crown of Aragon as well. Pere II's warfare with his half-brother, Ferran Sánchez, preceded his accession. Jaume I's division of his realms was essentially a dynastic one, never accepted as final by his eldest son. As a result, his younger brother of Majorca allied against Pere and with the French in 1285. In subsequent reigns the happy collaboration of Alfons II and Jaume II and the moderation, in regard to Majorca, of Alfons III limited the damage but both the ambition and the rifts of the dynasty made it very vulnerable to the demands of the nobility and the towns well into the reign of Pere IV. The death of the latter's brother-in-law, Jaume III of Majorca, in a vain attempt to regain that island in 1349 only came after the plague in 1348 had miraculously delivered the king from captivity by rebels first led into the field by his own brother, Prince Jaume.

In brief, the crown, in both Castile and Aragon, in the second half of the thirteenth and the early fourteenth century had more than enough to do to finish the consolidation of those realms, swollen by the rapid conquests of the preceding three decades. The addition of ambitious new undertakings strained the dynastic monarchy to breaking point. If legitimacy finally triumphed in both kingdoms it was due to the inconceivability of an alternative governmental frame and, in the final analysis, the irreducible loyalty of all sectors of Iberian society to those dynasties which had come to be seen as inseparable from ordered political life.

During the same period the Portuguese crown had been largely preoccupied by the circumstances of its emancipation from León–Castile. Its first king, Afonso Enríquez (1128–1185), had sought to bolster its independence by placing it under the suzerainty of the papacy. The results of that step had the most extraordinary repercussions as it put the Roman popes in a unique position to adjudicate the internal quarrels of the dynasty. Sancho I (1185–1211) had running battles with his bishops and the papacy during his reign but his last will also became a matter of dispute as his heir, Afonso II (1211–1223), quarreled with his sisters over the divisibility of crown possessions and the latter appealed to Rome.

That problem was negotiated but Afonso's disputes with the archbishop of Braga and other churchmen had led Pope Honorius III to move to declare him deposed just before the king's death. His son, Sancho II (1223–1248), also ran afoul of conflicting claims of crown and church and his rule was suspended by Pope Innocent IV who awarded the kingdom to Sancho's brother and the king died in exile in Toledo. Since Sancho had no children, his brother, Afonso III (1248–1279), was then generally recognized but would have his own problems with Rome. Disputes with the Portuguese clergy led to his excommunication by the papacy in 1277, a sentence still in effect at his death in 1279. In fact, his son and heir, Dinis (1279–1325), regarded the matter with some equanimity and the quarrel with Rome dragged on for some years yet. The Portuguese realm was to be delivered from the worst effects of papal jurisdiction by the long crisis that enveloped the latter institution beginning with the quarrel between Boniface and Philip the Fair of France that erupted in 1296.

The relative weakness of Portugal and its kings that permitted papal fulminations to be so uniquely effective there had determined much of its conduct in the peninsula as well and continued to do so. Relations with neighboring Castile were largely controlled by the momentary strength or debility of the latter. The dynasties continued not quite distinct as Afonso III married Beatriz, daughter of Alfonso X of Castile, in 1253 despite a papal interdict since he was already married. In return, the Castilian would recognize Portuguese claims to the Algarve. Born of the union, King Dinis would thus be grandson of Alfonso *el Sabio*. In turn, the daughter of Dinis, Constanza, would marry another of *el Sabio*'s grandsons, Fernando IV. Fernando's son, Alfonso XI, would marry Maria of Portugal, a granddaughter of Dinis by his son, Afonso IV. The Portuguese monarchs also sometimes collaborated in the work of the *reconquista* with their cousins of Castile. They sometimes allied with the disaffected in Castile or with Aragon to take advantage of their neighbor's internal crisis or to limit its strengths but such alliances proved ineffective. In fact, while the two realms remained legally and conceptually, in some places even geographically, distinct, in the politics of the peninsula they were almost inseparable.

The remaining Christian kingdom, Navarre, survived the near constant plans of Castile and Aragon to partition it largely because each found more important, or simpler, objectives. Fundamentally, one of its best guarantees was the rule of Aragon, properly speaking, by the dynasty of Barcelona after 1137 for the attention of that house was turned to the south and east. Castile was also busy in the south but not too much so to graft Basque Alava, Guipuzcoa, and Vizcaya, ever closer to itself. That process had affected Navarre about as much as had Aragonese preemption of the Ebro basin from Saragossa to the sea. Then, the restored line of the Navarrese house had perished with the death of Sancho VII (1194–1234). His sister, Blanca, had married into the house of the Champagne and four scions of that line had held Navarre in turn between 1234 and 1285. At that date, the heiress of Champagne and Navarre, Jeanne I, was married to Philip the Fair of France and thereafter four French kings in turn ruled Navarre, in absentia, until her granddaughter, Jeanne II (1328–1349), came to rule it jointly with Philip of Evreux, grandson of the Capetian Philip III (1270–1285) of France. By mid-fourteenth century it seemed that only geography stood between Navarre and a future as a province of France.

SOCIETY AND ITS CRITICS

From 1348 till 1352, and periodically thereafter for the next two centuries, Iberia and the rest of Europe were visited by the bubonic plague, or Black Death. Ever since authors have argued about the extent of the demographic havoc that it wreaked. The current consensus, allowing for regional differences, would place the toll of the fourteenth-century human holocaust at approximately one in every three persons alive in 1348. The overall demographic result seems to have been a steady decline in population for a half-century, which was only completely counteracted by about 1500 when European population generally had regained its late-thirteenth-century level.

Notwithstanding the recognition of the human, social, and psychological costs of a tragedy so immense, that no one who has read contemporary accounts can ignore, it is still clear that the fashion of attributing then-current social ills and problems simply to the "Black Death" just will not do. Western Europe was just then also experiencing a profound reorganization as well as, perhaps, an acceleration of its continuing historic evolution and it is difficult to separate entirely the effects of one from the other. Moreover, we ourselves too easily become partisans for one development or the other for it is, after all, our past and we wish to see the triumph of our present. Finally, the increased availability of paper and literacy during the age opens to us, principally through correspondence but also through judicial records, new windows through which we gaze eagerly without realizing fully the perspective of those peculiar apertures. The dullest of us may advert, occasionally, to the fact that judicial documents are "crisis" documents by definition. People do not take one another to court in the course of ordinary social cooperation. What we realize less often is that, human nature being what it is, people do not regularly utilize the personal or official letter as a vehicle of celebration. Almost always the letter is a happy harbinger of bad news, if not disaster, and the medium for personal railing against the ills and injustice that have recently beset the writer. In short, the form of the new testimony that the age just then began to furnish to posterity tends to magnify the problematic for us, if we are not careful, by testifying to it alone.

Throughout Iberia it is clear that villages will shrink or be deserted outright as the land devoted to agriculture contracts. But what is also evident is that this was not a new trend. Since the tenth century it had been typical of Muslim al-Andalus and, perhaps in the second half of the thirteenth century but certainly in the first half of the fourteenth, had begun to mark Christian Iberia as well. The successful *reconquista* of the latter and the population increase that drove it had by 1250 brought into cultivation a great deal of marginal land in the basins of the Duero and the Tajo that provided only the sparest sort of life for its cultivator. These areas received, after all, only 500 to 1,000 millimeters of rain annually. One need not predicate a Black Death to predict their eventual abandonment, especially if new lands became available. That, of course, is precisely what happened suddenly and on a large scale in the first half of the thirteenth century. What we simply do not know are the proportions of this occurrence which are due, respectively, to plague death and to migration from old land to new.

Nor can we sort out that proportion that was the result of the evolution of Iberian agriculture itself in the Middle Ages. The greater productivity of the new agriculture tended to make those same marginal lands increasingly uneconomic and that factor could not permanently be redressed by gradual population increase, especially if the latter found ready release in emigration. A sudden decrease in population would greatly aggravate it as farmers seized the opportunity to take up better lands left vacant by their previous occupier's demise.

The final elaboration of a mature system of irrigation also had its part to play. In al-Andalus it had promoted, from the tenth century, a concentration of both population and production in more easily watered lands. The more abundant production there permitted a diversification as well with former cereal lands being converted to grape and olive production as those water-seeking plants adapted readily to the dry environment. The Christian immigration into al-Andalus in the later Middle Ages certainly led to a limited revival of cereal farming in the basins of the Guadiana and the Guadalquivir, not to mention La Mancha, but it did not entail a complete return to the more simple agriculture of past centuries even so.

The most easily accessible of all of these modifications taking place in peninsular agriculture is the emergence of the great *Mesta* in the thirteenth century. The climate, soil, and topography of the peninsula naturally made it peculiarly apt for the raising of sheep and even cattle on a large scale and some transhumance had long been in practice. Still, in the thirteenth century and after, the new productivity of agriculture itself, the opening up of vast new lands, and the development of a particularly valuable new variety of sheep, the *merino*, by breeding with a North African strain led to a great expansion of the practice. The Castilian crown, Alfonso X in 1273 and Alfonso XI later, codified, enlarged, and protected the practices of the *Mesta*, the association of sheepowners and herders, turning it into a unified organization in the kingdom that yielded a most substantial crown revenue as well as wool. As that wool came to be the major export of the realm, it enriched other sectors as well. There can be little doubt that livestock grazing represented a change to the best use of the land in extended areas of the peninsula including the Portuguese Algarve and much of the crown of Aragon. Nevertheless, it collided often with the interests of the cultivator, sometimes displaced him, and gave rise to endless complaints and lawsuits.

Like much else that was taking place, this was often neither a comfortable nor a painless change. We are prone to see it as a retrograde one for we still cling to the myth of the "happy husbandman" enamored with his simple life and at one with nature. Since it was also a process which favored most directly the interests of the crown, nobility, church, and townsman at the expense of the little people of the time, we tend to find it objectionable on social grounds as well. Yet in economic and commercial terms the increase in stockraising clearly represented progress in the best sense of that much-maligned term. From the limited and impressionistic materials available to us it also seems to have added a considerable amount of animal protein to the popular diet. In so doing it was part of what appears to be a general improvement of the Iberian diet in the late Middle Ages.

In fact, most of the complaints about the agricultural changes of the day reach us from the *cortes*, nobles, the crown, church, and townsmen, who were precisely the privileged classes. They had to do with the undoubted inflation which raged between 1350 and 1450 at its most virulent. But the measures they advocated and sometimes attempted, control of prices but above all wages and the restriction of the mobility of the farming class, are interesting. They indicate the rise of agricultural prices, of the price of agricultural labor, and of the improved bargaining position of the cultivator. Such measures involved an even greater volume of complaint and litigation but their general lack of success probably is indicated by the absence of serious agrarian unrest except in Galicia and, rather later, in the crown of Aragon. The best evidence is that the income of the immediate cultivators of the land actually rose. While not much study has been devoted to such things in Iberia, it seems likely that, as elsewhere in western Europe, farmhouses themselves reflected the improvement in their increased size and the greater solidity of their structure.

For all of its human horrors, the Black Death contributed as well to alter the balance between rural and urban life in the peninsula. The plague struck with particular intensity in the congested towns and cities but did not lead thereby to anything like their decline. Instead, it seems to have helped to provide some opportunity for those being displaced from the land or fleeing it more or less willingly. If new villages have ceased to be formed in the countryside and older ones often disappear, the villages which survive have grown in average size. What is at work here is the continuing consolidation of life in Iberia which makes it at once more organized and complex institutionally and more closely interrelated and interdependent at every level. However, the substitution of legal, economic, and political constraints for natural ones is not necessarily more comfortable immediately, especially if the process is not understood. It is, however, more human.

Naturally, more information is available for the larger towns. In Barcelona a population of about 48,000 held steady all through this period only to decline in the period of civil war towards the end of the fifteenth century. Saragossa had actually begun to approach its population of the Muslim era by climbing back to about 20,000 inhabitants about 1480 from a likely 12,000 in the thirteenth century. Particular economic developments pushed Valencia to something like 75,000 as against a pre-plague high of 20,000 at best. Nor was this peculiar to the crown of Aragon. In Portugal Lisbon was so swollen from its population of 15,000 by immigration from the countryside that its new walls of the fourteenth century enclosed twice the area of the old ones, although their circuit contained much undedicated land. Toledo's population seems to have held steady at about 45,000, which fact calls our attention to the irregular fashion in which the new economy of Iberia was affecting its demography. That is, the greater integration of the peninsula in the western European economy was speeding disproportionately the development of those cities advantageously placed to participate in it. In Cantabria and Vizcaya to the north, Santander seems to have grown from 2,500 in AD 1300 to about 4,000 in 1500, and Bilbao, which had only just been founded by the former date, boasted some 5,000 souls by the latter. But then, they were products of the burgeoning trade with northern Europe.

That commerce continued to be based predominantly upon the export of natural products. Since the majority of these were by their nature bulky, transport costs rose very steeply if they had to be transported over any great distance. In itself, that simple fact dictated a future for the now politically and socially mature *mesetas* of *Castilla La Vieja* and *Castilla La Nueva* of a subsistence economy modified by the exchange, over short distances, of the products of a diversified agriculture. The wheat, wine, and olive oil of the *mesetas* became too expensive to pack or cart more than a hundred kilometers. This meant that they might often supply immediately adjacent fringe areas such as Asturias and the Bierzo but that their major products would not be widely distributed even in the peninsula. The seacoasts, down to the present day, would find it cheaper to import grain, wine, even olive oil, from abroad because of the relatively low costs of water transport. Even major technological advances, such as the introduction of the windmill in La Mancha during the fourteenth century, could not alter this dictate of geography.

In fact, agriculture was far from stagnant during the late Middle Ages, as is evidenced by the heavy investment in it by the nobility and townsmen. In both Navarre and Aragon proper the irrigation systems inherited from the Muslim period continued to be expanded and perfected along the course of the upper and middle Ebro. In Valencia a major new canal was dug to transfer water from the Júcar River to that of the Turia River where its use for irrigation was more critical. Where the prospects of successful commercialization offered, new crops such as saffron, honey, and a variety of specialty wines found more extensive and more intensive cultivation.

Ultimately, however, transport was the key and that meant that it was to be the basins of the Ebro and the Guadalquivir which were most fitted for the exploitation of their extensive hinterlands for purposes of trade. The wheat and wine of Aragon traveled the highway of the river down to Tortosa for export. On the other hand, its hides, iron, and armors, found only a limited export north over the Pyrenees by land. Barcelona could send its wool, textiles, its saffron, and its iron products, just as Valencia could merchandise its rice, paper, and silk, by sea to France, Italy, and North Africa.

Generally the late medieval trade of Iberia changed little in character from the thirteenth century except as it increased in volume. That increase was sufficient to move Pedro I of Castile (1350–1369) to introduce a heavier silver piece, the *real*, to supplement the gold coinage and the venerable *solidus* of antiquity finally disappeared as money of account. For Barcelona, the reannexation of the Balearics removed a troublesome competitor and restored a useful waystation on the searoads to both Africa and Italy. The greatest volume of its trade was with Italy but North

Africa, especially through Tlemcen, was important as well. The eastern Mediterranean was visited regularly but the volume was smaller. In all of this activity its sister port of Valencia was not yet a major competitor for shipbuilding was concentrated at Barcelona.

Just in this period when the *Libre del Consulat del Mar* assumed its final shape and began to be translated into the sailing vernaculars of both the Mediterranean and the Atlantic kingdoms, the crown of Aragon slowly lost ground to the rising power of Genoa at sea. To take advantage of the Atlantic trade Genoese carracks began to be built to 500 tons while Catalan ships seldom averaged more than 200. On their way to the Atlantic the Genoese established regular ports of call at Valencia; the whole of the overseas trade of Granada was in their hands, that meant entree for them to North Africa, and at Seville the Genoese strengthened their already commanding position. Indeed the most serious Iberian competitors of the Genoese were the Basques both at Seville and in the Mediterranean. Their ships had the audacity to regularly carry the salt of Ibiza to Genoa and the wheat of Provence to Barcelona, picking up cargoes of opportunity along the way.

The league of Basque ports known as the *Hermandad de las Marismas* from its founding in 1296 realized a brilliant future based upon the supply to the north of the iron mined in their hinterland and upon the wool of the *Mesta*. The latter, though bulky, was both light and valuable enough to make its travel to port on pack animals economic. In return, the Basque merchants sent south by the same route through Burgos and Medina del Campo the luxury goods, chiefly textiles, of the north of Europe to places as far distant as Seville. In 1351 Edward III of England concluded a treaty with the *Hermandad* but its future lay with France. Basque sea captains and merchants of Burgos quickly developed a carrying trade in the Bay of Biscay involving the wines of Gascony, the salt of La Rochelle, and the textiles of Nantes. Towards the end of the period, in 1419, the *Hermandad* defeated the German Hanseatic League at sea and excluded them from the Bay of Biscay. A series of treaties with France during the Hundred Years War consolidated their position in that kingdom for which they acted virtually as a navy, defeating the English fleet at La Rochelle in 1372, attacking and sacking Gravesend in 1380, and going on to control the English Channel itself. To secure help at sea, the English crown began to seek treaties with the mariners of Lisbon but the Portuguese were hardly a match for their rivals.

On the basis of their near monopoly of Castilian wool, their plenteous iron, and the control of the carrying trade of the Bay of Biscay, the merchants of Burgos extended their operations into the North Sea where the looms of Flanders were avid for their wool. The sea captains and the merchants of Burgos were to be found in Bruges in Flanders, Rouen in Normandy, and eventually in London as well. Curiously, in 1402 it was Norman adventurers sailing from La Rochelle who began the settlement of the Canary Islands in the name of the king of Castile. The Duke of Medina Sidonia himself stirred in 1449 to secure the royal license for fishing off the western coast of Africa.

Portuguese trade out of Lisbon grew slowly in the Later Middle Ages and was largely controlled by the Genoese. It too consisted in the main of natural products such as wine, olive oil, cork, and increasingly salt. Trade with England was substantial although much of it traveled in English vessels. But the ships of Lisbon did compete in a small way in the Mediterranean trade and, more importantly in the long run, Genoese sailors licensed by the crown began the exploration of the western coast of Africa. This was the age of Prince Henry the Navigator (1394–1460), son of King João I. Before 1450 the island groups of the Madeiras, the Azores, and the Cape Verdes, had been discovered and colonization was begun. By that time the gold of the African trans-Sahara was beginning to find a direct route to Europe as was the sugar of canes transplanted by the Portuguese to the Madeiras. The colonial world of the Atlantic was beginning to take shape.

Trade, at this level, was the business of merchants, nobles, and even kings and directly affected the life of the average cultivator of the soil very little. In the kingdoms of Castile and Portugal the business of trade was sufficiently marginal to the ordinary business of the realm that the towns themselves will increasingly fall under the competing jurisdictions of the nobility and the crown in the period. Except for Burgos and Medina del Campo and Lisbon they failed to develop a merchant class sufficiently powerful to defend their privileges. The *reconquista* was over so that their militias were no longer regularly needed. The increasing investment of the nobility in the agriculture of the countryside and the conversion of good parts of it to the stockraising which the nobility controlled entailed the shrinkage of municipal jurisdiction beyond the town walls. The greater involvement of the *caballeros villanos* of the towns themselves in the same pursuits led to their reinforced identification with the greater nobility and its interests.

Under the circumstances, town councils were increasingly dominated by a contracting number of "citizens" drawn from the lesser nobility and their patrons. They became even more oligarchic in character. Complaints against this ever narrower patrician regime could find redress only at the level of the crown itself. In the most outrageous cases of exploitation of municipal office, the crown began, from the time of Alfonso XI, to appoint *corregidores*, or royal inspectors to identify and remedy egregious abuses. Local justice was increasingly regulated by central codes and professional judges and lawyers and even then appeal of local decisions to the crown itself became more common. In particularly difficult and important instances, as at Seville in 1337, the king might simply arrogate to himself the right to appoint the *concejo* outright.

Even in the crown of Aragon, where long-distance trade was not largely in the hands of foreigners as at Lisbon or Seville and the native merchant community remained strong and active, it was not a happy era for municipal liberties. There too, especially at Barcelona, the development of long-distance trade had gradually split the commercial community into two distinct interests. Quarrels over policy between the *Biga*, or the great merchants, and the *Busca*, or local merchants and artisans, tore the city government between 1430 and 1450. The king intervened on one side or the other depending as his need for allies varied. Indeed, no Iberian monarch can be said to have had a consistent urban policy except that the towns should be in the hands of those most likely to vote the crown money.

Nonetheless, the tripartite government of the crown, separate for the realms of Aragon, Barcelona, and Valencia, insulated the urban patriciates of the latter two from the full influence of the great nobility of Aragon proper and gave the municipal fathers of the two cities a larger voice in their own realms at least. The banking crisis of the 1380s might lead to the failure of most private banks in Catalonia but by 1401 Barcelona had organized its municipal bank to manage city finances and to provide it with credit as needed. Typically, the period was one of impressive city building with Barcelona initiating its *Ramblas* as well as a mole to protect its port and a great new mercantile center. Gerona outgrew its Roman confines as Lérida and Tortosa did their Muslim ones. The renewed growth of Saragossa and Valencia has already been mentioned. The greater relative health of the towns of the crown of Aragon is demonstrated particularly by this spate of municipal building construction which simply has no analogue in the Castile or Portugal of the period unless one counts the construction of hospitals, frequently under town patronage. The *plaza mayor* of Salamanca, of Valldolid, and of other towns, of early fifteenth-century construction, were royal initiatives.

The chequered history of the Iberian towns in the Late Middle Ages was matched by that of its church. The heady days of the restoration entailed by the *reconquista* were over and only minor structural changes were made in the secular church. A bishopric was instituted for the newly colonized Canary Islands in 1351 and for newly Christian Ceuta in 1421. Aragon proper became a province separate from Tarragona under a new archbishopric at Saragossa so that its religious autonomy now mirrored its political autonomy within the crown of Aragon. Pope Benedict IX in 1390 was prevailed upon to raise the greatest city in Portugal and the favorite of the dynasty, Lisbon, to the archepiscopal rank.

The same sort of realignments, with political events determining religious ones, were enacted within the world of the regular clergy as well. The thirteenth century began with the spectacle of Pope Clement V being harassed into a shameful suppression of the Templars by the veritably demonic Philip IV the Fair of France. Both that event and its character encouraged major changes in Iberia. The papal intention had been that the possessions of the Templars should pass to the Hospitallers but in Aragon Jaume II preferred that they should go to the crown. Finally it was agreed in 1317 that the Hospital would indeed acquire Templar lands in Catalonia and in Aragon proper but that in Valencia a new native Order of Montesa would be created to receive them. Similarly in Castile it was the orders of Calatrava and Santiago which benefited from the Templars demise and in Portugal the new native Order of Christ. Half a century later, in 1372, the properties of the Hospitallers themselves in Castile would pass to Santiago and Calatrava in return for the cession of the latters' lands in Aragon to the Hospital.

Such structural changes, however, have not been what was meant as historians have almost unanimously agreed that the Iberian church was then in decline and in need of reform. Nor has the continuing virtual monopoly of high office in both the secular and the regular church in Iberia by the creatures of the great nobility or of the crown been so characterized. But then these latter are not really new but only become more obvious phenomena as the historical record becomes more full. We know much more about the "episcopal" relations of Gil Alvarez de Albornoz (1305–1363) who almost owned the see of Saragossa during the fourteenth century. We can follow the career of Albornoz himself as student in Toulouse, chaplain in the court of Alfonso XI of Castile, named by him to be primate of Toledo in 1338, fellow warrior at Río Salado in 1340, Algeciras in 1344, and Gibraltar in 1349, and refugee in the papal court at Avignon after 1350 when Pedro I acceded to the Castilian throne for having made the mistake of favoring Alfonso XI's mistress, Leonor de Guzmán, over his wife and Pedro's mother. Archbishop Gil would not be an ordinary refugee, of course, for Pope Clement VI would promote him to the cardinalate almost immediately and the cardinal would have a long and distinguished history in Italy as the conqueror, pacifier, and reorganizer of the papal states.

This lack of a proper institutional autonomy could only be felt as an abuse once the reformed papacy of the High Middle Ages had defined it in law and the fact is obvious that kings, nobles, and bishops themselves continued to prefer, except when it suited their particular interests, what a later age would call an Erastian model. That is, the control of the church had always been their prerogative and curtailment of the latter was tantamount to treason. What seems to be new is not the practice of the age but its occasional definition as abusive. So too with the host of complaints about clerical concubinage or outright marriage. From the eleventh century forward, the reform party in the western church insisted that celibacy on the monastic model was proper to the lower secular clergy as well. The evidence is that throughout the west the latter had simply refused to accept that decision and would continue to do so, in Iberia as elsewhere. Again, the "abuse" was intrinsic in a changed definition and the very denunciation of the former was a sign of vigor rather than relaxation. Clerical practice had not changed very much, one thinks. Much the same may be asserted in regard to the frequent denunciations of clerical illiteracy. It is impossible to believe or prove that the lower clergy were actually less educated than in some earlier, mythic "golden age." The better likelihood is that the very idea of a literate clergy, in something like the modern sense, that again was a product largely of the earlier reform movement, was gaining increased acceptance as a criterion in wider circles than ever before.

Clearly there were two major problems that plagued the Iberian church, as every other church in the west, in the late Middle Ages. One was an overcentralization of authority that was unworkable in either the political or the practical order. It gave rise to endless jurisdictional disputes at every level and consequent almost endless practical paralysis. It also promoted the indisputable abuse of absenteeism as those who desired to rise in the church sought out those distant centers of power and then, not remarkably, found them pleasant and declined to return even after their initial object had been obtained.

The second major problem was the wealth of the institutional church. Certainly it suffered in the age from a relative poverty for it shared the problems of other great landholders during a period of inflation, economic dislocation, and rapid economic change. Inflation is harder on the propertied than the debtors. Nevertheless, though contemporary churchmen complained about it bitterly, the whole non-verbal testimony of the age is to a continuing wealth. That is, after all, what most of the jurisdictional squabbles were about. Kings, nobles, and burghers continued to vie eagerly for the ability to find income for their familiars and retainers by placing them in church office. Now they were joined by popes and cardinals. Symptomatic were the quarrels over the *ius spolia*, the right to the personal estate of a deceased bishop. It was sufficiently lucrative for popes and kings to fight for it, legally sometimes, by force even to the point of murder in others as in the case of the estate of the bishop of Cuenca in 1346. And well might they quarrel. A Grand Master of the Order of Alcántara left personal possessions of over a million acres, sheep in the order of 200,000 and 2,000 cattle at his death in 1453. The archepiscopal see of Toledo held enormous land areas in the upper Tajo basin and La Mancha from the end of the twelfth century.

It has been said that, "in religion, nothing fails like success." The material riches of the Iberian church attracted the cupidity of all sectors of society from the highest to the lowest. The ineffectual strictures of clerical synods against clerical ostentation, gluttony, and avarice testify indirectly to the ability of ecclesiastical wealth to attract those who felt no particular religious calling. Obviously it stands behind another of the undeniable clerical abuses of the age, pluralism. It also largely accounts for the hordes of hangers-on, the not-quite-clerics, and the clerics in name only. For this reason it was even necessary for local synods to legislate that a priest must celebrate mass at least four times a year. The new literature emanating from the non-noble sector of society, of which the *Libro de Buen Amor* is the most famous example, leaves no doubt that public esteem of the clergy was quite low. A real question remains as to whether that attitude itself was new or merely the recording of it.

That the older monastic institutions experienced difficulty in recruit-ment is clear. Even the Franciscan and Dominican friars seem to have become less fashionable. Yet the genuine religious impulse continued to be felt. Much of what we know of clerical failings comes from the synods which legislated against them. Even the lordly Gil Alvarez de Albornoz found time to hold three such synods in the dozen years during which he presided at Toledo. Moreover, these are the very years in which the strictest of orders, the Carthusians, experienced their great growth in the peninsula. So too with the Hieronymites, another order of ascetics chartered in 1373, whose new monasteries in Iberia came to exceed thirty. Pilgrimage to the latter's monastery-shrine to the Virgin at Guadalupe in the Montes de Toledo almost competed with that to Santiago de Compostela by the fifteenth century. In the 1420s the Cistercians them-selves agreed on the need for greater austerity and Poblet was entrusted with leading a reform. Lay piety was newly demonstrated especially in charitable works such as hospitals of which dozens if not hundreds were founded in these times.

If we are at something of a loss to evaluate the condition of the Iberian church of the Late Middle Ages because its norms were changing and our own criteria are slippery, how much more is that true of the nobility. The very term raises our hackles. Our democratic proclivities are mortally offended at the notion of hereditary privileges as at that of private jurisdiction. Yet undeniably both spread and flourished. In all kingdoms of the peninsula the royal fisc shrank to their benefit and the lands which they extracted from a reluctant monarch increasingly were included in a *mayorazgo*, or entail, which meant that they could only be inherited en bloc by a single heir. Noble possessions were attempting to ape the indivisibility of the crown estates themselves. Together with the ownership of the land, they also vastly increased their political power over it as they purchased or wheedled or extorted grants of the royal jurisdiction over rural districts, villages, castles, monasteries, and even cities in Castile.

Despite our outraged sense of proprieties, it would yet be difficult to establish that the officials and agents or this or that noble house were less compassionate or more unscrupulous than those of the king himself. Indeed, they might well be the same people for both sold their offices and the great nobles were, more often than not, the primary officials of the crown as well. To separate the crown from the nobility was impossible for the king himself so long as the ancient regime endured. In government, as in religion, in economics, in society, in recreation, in procreation, they surrounded him. The king could not have conceived of such a separation much less desired it. They were literally his "cousins" to whom he married his bastards and not infrequently his legitimate children and whose children he sometimes married but more often took as mistresses. It was a poor lineage indeed that could not boast of some royal blood somewhere, at some time.

What was wanted was an association that recognized the paramount dignity in the life of the realm of the king and the direct line of the dynasty. To maintain that proper relationship an Alfonso XI would resort to the murder of an Alvar Núñez de Osorio. Pere IV of Aragon would order the great bell of the *Union* of Valencia to be melted and its liquor poured down the throats of its partisans. In 1360, Pedro I of Portugal and Pedro I of Castile would arrange an exchange of noble refugees who had fled to the lands of one from the other so that, repatriated, they could be executed as traitors to their king. Yet the contest was unequal. No king was to meet his end at the hands of a noble. Pedro I of Castile only perished by the dagger of his half-brother, Enrique of Trastamara. The nobility would not take to the field against their lord and cousin ordinarily unless they were led by another member of the dynasty with some claim of blood on the throne.

The nobility had no program against the crown except a passive one. They wanted to be left alone to enjoy their traditional dignities. When the crown was weak by virtue of a division in the dynasty itself, the accession of a minor, or a reverse in war, they were quite willing to offer their services in expectation of a generous reward in royal offices, lands, or pensions. There was an element of opportunism in all this, of course, yet all the same they were not asking for anything but that to which they held themselves quite sincerely entitled. Moreover, in so offering their services, they very often risked their fortunes, their families, and even their lives.

Of all of the kingdoms of Iberia the nobility became the most influential in Castile yet even there they suffered the most remarkable vicissitudes. In the course of the fourteenth century the biological failures to which every family was subject, the civil wars and those against Aragon and Portugal whose cost bore most heavily on a class military by definition, and the savage reprisals of Pedro I against the partisans of his opponents, left extant only eleven of the thirty-four lineages that had existed in 1300. Royal beneficence refilled the ranks of the *ricos hombres* under the Trastamaras from the lesser nobility in cases such as that of the Mendozas, the Manriques, and the Quinones. Access to the ranks of the lower nobility also continued to be surprisingly open. Customary exemption from general taxes was accepted by the royal courts as proof of nobility, it was often purchased apparently, and in times of war, the Trastamara awarded the status of *hidalgo* with a free hand in return for free military service to them. North of the Guadarrama, at least, *hidalguia* was so common that tax collectors and jurists protested against it regularly.

Royal government too continued to be surprisingly personal. There was a gradual growth of the royal bureaucracy everywhere but there continued gaps surprising to a modern. Armies, for instance, remained limited largely to the royal bodyguard and the garrisons of royal castles in peacetime to be filled out in wartime by contingents supplied by the nobility. In Castile the tax machinery had become somewhat more complex at the central level with the chancery, the *cámara*, and a *Casa de Cuentas*, cooperating in its administration but the *alcabala* continued to be farmed as were the customs dues. Jews or *conversos* continued to be the ordinary collectors. The branch most thoroughly professionalized was the administration of justice since the universities by then were supplying trained lawyers in good numbers. No realm had a capital for the kings continued to be itinerant and only the crown of Aragon had an adequate system of records which allowed its government to determine with some facility and accuracy what it had done in the past. Pere IV had instituted the office of royal archivist in 1346.

The closest approach to the sort of public regime to which we are accustomed to assimilate all government lay in the *cortes* of the various realms whose representative character forced the regular distinction between the persons acting and the kingdom in whose behalf they acted. However, the *cortes* remained emergency institutions. Therefore their evolution into permanent institutions of government was limited although the historic precedents that they established finally found fruition in the modern era. In Portugal, for instance, the *cortes* met very frequently during the early reign of João I (1383–1433) and most infrequently after 1402. But then, the illegitimate João had been recognized by the *cortes* of Coimbra against the claims of his own half-brother in a desperate struggle to prevent Castile from absorbing Portugal. His main support came from the cities of Lisbon and Oporto acting through the *cortes* and he agreed in return to convene it annually and to allow it to choose a treasurer to supervise the disbursement of the funds voted him. Once Castile was finally defeated and João firmly established on the throne he had little inclination to continue to have it meet and the frequency dropped from almost once a year, to biennially, then to triennially. Subsequent monarchs would summon it even less often.

The same pattern held elsewhere. Under Pedro I of Castile (1350–1369) the *cortes* met but once. Under his usurping successors, the Trastamaras, it met very frequently. Juan I (1379–1390) agreed that men chosen by the *cortes* could supervise the disbursement of funds it voted although that arrangement seems never to have become operative. The number of cities represented in the *cortes* rose to forty-nine in the reign of Enrique III (1390–1406) but a half century later would be a mere seventeen. During the reign of Juan II (1406–1454) representatives of the cities began to be appointed by the crown from among his own officials.

In the crown of Aragon, Catalonia, Valencia, and Aragon proper each had its own *corts* as it had its own institutions generally. This not infrequently allowed the crown the luxury of playing one against the other in order to secure support for the king's policies. Alternatively, the king could summon all three to meet together as it suited his purposes. Notwithstanding, the *corts* of Catalonia became the strongest such institution in the peninsula and achieved in the *Generalitat* a permanent body elected by the *corts* to administer between its meetings those funds which it had voted. This appeared in Catalonia already in the late thirteenth century and was imitated in Aragon in 1412 and in Valencia in 1419. Aragon also developed the office of a supreme justiciar chosen by the *cortes* and serving for life. Once again, the *corts* enjoyed its greatest influence and activity during the troubled period from 1350 to 1420 but was still sufficiently strong to attempt outright revolt against the crown in Catalonia after 1460.

THE MATURE TRADITION AND THE INTELLECTUAL LIFE

As did political and economic life, the world of culture in the Iberian Late Middle Ages built largely upon entrenched precedent. Learning continued to be distinctive of the clerical estate. Major new foundations were likely to fail, as with the universities that Pere IV attempted to found at Perpignan in 1350 and Huesca in 1354. On the other hand, the Castilian abbey of Sahagún had some success with the *studium* that it established at papal behest and that was intended to raise educational levels among the Benedictines generally. At Salamanca a faculty of theology was established in 1395 while the college of San Bartolome was endowed as the first residential hall there in 1401. Both went on to become distinguished. However, the most promising students still went abroad and in 1365 Gil Alvarez de Albornoz founded a Spanish College at the University of Bologna which would also have a long and rich career.

Among the clergy, the friars continued to be the most conspicuously literate. The Dominican, San Vicent Ferrer (d. 1419), has left hundreds of sermons and tracts, most of them dealing with the problems of reform and the conversion of Jews and Muslims. His fellow Dominican and inquisitor general of Aragon, Nicholas Eymerich (d. 1399), used his high scholastic training to compose a manual for inquisitors, the *Directorium Inquisitorum*, but he found opportunity as well to carry on a running feud with the intellectual heirs of Ramón Lull. His *Dialogus contra Lullistas* was probably directed to those who would or could not read it. After his initial success at the papal level, the crown took up the defense of Lull's tradition and secured its vindication while Pere IV forced Eymerich himself into exile. The Dominican Juan de Torquemada (d. 1468) fared better as a master of theology at Paris, later cardinal, and the author of more than forty books. He was chiefly famous for the defense of the extreme papal monarchy in his *Summa de Ecclesia*.

Franciscans proved to be quite as prominent. Certainly Anselm Turmeda, Majorcan and graduate of Bologna who rejected Christianity in disgust and fled to Tunisia, was. From that vantage point he wrote the *Disputa de l'Ase* in Catalan to demonstrate the superiority of brute animals to mankind. In a mode less misanthropic he did a *Refutation of the Partisans of the Cross* in Arabic. Somewhat more traditional, the Franciscan Alfonso de Madrigal (d. 1455) defended the conciliar view of church organization, *De Optima Politia*, from the vantage point of a chair of moral theology at Salamanca and survived to become bishop of Avila. Alfonso reflected as well a growing Italian influence in peninsular letters in that his treatise on the pagan gods of antiquity was influenced by Boccaccio's work on that subject. Another Franciscan, Francesc Eiximenis (c. 1340–1409), for a long time courtier to Marti I (1395–1410) of Aragon, wrote widely, authoring for one an encyclopedic *El Crestia* or complete guide for the Christian of which only four books out of twelve have survived.

The secular church was not scantily represented however. Juan de Segovia, who taught at Salamanca and went on to represent the university at the Council of Basle, displayed the tradition of scholarship long at home in the peninsula when he published a tripartite edition, since lost, of the Koran in Arabic, Latin, and Castilian, in collaboration with a Muslim scholar. The same sort of adherence to the Iberian tradition was displayed by Luis González de Guzmán, Grand Master of Calatrava, who sought out a Jewish scholar in 1422 to secure a new translation into Castilian of the Old Testament, complete with commentary. New currents were represented rather by the bishop of Burgos, Alonso de Cartagena (1435–1456). This *converso* bishop translated a number of Cicero's works into Castilian and some of Seneca as well.

Of course, the great novelty in the period was the number and the caliber of the laymen who participated in the world of intellectual exchange. One hallmark of the period was the transformation of royal and noble castles and fortresses into more comfortable and sumptuous palaces, from the Mendoza's Manzanares el Real north of Madrid to that of the Haro at Frías, to that great storybook confection of the crown, the *alcázar* at Segovia. The architectural shift spoke of the lessening need for protection as the crown began to approach that monopoly of warfare that marks the modern political order. But, even more remarkably, one begins to find reliable evidence of libraries in the possession of noblemen. Unlike the libraries of cathedrals and monasteries, these were not heavily marked by the Latin liturgical books and theological commentaries. The count of Benevente near León possessed more than 100 volumes including ones on chess, hunting, some of the Latin classics, and a wide variety of chronicles. The marquis of Santillana collected Castilian translations of classical works. Perhaps the book most sought after by the nobles was the geneological work of the son of the Portuguese King Dinis, the fourteenth-century *Livro das Linhagens*. Whether or not these works were read as well as collected, the very fashion of collecting them testifies to the growing sense that formal learning was no longer an adornment suitable simply for the clergy.

Inevitably their interests would change the emphasis in formal learning. Scriptural commentary tended to be replaced by the Romance, perhaps with little net gain. The poetry of love and nature became more common and began to be written in Castilian rather than the older Gallegan in both Castile and Portugal while that genre remained closely tied yet to the

Provençal in Catalonia. A great prince of the blood and nephew of Alfonso X of Castile, Juan Manuel (d. 1348), wrote naturally on the education of the young noble, on falconry, but also a collection of fables and moral tales, the *Libro de exemplos del Conde Lucanor et de Patronio*, derived from Arabic and Jewish as well as Christian sources whose emphasis was upon human nature and often an earthy human wisdom.

Of course such authors were much interested in the high politics of their own age in which they almost invariably participated. Pedro López de Ayala (d. 1407) who served both Pedro I of Castile and then abandoned him for his successor, Enrique II, ending as chancellor of Castile in 1398, has left us a *Chronicle of Pedro I*. It must be used with care, of course, but it is nonetheless an invaluable account. His *Rimado de Palacio* also drew upon much of the material of high politics of the age but this time satirically. By and large history was well treated by the lay authors of the time. From the Portuguese court of King Dinis we have the only surviving text and translation of the tenth-century *Crónica del moro Rasis*, done at his orders by Gil Perez. It was then incorporated in the *Crónica general* of 1344. Pere IV of Aragon had the *Crónica de San Juan de la Peña* written, had the tombs of Alfonso II and Jaume I rebuilt, and ordered the carving of nineteen statues of his predecessors on the throne for his palace in Barcelona. Clearly he had a sense of the political uses of history. But the greatest of the Aragonese historians of the time was Ramón Mutaner (d. 1336) who chronicled the rise of the Aragonese sea empire in the Mediterranean in which he was himself so often a participant. The medieval historiographical tradition remained healthy but now its major practitioners were nobles rather than monks.

Quite a different picture of the age and its interests comes to us from the pen of Juan Ruíz de Cisneros, the archpriest of Hita (1296–1353). He was himself the illegitimate son of a nobleman and became a cleric but his interests were with the lower classes of the time of whom he gives us a remarkable picture. His *Libro de Buen Amor* is a collection of tales and types in verse whose nature perhaps no subsequent commentator has managed to completely capture. Knowledgeable of Aristotle and the Arabs, the university and ecclesiastical milieu, the Bible and the streets, he combined them with a not-quite-innocence, a great good humor, and an active compassion, to produce a rowdy masterwork of western literature. Somewhat of the same genre was the *El Corbacho* of Alfonso Martínez de Toledo, archpriest of Talavera, writing about a century later. It has much of the same value for the historian of the manners of the age but it is less goodnatured and somewhat more pretentious in its learning. The author obviously knew Boccaccio's *Corbaccio*.

Just as different again were the poems of Ausias March (c. 1397–1458) a nobleman of Valencia and writing in Catalan. While influenced by the Provençal tradition as well as Dante and Petrarch, it was highly personal and introspective. Another Valencian noble, Joannot Martorell (c. 1413–1468), modified the medieval Romance form in his *Tirant lo Blanc* which put the knight-errant into the contemporary context of campaigns against the Ottomans in the eastern Mediterranean. In addition to drawing upon elements of actual Catalan history in that arena, he also utilized his materials to create a realistic context rather than one of some fantastic far country.

That the influence of the Italian Renaissance was beginning to make itself felt in Iberia will already be obvious from some of what has been said. That fractious notion has a variety of strands of its own, of course, and just as various was its impact in the peninsula. At one level it meant a new spate of translations of classical authors not previously known, or widely known. Such, for example, was the rendering of the Greek historian Plutarch at the request of Juan Fernandez de Heredia, Grand Master of the Hospitallers (1377–1396). Then again, it may be reflected in the conscious imitation of the ancients as with the *Livro de virtuosa bemfeitoria* of Pedro duke of Coimbra and younger son of João I of Portugal which took Seneca's *De Beneficiis* as its model. Or again, it may rather be the influence of the styles and the thoughts of Dante, Petrarch, Boccaccio, and company, whose works largely were translated into the peninsular languages during the first half of the fifteenth century. In this respect, as in others, the mental furniture of the educated Iberian was being more closely assimilated to that of the remainder of the western Europeans of the age.

7

THE PASSING OF MEDIEVAL IBERIA,
1248–1474

Despite all of the elements of continuity that marked the peninsula in the two centuries between the fall of Seville and the accession of the Catholic kings, some of its structures and verities were being altered beyond recognition. One of these was the role of Islam there. Though it was far from immediately clear, the thirteenth-century Christian conquest of Andalusia and Murcia was to be irreversible. It would take another century and Río Salado to demonstrate definitively that salvation was no longer to be looked for on the plains of Morocco, but the acuter minds of the age must have grasped that fact even sooner. Islamic Iberia was thrown back upon its own resources and they were to prove insufficient even so soon as the great revolts of 1264 in Andalusia and of 1274 in Valencia.

Both of those abortive risings were the result of the intrigues of Muhammad I (1237–1273) and of his son and successor Muhammad II (1273–1320) of Granada. In the first of them it was demonstrated fairly rapidly that the sinews of Spanish Islam alone continued to be no match for the combined might of Castile and Aragon which was hurled against them. The second rising was a reaction to the first invasion of Iberia by Banū Marin of Morocco but the rebels were ground down inexorably when aid failed to reach them from the Africans. The Marīnid had been called into the peninsula by the ruler of Muslim Granada but they could not be kept there when African events called them home to shore up the none-too-steady regime there.

The only independent Muslim power left in Iberia was to be the kingdom of Granada, that is, a principality which was constituted by a coastal fringe that stretched from north of Mojácar on the Mediterranean north of Almeria to Algeciras and Tarifa at the straits of Gibraltar, which fringe extended inland sometimes up to 100 kilometers and was largely protected by the mountainous character of the land that constituted great parts of it. As such, Granada was a tiny realm not exceeding 30,000 kilometers square by the most generous estimate. It was then not quite one-tenth the size of Castile and about a quarter the size of the crown of Aragon. Its population, swollen with refugees from Valencia, Murcia, and Andalusia, amounted to about 300,000. Therefore its population of ten per square kilometer mirrored the densities of Castile and Aragon in a terrain even less hospitable to agriculture.

By any measure, then, Muslim Granada was a tiny kingdom surrounded by formidable foes on whose lassitude or forbearance it must count to survive. It could and would attempt to play the one against the other and the North African Muslim realms against one or both. In the end all was to prove unavailing yet that end was successfully delayed for some two and a half centuries. During all of this time, Granada was, by Castilian reckoning, a vassal state and either paid or owed *parias* in amount set variously between 150,000 and 300,000 *maravedis* per annum. It would be a pretty task to compute how much was actually paid but it was sufficient to maintain the crown of Castile's gold coinage fairly stable through the economically troubled years of the period. Since the *parias* of Granada were also one of the most important items of the royal income and since they required no bureaucratic effort on its part to collect, needless to say Castile's interest in their collection was keen at all times and turned threatening almost immediately when they were not forthcoming.

The society upon whom this and other burdens ultimately rested was at least homogeneous as few Iberian Islamic societies had been. We hear virtually nothing of Mozarabs there. As for the other "people of the Book," Jews appeared to have numbered at best some one percent of the population, concentrated in the silk industry, gold- and silver-smithing, and small retail shops. Granada then emerges as the first of the peninsular realms in which that *convivencia* of Christian, Jew, and Muslim, supposedly typical of medieval Iberia, verged toward extinction. Doubtless it was a result of the population transfers stemming from the Christian conquest of Andalusia and Murcia in the thirteenth century. The character of Granada as a Muslim redoubt after 1248 would have made it increasingly uncomfortable for even native Christians and, in lesser measure, for Jews.

Given the extremely mountainous character of that redoubt, and the desert character of much land in the region of Almeria, there is no doubt that the realm was overpopulated. It had to import foodstuffs to exist and export specialty products to pay for them. Even from Castile in times of peace Granadan merchants purchased cereal grains and livestock but the great essential source of grain continued to be North Africa. All of Granada itself appears to have been turned into one great garden in which irrigation was pursued more intensively than before or since. This effort produced the silk, the sugar, and the dried fruits that were the staples of export as well as that proportion of the foodstuffs for which land could be spared. Of necessity, the export trade was in the hands of the Genoese from the beginning. They had the immunity at sea to attack that came from strength and the access to markets that Granadans themselves lacked.

Somehow or other this all worked for two and a half centuries. The society managed to support the city of Granada itself and its population of 50,000 not to mention the port cities of Almeria, Motril, and Malaga, that must together have constituted another 12,000 souls so that fully one-fifth of the population was urban. The trade and the taxes on it supplied the chief income of the monarchy and allowed it to pay the *parias* to Castile, to support a mercenary army, and simultaneously to raise that enormous wonder and pile, the Alhambra.

The government of Granada during this period supplies little in the way of novelty after the founding period. Initially and beyond self-interest, its success seems to have rested upon two pillars. Its founder, Muhammad ibn Yūsuf ibn Nasr was equally proficient as warrior and politician but the base upon which he built was his clan of the Banū Nasr, hence the term Nasrid. He brought it into collaboration and intermarriage with another clan, the Banū Ashqilūla, for additional strength. That was the stuff of Muslim politics. But Muhammad seems as well to have presented himself in a specifically religious guise as the one called to rescue Islam in Iberia. The circumstances of the middle of the thirteenth century are confused, of course, but the religious terminology and symbols adopted suggest a Sufic tone.

Obviously, the amalgam worked for the reign of Muhammad I was long and strong. Yet late in his reign he decided to change the bases of his government. To the extent he had ever embraced or endorsed it, he now renounced Sufism and its practices and beliefs in favor of that unqualified and unchanging Mālikite orthodoxy that had ever been the underpinning of the Muslim community in Iberia. He seems to have drawn back from the alliance with the Banū Ashqilūla as well and begun to concentrate power ever more in the hands of his own clan. The former, whose power was concentrated around Málaga, reacted by seeking assistance from Alfonso X of Castile but soon found that Muhammad I had more assets with which to play that game. As a result, the latter's son, Muhammad II

(1273–1302), was able to assume power on his father's accidental death, and himself to reign long and successfully. Nevertheless, the pattern had already emerged by which Castile, by far the strongest power in any event, would influence Granada by internal intrigue as well as by external pressure.

The entire period of Muhammad II's rule coincided with the great wave of Marīnid invasions of Andalusia with which he himself had much to do. It also had the advantage of coinciding with the time of troubles in Castile associated with revolt against Alfonso X and the briefer reign of Sancho IV (1284–1295) followed by the minority of Fernando IV (1295–1312). A combination of diplomacy and warfare allowed Muhammad to rid himself of the Banū Ashqilūla, they migrated to North Africa in 1288, and to avoid absorption into a Marīnid empire. Still, the kingdom had suffered its first great diminution. In the west, Tarifa had been lost to Castile and Gibraltar and Algeciras to the Marīnid. For practical purposes, Málaga had become its advance post.

Under a son, Muhammad III (1302–1309), the kingdom enjoyed a respite but by the end of that reign, indeed the cause of its end, Aragon and Castile had united forces against Granada, one besieging Almeria and the other Algeciras, temporarily back in Granadan hands. By this time, the latter kingdom disposed of a considerable force of Zanāta Berber mercenaries from North Africa as well as an annually reinforced group of religious Muslim volunteers from across the straits to engage in holy war with the Christians. That proved sufficient to rout the Aragonese before Almeria but the help of the Marīnids was needed to defeat Castile and their price was Algeciras and a variety of other western points. One further result was the assassination of Muhammad's *vizier* and his own deposition.

His brother, Nasr (1309–1314), replaced him but was himself deposed in a palace coup by his cousin, Ismail (1314–1325), who was supported by the Marīnid. The new emir of Granada was fortunate in the disarray of Castile at the time because of the long minority of Alfonso XI (1312–1350) who was but one year old at the time of his accession. In 1319 the Granadan inflicted a great defeat on forces led by two princes of the blood of Castile who ventured to invade his territories. Yet he was to perish in a plot of obscure nature. The conspirators made his young son, Muhammad IV (1325–1333), king and the new monarch ruled until Alfonso XI of Castile finally assumed the reins of power personally and decided to renew the *reconquista*. Muhammad reacted by deciding to appeal for Marīnid help. That decision apparently was offensive to some of his subjects and he fell to their daggers.

Nonetheless he was succeeded by his son, Yūsuf I (1333–1354), who had the misfortune to be contemporary to Alfonso XI of Castile in the period of his greatest power. Usually in alliance with the Marīnid, whose help was by now indispensable, Yūsuf fought and lost at Río Salado (1340), at Algeciras (1344), and might well have lost again at Gibraltar (1350) if the Black Death had not carried his adversary off and dispersed his army. All real hope now for rescue from North Africa was over. The Marīnid regime was in full decline at home in Morocco and their rivals at Tlemcen or Tunis were in hardly better condition. Yūsuf himself fell to the assassin's knife in 1354 in mysterious circumstances. What alone would protect Granada over the next half century was the succession crisis and civil war which began with the accession of Pedro I (1350–1369), the preoccupations of his executioner and successor, Enrique II (1369–1379), and the Portuguese war of his son, Juan I (1379–1390).

In Granada Muhammad V (1354–1391), son of Yūsuf, came to the throne and enjoyed a long and relatively successful rule by reason of the troubles of Castile. He too was deposed briefly, however, by palace coups which led to his replacement by his brother, Ismail (1359–1360), who was quickly murdered and then by a cousin, Muhammad VI (1360–1362), who was in turn assassinated by Pedro I of Castile during the course of negotiations. Muhammad V returned and a long period of peace followed. Yūsuf II (1391–1392) succeeded to his father only to be succeeded by his son, Muhammad VII (1392–1408), almost immediately. Active campaigning all along the frontier now began and Castile prepared for an assault on the mountain kingdom which was only prevented by the death of Enrique III (1390–1406). He left a son, Juan II (1406–1454), of but two years whose minority would continue until 1419. Nonetheless, the boy's uncle and regent, Fernando, began a major campaign which culminated in the capture in 1410 of Antequera, center of a fertile district and but forty kilometers north of Málaga itself. The conqueror would be known thereafter as Fernando de Antequera but fortunately for Granada he was shortly to have other preoccupations.

The subsequent history of Granada in the fifteenth century was one of continuing decline down to its final conquest in 1492. The history of border raids continued and the Muslims sometimes scored local successes of some importance but never enough to force Castile to grant them more than a short truce. Their enemy alternated between exacting *parias* from the hapless opponent and conducting destructive raids to destroy the fruits of their agriculture when they were slow in payment. The final capture of Gibraltar by Castile in 1461 had little more than symbolic value. There was no African power strong enough to employ it as a point of entry in any event.

The Granadans sought by every means to protect themselves but diplomacy and war proved equally futile. In the twists and turns of their policy the control of their own government changed some nine times in the period between the death of Yūsuf III (1408–1417) and 1452. Some of the emirs did manage to return to power after being deposed but the internal rivalries furnished regular opportunities for Castilian intervention on behalf of one faction or the other. After Antequera the only real question was when a sufficiently strong government would come to power in Castile and effect the conquest so obviously within reach.

THE MUDEJARS: LIFE AMIDST THE INFIDEL

If some 300,000 Muslims continued to live the precarious life in Granada in the Late Middle Ages, roughly another 600,000 spent their lives more peacefully as subjects of the various Christian monarchs of the peninsula. The region of Valencia constituted the most concentrated single population block with perhaps as many as 250,000 Muslims forming the majority of the total population there; large numbers were also to be found in Murcia but there were considerable numbers in Aragon proper as well. Few areas in the peninsula did not have at least a sprinkling.

Overwhelmingly it was, and continued to be, a farming community concentrated especially in those areas where the practice of irrigation made their long experience with that art particularly valuable. In the towns they continued to have their own small merchant class, bakers, butchers, grocers, and the like, essential in many ways to their life as Muslims. Mudejar art and architecture makes evident that their most widespread contribution to the Christian community all about them was as carpenters, plasterers, and tileworkers in the building trades but they also functioned as workers of precious metals and steels, as blacksmiths, carters, and textile finishers. It is easy to find communities numbering from 200 to 500 persons, whole villages in the countryside and *aljamas* in the towns.

According to the authorities on both sides they should not have existed, of course. Muslim religious teaching was unanimous that they had the duty to emigrate to Muslim territories. Only there could the full religious life be led since politics and religion were inseparable. The Muslim, for instance, had the religious obligation of paying taxes to the head of the dār al-Islam and to no other. Christian doctrine regularly distinguished between secular and religious society but the presumption was always that the society subject to the two laws was uniformly Christian. Rome and church councils periodically, then, called for the expulsion of Muslims on the grounds of the protection of the faith and morals of Christians. Up until the seventeenth century they were usually ignored for the

Muslim minority was too valuable to tax collector and lessor alike to be eliminated. Although generally it was tolerated, the practice of emigration was frequently sharply restricted or forbidden outright when it grew to a volume that alarmed the Christian authorities.

Although their condition was far from idyllic, the Muslim community of Iberia appears to have prospered in a modest fashion up until the expulsion. Certainly their numbers seem to have held relatively steady. The ideal of all concerned was that the two societies should be kept distinct. In a rough way that was realized in Muslim villages in the countryside and in the *aljamas* of the towns. Nevertheless, Christians sometimes lived in them and Muslims in Christian districts. Christians were forbidden as well to consult Muslim doctors or Muslims to hold political authority both of which were frequently transgressed. As separated, the Muslims were guaranteed the rule of their community by their own *qāḍī* under their own faith and law. By and large that guarantee was honored although difficulties inevitably arose and sometimes led to both individual and official violence.

In theory no new mosques were to be built but, in fact, they were when practical needs dictated. The call of the faithful to prayer by the *muezzin* was not to be tolerated, but clearly it was in practice. The prescription of distinctive garb for the Muslim was ignored. Muslims were, from time to time, required to attend harangues urging conversion but churchmen uniformly recognized that forcible conversion was illicit. Conversion was a rich source of trouble for both religions forbade it under pain of possible death. When the Muslim became a convert he became an outcast from his own community but was rarely accepted wholeheartedly in the new one. Sexual relationships across religious lines were viewed with only slightly less horror than apostasy and both communities punished their own with extreme rigor. Probably because the offense was much more common than outright apostasy. But again we must be careful to realize that most of the records we possess are produced precisely by the momentary breakdown of *convivencia* and that ordinary relationships may be presumed better. A happy exception to the rule is that official documents themselves make it evident that the Muslim was free to travel, even abroad with permission, and so the pious could and did satisfy the obligation of the pilgrimage to Mecca in fair numbers.

In return for this limited autonomy, the Muslim community was directly subject to the crown. Officials to oversee *aljama* itself were appointed by the crown as needed and appeals from their legal decisions were sometimes entertained. Both Aragon and Castile had a royal office of *alcade mayor* or supreme judge for all Mudejar communities of the realm and he was appointed by the crown. It does appear that he was ordinarily a Muslim himself. Some individuals were even allowed voluntarily to submit their cases to the Christian courts to escape the very harsh penalties of the *sharia*, the judicial code of Islam. The *aljama* was also collectively subject to a special royal tax that was a sign of their condition, the *pecha*. Ordinarily it was levied at the rate of one *maravedi* per family. As such it was not too onerous but in times of difficulty for the crown it might be levied more than annually and forced loans might also be extorted. In this respect, of course, the Muslim was not terribly different from the other subjects of the crown.

Muslim business men and artisans were subject as well to the *alcabala* after 1350 as was all business. Muslim farmers paid the customary dues to whomever held jurisdiction over the land that they worked. They were free to buy and sell land among fellow Muslims but selling to, or buying land from, Christians was subject to various restrictions. In particular, lands which could be proved never to have been in Christian hands were not subject to the church tax, the tithe. But lands once subject to the tithe always remained so even if purchased by a Muslim. In addition to giving rise to frequent disputes, such law acted to freeze lands in Muslim ownership and added to the usual conservatism of the countryside.

So the Mudejar Iberian community continued to exist relatively undiminished in numbers but it had been decapitated intellectually as well as politically. That is, the court and the aristocracy had been their great patrons of learning and now they lacked both. With the politicians of Islam, the judges, the doctors, the scholars, and the merchants, had fled to North Africa or Granada in disproportionate numbers and peninsular Islam was left impoverished and bereft of the structures to replenish its loss. Some education continued, to be sure, but slowly the knowledge of the sacred language itself was lost. Spoken Arabic continued to be a living language in Granada and in Valencia as well down to the conquest of 1492 and beyond. But in Castile, Portugal, and Navarre, Mudejars became Romance speakers. A small intellectual elite continued to read Arabic but increasingly its work was one of translation. When that select corps needed to be replenished a frequent device was to send the candidate to Valencia for instruction. Arabic was becoming a school language elsewhere.

To carry on the ordinary business of life Muslim law codes, in the form of the *Leyes de Moros*, was being translated into Castilian apparently by the fourteenth century. In the fifteenth century Isā ibn Jābir, *imām* and *faqīh* in Segovia, published a *Breviario* of the pious Muslim. Although himself a religious figure, Isā had already cooperated with Juan de Segovia to translate the Koran, the sacred text itself, into Castilian. Popular literature as well existed although without any great originality in the so-called *aljamiado.* That is, increasingly translations or compositions were written, both prose and poetry, using the Arabic script but the Catalan, or Castilian, Galician, or Portuguese language now native to the author. Most of the materials were pious stories, of Muhammad, or the Biblical Joseph, or Solomon, but Alexander the Great was also represented. The pieces sometimes dealt with calendars, or homely medical lore, but in others with love stories, both traditional Arabic ones and some even borrowed from current Christian popular literature. Much of this material remains to be investigated but it seems unlikely that it will ever be found to constitute a great literature.

Even in independent Granada the drain of the most cultivated spirits toward North Africa is to be noted, continuing a trend which had begun in Muwāhhid, or even Murābit, times. To the extent that there was religious variety in Iberian Islam, eastern Andalusia was its home. Ibn Arabī (1165–1240) had been born in Murcia, educated in Seville, and died in Damascus. Credited with more than four hundred works from love poetry to treatises on the mystical life, his tomb in Syria is still venerated by the pious. Last in this line was Ibn Abbād (1332–1389), born in Granada at Ronda, who finished his life as *imām* of the principal mosque in Fez. In addition to his treatment of the mystical life in the *Commentary on the Maxims of Atāllah*, he left a collection of homilies that were long used after his death. Ibn al-Khatīb (1313–1374), born in Granada, was a more secular figure who served as *vizier* for the Nasrids but ended a refugee in Tlemcen where he was strangled as a courtesy to the Granadan authorities. He had written with distinction on music, Sufism, medicine, politics, and history. His former protégé, successor as *vizier*, and final nemesis was ibn Zamrak (1333–1393), a poet of nature many of whose verses can be found on the walls of the Alhambra.

But perhaps the last great intellectual figure of Iberian Islam was ibn Khaldūn (d. 1406), scion of one of those numerous Andalusian families who sought refuge in North Africa after the conquest of Seville. He was born at Tunis and died in Cairo but he also served the Nasrids of Granada for a time. His great work was the *al-Muqaddimah* and the *Kitāb al-Ibar*, together a philosophy or sociology of history followed by a universal history in three books of seven volumes. In the originality and brilliance of his thought he was a melancholy example of the still unrealized potential of al-Andalus.

TOWARDS THE DESTRUCTION OF IBERIAN JEWRY

The political collapse of the Muwāhhid in the mid-thirteenth century implied little in the way of change initially for the Jews of the peninsula.

From what we can gather from the *Libros de Repartimiento* the Jewish quarters of the major towns of Andalusia survived and the more important Jewish courtiers of the kings were rewarded with houses and lands in the newly conquered territories as well. Indeed, the most important *juderias* of Iberia had already long been located in the north due to the relative intolerance of Murābit and Muwāhhid in al-Andalus.

By way of contrast, the Jews were far less numerous than the Mudejars in any event. The best current estimates would put their total numbers in the peninsula as not more than 50,000. The largest individual community in Castile was that of Toledo which numbered perhaps 2,000. Seville had 1,000 and Burgos about 600. In the crown of Aragon the Jews of Barcelona numbered about 1,000, Valencia 1,200, and Saragossa about another 1,000. Nevertheless, they lived subject to the same basic conditions as did the more numerous Mudejars. That is, theoretically they were a people apart, living in their own communities under their own law and officials and practicing their own faith, but that not so ostentatiously as to perturb their Christian neighbors. Actually these regulations were observed with as little rigor as were those governing the Muslims. Like the Mudejars, Jews also were subjects of the crown in a particular sense and paid a special tax in recognition of that fact.

There is a nice problem then as to why the fortunes of the two groups should have taken such different courses over the next two centuries. The documents make it clear that the usual frictions and prejudices arising from distinctly different cultural groups living in close proximity were present in both cases. Ambitions, rivalries, and cupidities, were regularly translated into ethnic antagonisms in both cases and usually that meant that the minority suffered and lost in some measure. But the fourteenth century will be disastrous for the Jews and only mildly uncomfortable for the Mudejars despite the fact that the latter are fifteen times more numerous and that their co-religionists in Granada were current and active antagonists of all things Christian. Obviously the continuing onslaught against the Jew was not a reaction to a perceived threat in any ordinary sense.

In the last quarter of the thirteenth century Alfonso X could summarily hang his chief tax collector, a Jew, and suddenly impose a double tribute on the entire Jewish community of the realm. There was a history of the Jew as scapegoat and possibly more of a history than the surviving records tell us. It would seem to speak more to political expediency than to settled policy. But what began in the fourteenth century appears to be different. A permanent rather than an occasional hostility to the Jew, precisely as Jew, emerged and gradually took on the aspect of a constant condition of life. At the same time, hostility to the Mudejar was of the older, occasional variety.

Old and official hostility was gradually intensified. The Christian church in the west had long sought an end to Jews in a position of power over Christians. In 1263 the crown of Aragon had allowed the preaching in synagogues by Dominicans with the purpose of converting the Jews. The Council of Zamora of 1313 reiterated the old demands of the church as to the segregation of Jews, the wearing of a distinctive badge, the payment by them of the church tithe, and the rest. But increasingly the voice of the church was seconded by that of the *cortes*. In response to it Sancho IV of Castile promised to rid the royal curia of his father's, Alfonso X, Jewish financiers. He did not but the demands continued. In Aragon the crown in fact did cease to employ Jews as its chief financial officers in the time of Pere III under pressure from the *corts*. But in Portugal the older practice endured down to the end of the fifteenth century. After the accession of Pedro I of Castile in 1350 part of the propaganda of the rebel Trastamara faction against him was that he employed and befriended Jews.

This sort of heightened anti-Semitic agitation among the privileged classes must have had some resonance among the populace at large. But when the attack came it was a popular phenomenon which responded to no official program whether of church, crown, or *cortes*. A mob attacked and destroyed the *aljama* of Estella in Navarre in 1328. Another attacked that of Gerona in Catalonia with less success in 1331. Royal troops massacred some Jews in Toledo in 1355. But the final storm broke in Seville where the archdeacon of Ecija, a member of the cathedral chapter there, had been rabid in his preaching against the Jews since 1378. There on June 4, 1391, a mob sacked and burned the *aljama* and its synagogues and such Jews as survived were forced to accept baptism. As the news spread 250 Jews were killed in Valencia, 300 in Majorca, 400 in Barcelona. Reliable numbers elsewhere are lacking but at Gerona, Huesca and Lérida, at Burgos, Madrid, Segovia, and Cuenca the pattern was the same. Only in the smaller villages do the Jews seem to have gone unscathed. Typically, the larger the town, the greater the violence, which suggests that the discontents of an urban proletariat are primary to the phenomenon. It would also help to explain its absence in relatively underdeveloped Portugal.

The first reaction of the crown and often of the municipal authorities was to protect such Jews as they could. That the *juderia* of Saragossa subsequently became the most vigorous one in Iberia was due to the fact that King Joan of Aragon was there at the time to protect it. Some *juderias* were restored and some property also. Some looters were hung.

But San Vicent Ferrer traveled through Castile and Aragon in the following decades capitalizing on the fears of the Jewish population to secure additional conversions. He inspired new anti-Semitic legislation in Castile in 1412 and inspired a great debate over Judaism and Christianity at Tortosa in 1413. Everywhere the crown found itself at least temporarily forced to adhere rather more fully to the ideal strict segregation of Jewish from Christian communities long advocated by churchmen and the exclusion of Jews from most official positions, from the learned professions, and even from such trades as had a Christian clientele. On the other hand, those concessions of the crown were made simpler by the fact that places in such positions, professions, and trades, were often assumed by the *conversos* or "new Christians."

What had changed and to what extent is not easy to say. The total number of Jews murdered in 1391 is, like the total number terrified into emigrating, or the total number "converted," almost impossible to estimate. The best guess may be that the Jewish community in Iberia, outside of Portugal, lost something like 40 percent of its membership to the combination of the three. At least that can be estimated if one calculates back from the number of Jews expelled in 1492 and predicates that the Jewish community experienced something like the same population growth general in fifteenth-century Iberia. It would seem to be the curious fact that the number of Jews then expelled correlates quite closely with the number estimated to have existed there in 1300.

The events of the turn of the century, then, had profoundly shaken but not destroyed the Jewish community. In some measure it was turned rather more in upon itself but, at the same time, relations with the *conversos* were frequently close, too close for the liking of Christian churchmen. For Christian Castile and Aragon the problem of *convivencia* with the Jews remained and soon enough assumed much of its previous dimensions. More, to it now had been added the problem of assessing the sincerity of the "new Christians." The very circumstances of their conversion made all concerned wonder about its quality and if they remained secret adherents to Judaism; the preference accorded to them by the authorities was yet more maddening. When they became secretary to kings as did Juan de Coloma of Aragon or bishop of Burgos as did Pablo de Santa María, it began to seem a conspiracy of the wellborn to restore the bad old custom in a new guise. The problem of the *conversos* would eventually be addressed by the equally sinister means of the inquisition and the *limpieza de sangre* in the èra of the Catholic kings as the problem of the Jews would be by the expulsion.

The blighting of the intellectual life of Iberian Jewry was not as severe as that which affected the Mudejar community. It had its costs of course.

The Rabbinic scholar Simon ben Zemah Duran of Majorca finished his life in Algeria. The Barcelonan Talmudic scholar, Hasdai ben Abraham Crescas (1340–1410) lost his only son in 1391 and migrated to Saragossa. Israel ben al-Nakawa of Toledo who wrote on ethics, the *Menorath ha-Maor* or *Lamp of Illumination*, was killed there in 1391. But Iberian Jewry was not handicapped by the close relationship of political and religious life that marked Islam and there was no wholesale exodus of its intelligentsia on the order of the Mudejar experience.

Instead the Jewish learned tradition continued to be marked rather by the logic of its own internal development. Secular poetry still treated such themes as love and friendship as in the case of Solomon ben Rueben Bonfed (1380–1450) who even composed a poetic history of poetry. Abraham Bibago wrote commentaries on the *Analytics*, the *Physics*, and the *Metaphysics* of Aristotle, as well as on the medical works of Averroes. Isaac ben Joseph Israeli put together a treatise on astronomy and the calendar, *Yesod Olam* or *Foundation of the World*. Joseph ben Tzadik of Arevalo published a world chronicle after the fashion of Christian historiography.

More typical, however, was a turning away from rationalist thought towards mysticism which also marked developments in both Islamic and Christian thought during the period. Frequently this took the form of attacks on the great Moses Maimonides and his *Guide for the Perplexed*. Hasdai Crescas in particular composed his *Or Adonai*, or *Light of the Lord*, as a replacement to, and refutation of, that work. In the Jewish community the influence of Maimonidean rationalists was combated by social ostracism and a good deal of satirical polemical literature in poetic form was produced.

Perhaps the most remarkable feature of intellectual life was the growing preoccupation with the lore of the *Kabbala*, or *Tradition*. This was a body of thought that held to the existence of a secret tradition of Hebrew learning, separate from the Bible or the Torah, which had been transmitted orally among the elect of Jewry from the most ancient times. In some respects it resembled Neoplatonism with its emphasis on the universe as an emanation from the godhead and on the role of angels as demiurges midway between God himself and his creatures. It also featured an arcane knowledge which dwelt on the symbolic and even magical properties of Biblical phrases and the letters of the Hebrew script. This school first emerged clearly with Moses of León (1250–1305) who claimed to have made a marvelous discovery of its canon, the *Zohar*, that had been magically transported from Palestine to Spain in a fashion irresistibly suggestive of the earlier development of the Santiago legend. The school of the *Kabbala* obviously predated the events of 1391 but the fourteenth- and fifteenth-century experiences of Iberian Judaism would provide fertile soil for its spread as a reaction to that accommodation and interaction with Islamic and Christian thought more typical of the earlier Iberian period.

THE AGGRANDIZEMENT OF CASTILE

Certainly from the time of Fernando I (1037–1065) and perhaps from the appearance of the older Kingdom of Asturias, León–Castile had always been the largest and most populous of the Christian societies of the peninsula. The dictates of geography and of political opportunity had determined that it would profit most from the long decline of Islam as a political force there. Despite the secession of Portugal and the remarkable creation of the crown of Aragon in the twelfth century, Castile had remained the demographic, geographic, and political behemoth into the fourteenth century. Not infrequently, as with Alfonso VI (1065–1109), Alfonso VII (1126–1157), and finally Alfonso X (1252–1284), it had asserted its claim to an imperial status which implied a rightful hegemony in Iberia. Nevertheless, the realities of geographical and political life there had seldom allowed that ambition more than a momentary realization. But in the fourteenth and fifteenth centuries the dynamics of dynastic monarchy were to finally result in the creation of a kingdom of Spain under the Catholic kings.

After the disorder of the final days of Alfonso X, the short reign of his rebel son, Sancho IV, and the regencies of Fernando IV and Alfonso XI, the brilliant reign of the latter demonstrated yet again the potency of Castile in the peninsula. Before his death in 1350 Alfonso had cleared the Marīnid from Andalusia and in so doing asserted once again the leadership of Castile in the great enterprise of the *reconquista*. Only his spectacular infidelity to his queen, Maria of Portugal, daughter to Afonso IV (1325–1357), could have caused the renewal of dynastic conflict which threatened that dominance. As a result of his long and public relationship with Eleanor de Gúzman, the king left his heir, Pedro I (1350–1369) the most serious sort of rivals in his half-brothers Enrique and Fadrique of Trastamara. Pedro I in turn would contribute his share of dynastic disruption by deserting his own wife, Blanche of Bourbon, to live publicly with his mistress, Maria de Padilla.

His half-brothers were soon in revolt against him but despite handicaps of his own making, Pedro defeated them easily. Enrique took refuge in Aragon and in 1356 what is usually called a war began between the two largest of the peninsular realms. At issue were the provision of assistance to rebels against the other by both monarchs, the possession of northern Murcia by Aragon since 1304, and trade disputes. It went on until 1365 but consisted actually of a series of individual campaigns, after the fashion of wars at that time, with a corresponding variety of short truces and peaces. Yet the superiority of Castile on the field was evident to all and Pere IV decided in 1365 to join his suit to that of Enrique of Trastamara who had sought the assistance of the French king, Charles V. Since Pedro of Castile was allied with his English enemies, Charles agreed and Enrique of Trastamara returned to Iberia in 1366 at the head of a French mercenary army paid by Aragonese gold, in what the pope at Avignon portrayed as a "crusade." After still another three years of fighting, during which Pedro was forced to secure the intervention of Edward, the Black Prince, at great cost, the king was finally defeated and stabbed to death by his own half-brother to whom the French mercenary captain, Bertrand du Guesclin, had betrayed him.

This was perhaps a fitting end for a king who had earned the name of "the Cruel" by his political murders and reprisals, but it changed very little except to bring another branch of the dynasty to the throne. Both the dynasties of Aragon and of Castile had squandered much of the royal resources to the profit, principally, of the nobility of both realms. Still, Enrique II (1369–1379) took up the mantle of kingship and sought to restore the fisc and royal jurisdiction in quite the manner of the brother whom he had murdered.

Even while so occupied the Trastamara was sufficiently strong to repel the attacks of Fernando I of Portugal (1367–1383) who had his own if distant claim to the crown of Castile. Enrique invaded Portugal in 1373, defeated Fernando, and forced the betrothal of the Portuguese's daughter to his own bastard son. Two years later he secured the marriage of an Aragonese princess to his son and heir, Juan, while his daughter was married to the heir of Navarre. Meanwhile Basque fleets were cooperating with the French and ravaging the coasts of England.

Enrique's son, Juan I (1379–1390), was to continue his father's policies and to attempt as well the absorption of Portugal. Fernando I of Portugal had been an ally of Pedro I and of England in the time of Juan's father and of John of Gaunt, brother of the English king and Duke of Lancaster, who had married the daughter of Pedro I, Constancia. Fernando took advantage of the death of Enrique to ally with England once again but Juan defeated him easily and arranged his own marriage to Beatriz, daughter of Fernando, in May of 1383. When the Portuguese king died five months later, Juan asserted the rights of his wife as queen but a revolt in Portugal followed. An illegitimate half-brother of the dead king, João I (1383–1433), was named first regent and then king. Generally, the church and the cities of Lisbon and Oporto supported João while the nobility supported Juan I.

Juan invaded Portugal but an outbreak of the Black Death destroyed most of his army besieging Lisbon in 1384. When Juan could return to the attack in 1385 a small English force had arrived to assist the Portuguese. At Aljubarrota on August 14, 1385, the new tactics they had introduced and a Castilian frontal assault on prepared positions protected by archers led to a crushing defeat of the latter and their Portuguese allies. In 1386 John of Gaunt landed at La Coruña and overran Galicia. He now married his daughter, Philippa, to João of Portugal in exchange for assistance and in 1387 the two invaded Castile but without success. Juan I proceeded then to buy off the Duke of Lancaster for a huge sum and to agree to marry his son and heir, the future Enrique III (1390–1406), to Catalina, Lancaster's daughter and the granddaughter of Pedro I. Juan also was forced to sign a truce with Portugal but his own death in 1390 and the succession of an eleven-year-old son would in fact secure the immunity of that kingdom from renewed Castilian attack for a long time to come.

The battle of Aljubarrota, twenty-four kilometers southwest of Leiria, is usually regarded as having sealed the independence of Portugal from Castile and it would be foolish to disregard its importance. Nevertheless, the dynastic alliance of the Portuguese monarchy with the English was not maintained. Rather, João's son and successor, Duarte I (1433–1438), would marry Leonor, daughter of Fernando de Antequera, and so the close connection with the dynasty of Castile would be maintained. Of necessity then, Portugal would be involved in Iberian dynastic politics and, in an age when dynasty meant more than mountains, liable again to fall subject to a Castilian claim that it could not resist out of its own resources. In 1580 during the reign of Philip II that is precisely what would befall it and for sixty-odd years thereafter it would be a part of the Spanish Empire until a general European war restored its independence.

Beginning with the accession of Enrique III (1390–1406) the consolidation of Iberia took a different, unforeseeable turn. He followed a predictable internal policy hoping to bring the great nobility under more control. To that end, he avoided war with his neighbors even under much provocation. However the king died young and left a son, Juan II (1406–1454), of not quite two years. A long regency was in prospect but the late king's brother, Fernando, rapidly consolidated power in his own hands as regent and fought a popular and successful war with Granada, triumphing at Antequera in 1410. Fernando of Antequera ruled Castile as regent until his own death in 1416. But in 1412 he had become Fernando I of Aragon as well.

After the death of the great Pere IV (1336–1387) the crown of Aragon had been held in turn by two of his sons, Joan I (1387–1395) and Martí I (1395–1410). While Joan inherited the empty treasury and a crippled internal jurisdiction, both legacies of Pere IV's disastrous Castilian wars, he himself did nothing sufficiently energetic to either remedy or worsen the situation. His brother Martí had some success in the recovery of alienated crown lands and jurisdiction and rather more success abroad in Sicily and Italy. Before he became king Martí led an expedition in 1392 that restored control in Sicily to the elder branch of the house of Aragon in the person of his son, Martí the Younger. His son also commanded the Sardinian expedition of 1409 that almost completely restored Aragonese power over that restive island. Unfortunately the younger Martí contracted malaria there and died. Ten months later in May of 1410 Martí I died without leaving a direct heir.

When the direct, male line of the counts of Barcelona thus came to an end there was no dearth of claimants but political conditions quickly reduced the viable candidates to two. One was Jaume, count of Urgel, and greatgrandson of Alfons III (1285–1291). The other was Fernando de Antequera, son of Juan I of Castile and of Eleanor, sister of Martí I. Precisely because the *corts* of the realm had secured so much authority over the past century the question of recognition of a successor was bound to be theirs. Eventually it was decided that the three *corts* of Catalonia, Aragon, and Valencia, would each name three representatives to a commission that would decide the question by a two-thirds majority.

In the political contest that ensued, Fernando proved not only to have the advantage of a great fortune to buy support and a reputation as warrior gained at Antequera. He was also the favorite of Vicent Ferrer and the Catalan claimant to the papacy, Benedict XIII. Moreover, Fernando displayed a much greater energy and firmness in pursuing the crown. Jaume was an early favorite of the *corts* of Catalonia and Valencia largely because his absence of resources outside Catalonia itself promised to make him easier to control. In the so-called *Compromiso de Caspe* of 1412 the Castilian was elected and the dynasty of Castile gained the throne of Aragon.

That fact itself and a healthy heir were to be Fernando's sole legacies to the crown of Aragon. His four years of rule were too brief to leave much impress on the welter of competing jurisdictions there. His son, Alfonso V (1416–1468), who succeeded him is better known as an Italian prince than an Iberian one. Alfonso began by solidifying the Aragonese positions in Sicily, Sardinia, and even Corsica which had been a possession in name only since 1297. He also carried out the conquest of the Angevin kingdom of Naples between 1436 and 1443 although in all of this he continued to incur the enmity of Genoa which was usually therefore at war with Aragon. The Castilian Trastamaras then fully adopted the established policy of Aragonese empire in the western Mediterranean and carried it to that point at which it would become part of the Spanish Empire.

In that pursuit, Alfonso V himself largely abandoned Iberia for Italy. He had married his first cousin, Maria, sister of his former ward, Juan II of Castile (1406–1454), and she became his very capable viceroy in the peninsula. After 1436 that function was assumed by Alfonso's brother who was also to succeed him as Juan II (1458–1479) of Aragon. The latter was the father of Fernando of Aragon. The former had long experience of Aragonese policies before his actual accession of course, yet his reign there was long and stormy. From 1462 until 1472 he faced revolt in Catalonia although he was able to retain the support of Aragon proper, Valencia, and Majorca. Ironically the Catalan *corts* sought the support of his own son, Carlos, against him, then that of his cousin Enrique IV of Castile, and finally that of René of Anjou, count of Provence. In desperation Juan II was forced to ask help of Louis XI of France which that monarch furnished but in the process annexed Roselló and Cerdanya. Still at his death Juan had not been able to reclaim the two territories and would leave that task, and the ensuing enmity with France, to his son Fernando.

But Juan II of Aragon had also been king of Navarre from 1425 for he had married Blanche, heiress to that modest kingdom in 1420. The house of Evereux that had succeeded there in 1328 was a cadet branch of the Capetians of France. Its kings had attempted to take advantage of the Hundred Years War and its peninsular extension without success. When the male line failed in 1425, one of the most powerful members of the Trastamara dynasty in Castile became its king by marriage and a son, Carlos, had been born to Blanche and him. At his wife's death in 1441 Juan refused to acknowledge his son as either king or his successor in Navarre. That made his son a rebel who plotted against his father until his own death in 1461 and gave the rebellious *corts* of Barcelona an opportunity to use him against his father. Eventually, Juan recognized instead his daughter Leonor as heiress and permitted her marriage to Gaston, count of Foix. But in 1512, Juan's son by his second marriage to the Castilian noblewoman Juana Enríquez, Fernando II of Aragon, was to reclaim that portion of his father's lands.

But Juan II of Aragon had long been more interested in his Castilian inheritance than in the former throne to which he came only at his brother's death. In that realm the long minority of his namesake provided the opportunity for the regents and great nobility to enrich themselves out of the crown's income. That was the beginning and the end of the nobility's program. To displace the monarchy would have been unthinkable. Therefore it was essential to control it in one's own interest. The obstacle to that intention was their own mutual rivalry and jealousy of course. The leading contenders in this effort to control the king after 1416 were precisely the sons of Fernando de Antequera, the *infantes de Aragon*, Juan and his brother Enrique. But even they were sometimes as much rivals as brothers.

When Juan II of Castile came of age, fourteen, in 1419 he had no particular desire to rule personally but he did desire someone who would rule in his interest. He soon found such a person in the illegitimate son of a minor noble, Alvaro de Luna. Until his judicial murder in 1453 Luna did just that; he became Constable of Castile and Grand Master of the Order of Santiago, and rich almost beyond imagining; his brother, Guter Alvarez, became archbishop of Toledo (1442–1446). Luna was that worst of obscenities in the view of the *ricos hombres*, a man of no lineage who preyed upon an irresolute king.

First Luna divided the *infantes de Aragon* and then forced them into a position in which they had to invade Castile from Navarre in 1429. That lost them the sympathy of everyone and their lands were confiscated. But the favorite's own position was never safe from noble intrigue and from 1439 divisions in his party allowed the *infantes* to reassert themselves. When the king himself was captured at Medina del Campo in 1441 the rule of Juan of Navarre became so obvious that the heir to the throne himself took the field with Luna and the *infantes* were defeated at Olmedo in 1445. Enrique died of his wounds and Juan was driven back to Navarre and to an eventual future as ruler of Aragon. But of its nature, Luna's power could never be complete or secure. Juan II's heir, the future Enrique IV (1454–1474), now became jealous of the power of Luna over his father and led the conspiracies against him. Luna also erred when he arranged the marriage of Isabel of Portugal to his royal master. The new queen soon became one of the most ardent plotters against the great minister.

Finally Alvaro de Luna fell to the one force always capable of his destruction. Juan II ordered his arrest and he was beheaded in Valladolid in 1453. Within a year the king himself had followed his great minister to the grave and his son, Enrique, succeeded him peacefully. But Enrique would himself find a favorite to guide the crown, Juan Pacheco who would become Marquis of Villena, his brother the Grand Master of the Order of Calatrava, his uncle Archbishop Carrillo of Toledo (1446–1482). Before long the grandees of the realm were plotting against this new upstart. Sometimes assisted by the king or his minister, who worked somewhat less well together than his father and Luna had, the plots gradually made headway until in 1464 a great noble manifesto attacked the king and in 1465 he was deposed in absentia at Ávila. The Marquis of Villena who had joined the rebels was the most dangerous of them.

Of course no noble rising could hope for success without the support of the dynasty and so the young half-brother of Enrique, Alfonso, was crowned king there. The claims of Enrique's own daughter by Juana of Portugal, the younger Juana, were set aside on the grounds that the king was impotent and that the child was illegitimate, born of the adultery of his wife and his new minister, Beltrán de la Cueva. The civil war that followed was stalemated when the young Alfonso XII, as his supporters called him, died in 1468. The rebels now looked to the half-sister of Enrique, Isabel, to play the same part and she was indeed proclaimed queen in Seville. But the king had the better cards to play. He met with Isabel outside Ávila and agreed to recognize her as his heir to the crown of Castile.

Part of that agreement stipulated that Isabel was not to marry without his consent. But at this time Juan II of Aragon badly needed help against the Catalans. His son and heir, Fernando, was advanced as a bridegroom with assurances that Isabel would have a free hand in the government of Castile. The match pleased her and her supporters but Pope Paul II refused to provide the necessary dispensation so that the two cousins might marry. Two years later his successor, Pope Sixtus IV, would do so. In the meantime a papal bull was forged and the royal cousins were wed at Valladolid on October 18, 1469, while Enrique IV was in Andalusia.

The king reacted strongly against the marriage but the march had been stolen and the two young dynasts had strong support. By dint of delay and negotiation they managed to survive until the king himself died in 1474, defeated by this final conspiracy of his house against him. But the end product of this infinite skein of intrigue and ambition was that medieval Iberia had all but perished and that modern Spain was in gestation. A single dynasty had gained the power of direction over both Castile and Aragon and the further consolidation of the peninsula under its government was all but inevitable.

AN INTRODUCTORY BIBLIOGRAPHY

The following annotated list makes no pretence of being either comprehensive or scholarly in the fullest sense of the word. Therefore it includes no list of critical editions of the sources or of the periodical literature. It is designed, as is this book hopefully, to give the intelligent and interested reader with scant previous knowledge of the Iberian peninsula both a sense of what was going on in that fascinating place during the medieval period and an easy road to such modern scholarship as will satisfy further interests. Because an English-speaking public is primarily intended, I have cited works in English where possible and responsible. Nevertheless, a great deal of the best scholarship is in the peninsular languages and I have not hesitated to include these works. In fact, no bibliography worthy of the name could be compiled without them.

GENERAL SURVEYS

Still the most useful survey of the entire subject in English is Joseph F. O'Callaghan, *A History of Medieval Spain*, Ithaca, N.Y., 1975. By design it is fuller in materials than this volume. Despite the title, Gabriel Jackson, *The Making of Medieval Spain*, New York, 1972, deals mostly with the period after the fall of the caliphate. The same may be said of Angus Mackay, *Spain in the Middle Ages*, New York, 1977. Among the shorter Spanish histories Luis García de Valdeavellano, *Historia de España*, 2nd ed. Vol. 1, Madrid, 1973, is the simplest to use for its old-fashioned attention to names and dates and political history. José Angel García de Cortázar y Ruiz de Aguirre, *Historia de España Alfaguera. Vol. 2: La epoca medieval*,

Madrid 1973, and José Luis Martín, *La península in la Edad Media*, Barcelona, 1976, are more interpretive and less directly informative for the beginner. Treatment in the grand manner may be had in Espasa Calpe's series, Ramón Menéndez Pidal, ed., *Historia de España*, 18 vols., Madrid, 1957–90, which is still appearing but contains serious gaps and the original volumes now are quite old. They are still useful, however, for their determined attention to detail and breadth of coverage from political history to archeology and art history. Jaime Vicens Vives, ed., *Historia de España y America social y económica*, Vols. 1 and 2, 2nd ed., Barcelona, 1971, contains a plethora of information difficult to come by elsewhere. Ruth Way, *A Geography of Spain and Portugal*, London, 1962, is particularly necessary for readers who have not visited the peninsula.

LATE CLASSICAL AND VISIGOTHIC PERIOD (CHAPTERS 1 AND 2)

The Visigoths have gone somewhat out of style these days except perhaps in England. E. A. Thompson, *The Goths in Spain*, Oxford, 1969, remains indispensable. Nonetheless, Luis A. García Moreno, *Historia de España visigoda*, Madrid, 1989, is by far the best present treatment. Also, see the same author, *El fin del reino visgodo de Toledo*, Madrid, 1975. José Orlandis, *Historia de España: La España visigotica*, Madrid, 1977, is a bit out of date now. P. D. King, *Law and Society in the Visigothic Kingdom*, Cambridge, 1972, is the best of careful scholarship if, perhaps, too ready to believe that law gets regularly applied. Edward James, ed., *Visigothic Spain: New Approaches*, Oxford, 1980, lives up to the title. Ricardo García Villoslada, Manuel Sotomayor y Muro, Teodoro González García, and Pablo López de Osaba, *Historia de la iglesia en España*, Vol. 1, Madrid, 1979, treat that most necessary institution for the Roman and Visigothic periods in a ponderous and quite traditional fashion but the basic information is provided. José Orlandis, *La iglesia en la España visgótica y medieval*, Pamplona, 1976, supplies a briefer introduction. Aloysius K. Siegler, *Church and State in Visigothic Spain*, Washington, D.C., 1930, remains a formidable study of that subject. Angel Montenegro Duque, Jose María Blazquez Martínez, and José María Solana Saínz, *Historia de España: España romana*, Madrid 1986, provides a survey of the latest scholarship, Roger Collins, *The Basques*, Oxford 1986, reminds effectively that the peninsular evolution remains complex and thorny.

THE PERIOD OF MUSLIM DOMINATION (CHAPTER 3)

Given the general lack of familiarity of English-speaking peoples with the world of Islam, the neophyte may consult with profit Gustave E. von

Grünebaum, *Medieval Islam*, Chicago, 1953. *The Cambridge History of Islam*, Vol. 2, Cambridge 1970, supplies, amidst much else, a brief history of Islam in western North Africa. Anwar G. Chejne, *Muslim Spain; Its History and Culture*, Minneapolis, Minn., 1974, is the best short survey in English. W. Montgomery Watt, *A History of Islamic Spain*, Edinburgh, 1965, is handy and unfailingly intelligible for the newcomer. Roger Collins, *The Arab Conquest of Spain*, Oxford, 1989, is the most recent and authoritative treatment of that subject. The same author, *Early Medieval Spain*, New York, 1983, handily puts the former in a somewhat larger context. Andrew M. Watson, *Agricultural Innovation in the Early Islamic World*, New York, 1983, calls careful attention to a subject ordinarily treated with platitudes. Juan Vernet, *La cultura hispanoárabe en Orient y Occidente*, Barcelona, 1978, supplies many specifics and complements Chejne.

A yet wider context for events is supplied by Archibald R. Lewis, *Naval Power and Trade in the Mediterranean, A.D. 500–1000*, Princeton, 1951. Eliyahu Ashtor, *The Jews of Muslim Spain*, 3 vols., Philadelphia, 1973–84, tr. Aaron Klein and Jenny Machlowitz Klein, treats that essential component of Iberian Islamic society. Unfortunately there is presently no satisfactory work which devotes similar attention to its Mozarab analogue. For the nascent independent Christian societies of the north the classic study is Claudio Sánchez Albornoz, *Orígenes de la nación española*, Oviedo, 1972. Abilio Barbero and Marcelo Vigil, *Sobre los origines sociales de la reconquista*, Salamanca, 1974, suggests alternative methods for considering and supplementing the traditional data without arriving at a very satisfactory synthesis. Antonio C. Floriano Cumbreño, *Estudios de historia de Asturias*, Oviedo, 1962, is probably the easiest approach to what remains a major historical problem.

Farther east in the peninsula Thomas N. Bisson, *The Medieval Crown of Aragon*, Oxford, 1986, is lucid throughout and sensible on beginnings as well. Antonio Ubieto Arteta, *Historia de Aragón: Orígenes de Aragón*, Saragossa, 1989, surveys the entire region until AD 1000. Maria J. Viguera, *Aragón musulmana*, Saragossa 1988, takes the other perspective. Portugal is adequately served in English by A. H. Oliveira Marques, *History of Portugal*, Vol. 1, New York, 1972. The period up to the beginning of the fifteenth century is provided by Joaquim Veríssimo Serrão, *História de Portugal*, Vol. 1, 3rd ed., Lisbon, 1979–80. That to the beginning of the fourteenth century is done in much more detail by José Mattoso, *Identifição de um país: Ensãio sobre as origens de Portugal, 1096–1325*, 2 vols., Lisbon, 1985–6.

THE CHRISTIAN RECONQUEST AND THE CENTRAL MIDDLE AGES
(CHAPTERS 4, 5, AND 6)

For the military aspect one cannot do better in English than Derek W. Lomax, *The Reconquest of Spain*, London, 1978. Longer and more concerned with the institutional basis is James F. Powers, *A Society Organized for War*, Berkeley, 1988. The application of that power is still best examined in Ambrosio Huici Miranda, *Las grandes batallas de la Reconquista durante las invasiones africanas*, Madrid, 1956.

The Muslim society, its defenders, and its appropriators from North Africa may be examined first of all in David Wasserstein, *The Rise and Fall of the Party Kings*, Princeton, 1985, and then in the UNESCO *General History of Africa*, Vols. 4 and 5, Paris and Berkeley, 1984 and 1988, for the Murābit, the Muwāhhid, and the lesser dynasties. Charles-André Julien, *History of North Africa*, trans. John Petrie, London, 1970, remains a classic treatment with the additional advantage of brevity. Jacinto Bosch Vilá, *Los Almorávides*, 1956, reprint Granada, 1990, is the only full modern history. Ambrosio Huici Miranda, *Historia politica del imperio Almohade*, 2 vols., Tetuan, 1956–7, does the same for their successors.

For the Christian realms we have the volumes of Antonio Ubieto Arteta, *Historia de Aragón: La formación territorial*, Saragossa, 1981, and *Historia de Aragón: Creación y desarrollo de la corona de Aragón*, Saragossa, 1987. Ferrán Soldevila, ed., *Historia dels Catalans*, 3 vols., 2nd ed., Barcelona, 1962–4, should be supplemented with the brilliant essay of Pierre Bonnassie, *Cataluña mil años atrás, siglos X–XI*, 1975–6, trans. and repr. Barcelona, 1988. For the realm of Valencia after its reconquest one may begin with Robert I. Burns, *The Crusader Kingdom of Valencia, Reconstruction on a Medieval Frontier*, 2 vols., Cambridge, Mass., 1967. Curiously there is no satisfactory history of that entity we call variously the kingdom of Asturias, of León, of León–Castile, and finally simply of Castile. Some of the individual monarchs have been treated: i.e., Bernard F. Reilly, *The Kingdom of León–Castilla under King Alfonso VI, 1065–1109*, Princeton, 1988, and *The Kingdom of León–Castilla under Queen Urraca, 1109–1126*, Princeton, 1982; Julio González, *Regesta de Fernando II*, Madrid, 1943, *Alfonso IX*, 2 vols., Madrid, 1944, and *El reino de Castilla en la época de Alfonso VIII*, 3 vols., Madrid, 1960; and Antonio Ballesteros, *Alfonso X, el Sabio*, Murcia, 1963.

For institutional studies of the Christian realms we are very well served by modern scholarship. Charles E. Dufourcq and Jean Gautier-Dalché, *Historia económica y social de la España cristiana en la Edad Media*, Barcelona, 1983, is basic. Salvador de Moxó, *Repoblación y sociedad en al España cristiana medieval*, Madrid 1983, hardly less so. José Antonio Maravall,

Estudios de historia del pensamiento español, Vol. 1, Madrid, 1973, surveys most aspects of things intellectual. There simply is no good, single-volume history of the Iberian church. Javier Fernández Conde, ed., *La historia de la iglesia en España*, 7 vols., Madrid, 1979–83, is old-fashioned in conception but contains a great deal of information. Fortunato de Almedia, *História da Igreja em Portugal*, Vol. 1, new ed., Oporto, 1976, is its opposite number. Evelyn S. Proctor, *Curia and Cortes in Leon and Castile, 1072–1295*, Cambridge, 1980, is essential but needs to be supplemented by Joseph F. O'Callaghan, *The Cortes of Castile–Leon, 1188–1350*, Philadelphia, 1989.

At the introductory level, a beginning can be made on Islamic institutions with Thomas F. Glick, *Islamic and Christian Spain in the Early Middle Ages*, Princeton, 1979. Jewish ones with Yitzak Baer, *Historia de los judíos en la España cristiana*, trans José Luis Lacave, Madrid, 1981, as well as Salo Wittmayer Baron, *A Social and Religious History of the Jews*, Vol. 10, New York, 1965.

THE LATE MIDDLE AGES (CHAPTER 7)

In English the absolutely indispensable work is J. N. Hillgarth, *The Spanish Kingdoms, 1250–1516*, 2 vols., Oxford, 1976–8. Julius Klein, *The Mesta: A Study in Spanish Economic History, 1273–1836* is the classic study. Earl Hamilton, *Money, Prices, and Wages in Valencia, Aragon, and Navarre, 1351–1500*, Cambridge, 1936, has not been replaced. P. E. Russell, *The English Intervention in Spain and Portugal in the Time of Edward III and Richard II*, Oxford, 1955, is very good on the civil wars. Philip Ziegler, *The Black Death*, London, 1969, is a general study. Most of the more general works listed under previous headings will continue to be useful.

Spanish Islam in the Later Middle Ages is currently being served well in English. John Boswell, *The Royal Treasure: Muslim Communities under the Crown of Aragon in the Fourteenth Century*, New Haven, 1977, has been followed by L. P. Harvey, *Islamic Spain, 1250 to 1500*, Chicago, 1990, and by James M. Powell, ed., *Muslims under Latin Rule, 1100–1300*, Princeton, 1990. Miguel Angel Ladero Quesada, *Granada, Historia de un país islámico, 1232–1571*, Madrid, 1969, is authoritative.

INDEX

Coria, 115, 132
corregidores, 178–9
Corsica, 168, 206
cortes, 152–3, 164, 184–5, 200, 206, 207
count of Spain, 9
countship, 20, 23, 29, 37–8, 61, 95
Covadonga, 74–5
Crestia, El, 187
Crónica de San Juan de la Peña, 188
Crónica del moro Rasís, 188
Crónica general, 188
Cuart de Poblet, 98, 100
Cuenca, 134, 141, 182, 200
Cullera, 111
curia regis, 94, 151
Cutanda, 110

Dante, 189
Daroca, 81, 83, 110
De Adventu Antichristi et Fine Mundi, 158
De Beneficiis, 189
De Intellectu, 127
De Motu Stellarum, 127
De Optima Politia, 187
De Quinque Essentiis, 127
De Rebus Hispaniae, 156
De Viris Illustribus, 30
Decius, 6
Decretals, 157
Denia, 65, 98, 131
Desiderius, 30
Despeñaperros, 134, 136
dhimmi, 59–61, 79
Dialogus contra Lullistas, 186
Diego Gelmírez, 108, 126
Dinis I, 150, 151, 155, 171, 187, 188
Diocletian, 6, 7
Dioscorides, 71
Directorium Inquisitorum, 186
dirhem, 57
Disputa de l'Ase, 186
Djahira, 123
Dolce, 112
Dominic González, 127
Dominicans, 149, 155, 182, 186, 200
Donatus, abbot, 33
Duarte I, 205

Dunash ben Labrat ha-levi, 72
dux, 23, 37, 42, 49

Ecija, 52
Edward I, 163
Edward III, 177
Edward, the Black Prince, 204
Egica I, 35, 36, 46–9
Eleanor, sister of Martí I, 206
Eleanor, wife of Alfonso VIII, 132
Eleanor de Guzmán, 203
Eleanor of Aquitaine, 132
Elements, 71, 127
Elipandus, 74
Elizabeth, 93
Elvira, city of, 6, 56, 66, 73, 84
Elvira, daughter of Alfonso VI, 93
Empúries, 112, 166
Enrique I, 136, 137
Enrique II, 188, 194, 203, 204
Enrique III, 183, 185, 194, 205
Enrique IV, 207, 208–9
Enrique, son of Fernando de Antequera, 208
entail, *see mayorazgo*
Ervig I, 35, 36, 45–7
Especulo de las leyes, 156
Estella, 200
Etymologies, 31–2
Euclid, 71, 123, 127
Eudes I Borrell, 93
Eugenius III, pope, 115
Eugenius I, bp. of Toledo, 32
Eugenius II, bp. of Toledo, 32, 43
Eulogius, 74, 83
Euric I, 11, 36
Evereux, 207

Fadrique, 203
Fafila, 75, 76
familiares, 151
faqīh, 55, 124, 197
Faro, 137, 138
Fātimids, 56, 64, 65, 85, 87
Felix, 74
Fernán González, 85
Fernando I of Aragon, 194, 205, 206
Fernando I of Castile, 92, 96, 104, 113, 203

Medieval Russia, 980–1584
JANET MARTIN

The Wars of the Roses: Politics and the Constitution
in England, *c.* 1437–1509
CHRISTINE CARPENTER

Other titles are in preparation